In 1931, Gil Schmerler's aunt Henrietta, age 22, was raped and murdered on an Indian reservation while conducting an anthropology study. Most newspapers, acclaimed anthropologists, and subsequent mystery writers spun stories that blamed the victim, portraying Henrietta as inviting the attack to some degree. Nearly a century later and after several decades of research, primarily of federal investigations and the trial of Golney Seymour, Schmerler shapes a more accurate portrayal of both the event and his aunt. His labor of love has produced a fascinating story, intricately researched and beautifully told.

—Paul Levy, lawyer, social worker, teacher, and
author of *Finding Phil: Lost in War and Silence*

Despite a long and circuitous research journey, filled with innumerable roadblocks along the way, a nephew, Gil Schmerler, in partnership with his sister Evelyn, has at last been able to tell the whole story of their aunt, Henrietta Schmerler, who began unknown and a complete mystery to them. Henrietta's rape and death in 1931, while doing anthropological fieldwork among the Apaches, originally was a sensational news story coast to coast. But whose narrative of what actually happened would dominate since competing parties had much to lose depending upon how Henrietta's actions were remembered? In most cases, from the FBI to Columbia's fledgling Anthropology Department, some version of 'blame the victim' prevailed. In setting the record straight, Gil goes well beyond his own well-documented account, including how the murderer was caught and subsequently found guilty, to raise important questions about how public institutions are never neutral in the ways they shape and report the 'meaning' of events. His is an achievement deserving of wide dissemination.

—Gordon Pradl, Professor Emeritus at New York University, author of *Literature for Democracy*

A fascinating read, suspenseful and well-crafted. What begins as a chronicle of dedicated research on the mystery surrounding a beloved family member's murder in 1931 becomes an illuminating look at the institutional and cultural dynamics of an intriguing historical era. The story offers insightful portraits of the early years of reservations as a solution to white and Native American relations, the practices and ethical dilemmas of the emerging discipline of anthropology within the halls of academe and in the field, rivalries among federal and local law enforcement and government agencies, and the elusiveness of truth and justice. A rewarding journey for the reader.

—David Potter, former president of Delta State University and of North Georgia College and State University, previously chair of anthropology at Denison University.

HENRIETTA SCHMERLER

AND THE **MURDER** THAT PUT

ANTHROPOLOGY ON TRIAL

Gil Schmerler

ISBN 978-1-365-96408-4

Design by Niki Harris Graphic Design, Eugene, Oregon

Henrietta Schmerler's article, "Trickster Marries His Daughter," published in the Journal of American Folklore, Volume 44, April-June, 1931, No. 172., is reproduced (page 267) by permission of the American Folklore Society, *afsnet.org*.

Photos on pages 51, 89, 182, 185, 187, 189 appear through the generosity of Richard S. Mickle.

Other photos and clippings are reproduced from the Schmerler family archives.

Additional material regarding this story can be found at *henriettaschmerler.com*

Contents

Acknowledgments

Writing that's spanned three decades owes a powerful debt to dozens—maybe hundreds—of people. Readers of countless drafts, small portions and large. Literary agents who've inspired us mightily (and sometimes, admittedly, left us dispirited). Friends whose houses and cottages I've commandeered to try to write in for a few days or a week. Aging relatives who tried desperately to recall the subject in the years and days before Henrietta headed west. Apache sources who helped us retrieve the story of her time on the reservation—including some who worried that we were just two more Easterners from a very different world, ready to exploit Apache history once again. To almost every person who ever asked me to describe the story I was working on, who renewed my excitement and enthusiasm every time: you probably are not even aware of the effect you had.

And then there are the people I specifically want to name, who had out-sized influence and provided immeasurable impetus:

Evelyn Kamanitz, first and foremost! The originator and heart of this search, my partner in this journey from beginning to end. That her name is not listed as a co-author of this book is her decision, but her influence is boundless. When "we" is referred to in this book, it is Evelyn and I—sister and brother—who are meant. The journeys we took—to museums, archives, and particularly to the White Mountain reservation—were quite literal, as well as figurative.

Gordon Pradl came to this project late in its writing, but had a hugely disproportionate effect on its being completed. (In fact, I'm sure I'd be making excuses right now for why I couldn't finish it this year...) I relied heavily on his keen editorial eye and organizational skills in the book's latter stages.

Paul Levy and I spent a summer week together in 2012, with the original intent of each finishing our own book, and maybe helping each other. Paul finished his before we even got together, and not only inspired me with his writing brilliance and self-publishing success, but helped me rethink more than one major portion of the book.

Elizabeth Segal was an admirer of the Henrietta story long before I put her professional proofreading skills to important use, and her editing can be felt in the tighter and (mildly) shortened pages you're about to read.

Anne Atkinson, my partner in all things, put aside her legal responsibilities whenever I needed a sharp (and logical) eye on the writing, undoubtedly understanding there would never be total equanimity in our lives until this project was done.

Irv Nathan was my guide and advocate through the difficult two years it took to pry the Henrietta file loose from the FBI. We managed to make a bit of judicial history in the process, and Irv's eminent legal career survived!

Willie Schmerler, our younger brother, made a number of extremely helpful interventions along the way, particularly when it came to the court proceedings—and then brought indispensable perspective and care to the manuscript in its later stages.

There were many other important influences, and even beginning to name them will undoubtedly lead to slighting additional people who helped shape this book: Jennifer Robinson, Larry Kamanitz, David Potter, Hilde Weisert, Hope O'Keeffe, Rima Shore, Dik Mickle, Niki Harris, are just the first names in what would be a very long list.

Of course, this book would never have happened without Sam Schmerler, Henrietta's brother and our father, who suffered through the events in real time and then through much of the writing, but did not live long enough to see this book completed. It is dedicated to him.

Prologue/Overview

A Discovery at Belle's

When you pick your way through the weeds and move aside the fallen rusted plant stand blocking your path through the door, you step onto the terrace and behold a magnificent view of lower Manhattan, the twin towers of the World Trade Center gleaming in the sunlight directly before you. You make the mistake of resting your hands on the railing, and cobwebs stick to your fingers and sleeve.

Back inside, what bothers you most is the stopped-up sink. Little things float on the brownish green water. You open one kitchen closet cautiously; brown paper bags, dirty mops, plastic wrap, and hundreds of useless kitchen aids are crammed helter-skelter into every available centimeter of space, threatening to cascade out if one item is touched. Strangely, no insects are in sight.

It had been less than six weeks since Belle Meller had lived in this apartment. She had fallen down the steps of the IRT subway on April 1, 1985, and died two days later of a brain hemorrhage, 87 years old. Belle always used the subway; she refused to take cabs because they were too expensive; she would only ride in an automobile when some hopeful foundation sent a car to bring her to their offices. She left four and a half million dollars to the Chaim Weizmann Institute in Israel.

Belle, our father's older sister, was an insomniac. Since she slept during the day, we'd visit her in her penthouse apartment in the late afternoon. There was always an eerie, dark, and dusty feel to her apartment. Although she owned a great deal of real estate in Manhattan and Atlantic City, she saved toys and cereal boxes and "pretty ribbons" from packages to give us children as gifts.

More than twenty-five years before her death, Belle cut off all communication with our family, for mostly-imagined slights. Our father never accepted the separation, continuing to write letters and leave notes long after it became evident she would not respond. When her husband Irv died in 1973, he had been having lunch with a nephew. The nephew went to Belle's apartment to inform her of his death, but was forced to shout the news through a closed door. "Don't tell anyone. I'll take care of it," said Belle. So she lived for twelve years, alone, isolated, and profoundly eccentric. Her neighbors reported that she wore the same clothes every day. She rode the subway at night and carried three-figure bearer bonds in her pocketbook. No one could enter her apartment, and since the toilet had long since ceased to flush properly, she brought a bucket of water up each night.

When she heard of Belle's death in spring of 1985, Evelyn urged our father to visit the apartment to see if there was anything of interest there. He didn't want to go at first, declaring such concern to be "morbid" or "ghoulish." But then he remembered the book of Herbert Spencer his father had translated into Hebrew, and decided to go to see if the original copy was there.

The apartment had been gone through by the team of lawyers representing her estate. While they admitted they had displaced a few items, they assured us this was, in fact, the general condition in which Belle had left it. They had told us the place was in "bad shape" and used the expressions "dirty" and "chaotic"—but nothing could prepare us for the filth and squalor we came in upon.

The dust was literally a quarter of an inch thick in many places. Virtually any item you picked up—even after it had been "dusted"— left a lasting residue on your hands. We subsequently reported to each other that more than twenty-four hours and numerous washings later, our hands still felt grimy.

Belle had apparently been sleeping in a chair. There was a single pathway through the piles of junk from that chair to the door. Odd possessions intermingled: amid the Harvard classics and works of early twentieth century philosophy lining the bookshelves were four-year-old copies of the *New York Post*, directions for toaster operation, and pieces of knotted twine. Expensive antique furniture was covered by unopened boxes of men's handkerchiefs and four flashlight and battery packages, undisturbed in their original plastic wrappers. The ornate light fixtures were bare, and faded and torn tapestries hung on the wall. And even though she had long been estranged from virtually every family member, we found the postcards from our father, a letter even from our mother, who had died ten years earlier, and the invitation we had sent Belle a few years earlier to the surprise seventieth birthday celebration for our father—she had carefully labeled the card "Sam's birthday." Our grandfather's Spencer volume was there, too.

Evelyn opened a stained-glass cabinet hidden away in a corner. She gingerly removed a cardboard box. Inside the box, with tags affixed, were Indian beads, a flashlight, a torn leather pocketbook, several wooden blocks, a beaded headband. With a shudder, Evelyn suddenly understood that these were items connected to the murder of our Aunt Henrietta, probably exhibits from the trial. She pulled out a stack of letters, in various states of decay, addressed to family members and invariably signed "Hen." There was a black scrapbook overstuffed with yellowed and crumpled newspaper clippings, headlines blaring about a co-ed's disappearance and murder in Apache country. Evelyn picked up a curious piece of tough yellowish leather-like material, realized it might be part of some old buckskin dress—worn, in fact, by our aunt at the time of her murder!—and dropped it hurriedly.

Back home in Baltimore, reading the letters, Evelyn found herself in another world: the harsh, mountainous Indian country of Arizona in 1931, with a spunky and altogether likeable young anthropologist trying anxiously to communicate her excitement and fear to the folks 2,400 miles across the country. As we were growing up, our father had told us that his older sister had been killed on an Apache reservation many years before, but offered no further details. Evelyn looked again at the exhibits and the clippings, and saw a story that needed to be told. She recruited one of her brothers to help with the research and writing, and a second adventure was begun.

Overview

On July 24, 1931, Henrietta Schmerler, a Columbia University graduate student, was found raped and murdered on the White Mountain Apache reservation in Arizona. Her death set in motion a massive manhunt which culminated in the capture and conviction of a twenty-one-year-old Apache.

The incident was reported in sensationalized headlines around the country and would change forever the way in which social scientists conducted their studies of indigenous peoples. It has since been resurrected every few years for lurid treatment in detective magazines—as a classic tale of sex, violence, and pursuit—and in academic writings as an anthropological object lesson.

Many years later, the story captivated a niece and nephew, when they came across unpublished letters written by their aunt on the reservation, and, subsequently, documentation of events greatly at variance from those that were publicized. A new picture began to emerge: of an intensely earnest and ambitious young woman, struggling against the odds to do difficult and important work, victimized as much by powerful social and cultural boundaries as by the individual aggressor who ultimately took her life. They uncovered, among many other things, self-protective anthropologists, a sometimes bumbling FBI, a surprisingly scrupulous legal system, a yellow and culturally-distorted press, an historically beleaguered and insular Apache people, and a public willing to believe the worst about this female victim.

We know some things with certainty: Henrietta was bright, personable, and ambitious. She received the backing of the Columbia University anthropology department to do summer field work— alone—among the White Mountain Apache. She worked diligently for three and a half weeks on the reservation collecting Apache lore and studying tribal customs. Her battered body was found beside a trail which led from the cabin in which she lived to the dance at which she had been expected.

An arrest made over three months later led to the indictment and conviction of a young, married Apache man. There was much behind-the-scenes discussion about the appropriateness of Henrietta's behavior on the reservation. Attempts to introduce suggestions of improprieties were unavailing in court, yet many people formed their opinions of Henrietta and what they saw as her contribution to her own murder based on these stories. Even her guides and mentors in this fated adventure—legendary anthropologists like Margaret Mead, Ruth Benedict, and Franz Boas—were quick to accept the rumors as truth.

It was widely believed that the murderer was hunted down brilliantly and efficiently by a dedicated lawman; that there was a thorough and impartial trial insulated from public prejudices; that the convicted man served his time repentantly and returned to the reservation rehabilitated; and that Henrietta's murder was but a grievous aberration, an isolated historical footnote.

We view much of this through a very different lens.

We see a gap between the public and private reactions to the crime. We examine the heralded professionalism of the law enforcement people in solving the murder—and wonder why it took so long. (We also wonder why the FBI, sixty years later, expended so much effort to keep Henrietta's file from us.) We watch the Bureau of Indian Affairs and its agents respond nervously, believing ever-precarious Indian-Anglo relations were at stake. We see the Apache retreat into a closed, defensive posture, threatened once again by the white man's justice and values (and experience some contemporary manifestations of this ourselves). Most incongruously, we witness the anthropologists rapidly distancing themselves from Henrietta, who until her death was a rising star among them.

Henrietta's younger brother, Sam, places pebbles on Henrietta's gravestone in Staten Island around 1997; Sam's daughter Evelyn and son Gil (author) at the grave in 1992 (facing page).

English inscription on
Henrietta's gravemarker:

Henrietta Schmerler
Student and Pioneer,
She hoped to further knowledge
and lost her life among the
Apache Indians at White River,
Arizona, while exploring their love
under the auspices of
Columbia University.

* * *

Cut is the bough
that might have grown
full straight...

People Involved

Henrietta's Family
Elias Schmerler (father)
Bertha Klepper Schmerler (mother)
Belle Schmerler Meller (sister)
Tillie Schmerler Wilkes (sister)
Fabius Schmerler (brother)
Sam Schmerler (brother)
Ruth Schmerler Neumark (sister)

Henrietta's NYC Acquaintances
Bertha Cohen
Freda Fine
Anita Bell
Tony Gallerini
Edith Weil

Anthropologists (Columbia University)
Franz Boas (department chair)
Margaret Mead
Ruth Benedict
Gladys Reichard
Ruth Underhill
Jules Henry Blumensohn

Government Officials
C. J. Rhoads (U.S. Commissioner of Indian Affairs)
H. J. Hagerman (Special Commissioner To Negotiate with the Indians)
C. Norris Millington (Asst. U.S. Commissioner of Indian Affairs)
Senator Carl Hayden (D-Arizona)
Governor George W. P. Hunt (Arizona)
Vice-President Charles Curtis

White Mountain Apache
Golney (Max) Seymour
Robert Gatewood
   (Golney's brother-in-law)
Bessie Gatewood (Golney's sister)
Elizabeth Seymour (Golney's wife)
Samuel Seymour
   ("H-4," Golney's father)
Alma Seymour (Golney's mother)
Jack Keyes
Jack Perry
Amos Massey
Mary Velesques (Riley)
Simon Wycliffe
John Doane
Claude Gilbert
Peter Kessay (Riley—later name change)
Silas Classey
Dan Cooley
George Wallen
George Clantz
Edith Sanchez
Bessie Sanchez
Walter Anderson
Edgar Perry
Nelson Lupe (tribal chairman)
Mary Enfield (tribal secretary, 1980s)
Ronnie Lupe (tribal chairman, 1980s)

Non-Apache on Reservation
William Donner (superintendent)
Chester Cummings
   ("government farmer")
Reverend Edgar E. Genther
Francis Warner
Willard Whipple
Johnny Lee

Jesus Velesques
William Moffitt
Sid Earl
Gertrude Cobb (secretary to
  reservation superintendent)
Dr. John Hupp (doctor
  in Whiteriver)
Dr. Ray Ferguson (doctor
  in Fort Apache)

Tribal Law Enforcement
William "Tulapai Bill" Maupin
George Woolford
Ted Shipley

Golney's Trial
Judge Albert M. Sames (presiding)
John Dougherty (defense attorney)
John Gung'l (U.S. Attorney,
  prosecutor)
Clarence V. Perrin (Assistant
  U.S. Attorney)
Donald McIntosh (interpreter)

FBI
J. Edgar Hoover (Director)
R. H. Colvin (Special Agent
  in Charge, El Paso)
J. A. Street
John K. Wren
L. C. Taylor

FOIA Lawsuit (1980s)
Judge Gerhard Gesell (U.S.
  District Court)
Irv Nathan (of counsel)
Hope O'Keeffe (of counsel)
John Schnitker (attorney for
  Justice Department)

David Sentelle (D.C. Circuit
  Court of Appeals)
Laurence Silberman (D.C.
  Court of Appeals)
James Buckley (D.C. Circuit
  Court of Appeals)

Historians/Writers/Archivists
Karen Louise Wyndham
Jen Spyra (*Columbia Spectator*)
Maida Tilchen
Hilary Lapsley
Edmond Van Tyne (*True Detective*)
West Peterson (*Saga*)
Edward Radin (*Sunday Mirror*)
Alan Ferg

Others
James McNeil (stage driver)
Tom Dosela (interpreter)
Charles Firth (surveyor)
Frank Fackenthal (Secretary
  of Columbia University)

Part One:

HENRIETTA'S JOURNEY

Elias Schmerler, Henrietta's father.

Bertha Schmerler, Henrietta's mother.

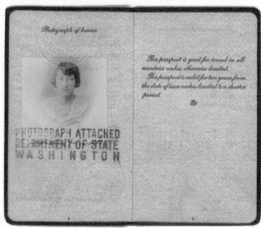

(Facing page) Four family snapshots of Henrietta—in winter dressed as an Indian; with her younger sister Ruth; with her older sister Belle and Belle's husband Irv Meller; posed alone. (This page) Studio portrait of Henrietta; her 1929 unused passport.

Chapter One

Roots

Of all Elias and Bertha Schmerler's gifted, eccentric offspring, Henrietta stood out, even before her sensational death.

Henrietta was the one, in a family which often defined itself by the father's scholarly pursuits, who actually set off to make a place for herself in the loftiest reaches of academe. When her mother died in 1928 and her father went into a self-pitying tailspin, she was the one who anchored the household and nurtured the youngest children. And it was her vitality and intensity and generosity which still held sway over the family survivors' imaginations more than seventy years after she was gone.

She was a lively, curious child, with a frequent, bright, broad smile that made you forget entirely the plainness of her facial features.

When Henrietta was two years old—it was 1911 and Taft was still president and the Triangle Shirtwaist factory fire had just left 146 people dead in New York City—she invented songs about being a princess and ruling over a purple kingdom. She talked a lot about making all the people and animals happy, and no one ever dying. She read voraciously—from the age of three—and made up stories of her own on every conceivable subject.

It was about this time that the growing Schmerler family moved from Bedford Stuyvesant, where they lived when Henrietta was born, the fourth of six children, to a luxurious home occupying half of a whole block in Borough Park, Brooklyn. The children's clothing manufacturing business that Elias co-owned had boomed in recent years. He had started out as a pushcart peddler upon his arrival in America from Austria only slightly more than a decade before, around the turn of the century, selling "sundries," including needles, pins, thread, and ribbons. Now, he had made it to the point where, as they reported, he was the richest father in his children's elementary classes.

Elias was proud of the new three-story, eight-bedroom frame house and its big lawn, fountains, fish pond, and thirty-foot-long glassed-in porch with—his special favorite—an imported palm tree rising to the roof. And he relished providing his wife with a cook and maid, and being able to employ for himself a chauffeur named Charlie Black. He didn't speak of how much this new affluence meant to him—he never talked about feelings until years later when his wife and daughter and business died in quick succession and he was feeling very sorry for himself—but his family and friends knew.

Even at his most successful, Elias never viewed himself as primarily a merchant. Bertha used to tell of catching him in his pushcart days sitting on a curb, reading a book, and insisting he get back up alongside his cart. He became a self-taught Hebrew scholar and translator, numbering among his several published works a translation of Sir Herbert Spencer's *Ethics* and a biography of Heinrich Graetz, who wrote a definitive history of the Jews. The study in his new house was lined wall to wall with books, in German, Hebrew, and English. When he was working, the room was, according to house rules, off limits to all but himself.

He was a stern, aloof, sometimes harsh man. "Austere" is a frequent description of him, particularly from younger relatives. "We're going to the Schmerlers'—be very quiet," his niece Gertrude remembers being warned. And they always were.

But boating or fishing on a cool, still mountain lake in the Adirondacks was soothing to Elias. He relaxed, spoke more softly, and even wore a faint smile on his face. Many memorable family weekends were spent driving around the mountains looking—always without success—for a country farm to purchase. Each child had a favorite memory of their father's occasional flashes of warmth—laughter at a joke, concern for an injury, pride in an accomplishment—but they stood out for their rarity.

Bertha was, in contrast to her husband, gentle and soft-spoken. She loved singing and teaching German songs to her children. Her children remember being frightened by occasional heated arguments between their father and mother, he loud and volcanic, she quiet and subdued. The arguments did not last long. Bertha invariably acquiesced.

At eleven, Henrietta published in the *Brooklyn Eagle* a tale called "How the Indians Came to North America." Imaginatively combining mythology, history, and personal invention, she wrote of Mindanaon, a lovely "princess in India," who persuaded her daughter to flee across the Bering Straits in a canoe to avoid the repulsive monster who was the child's father. Kattetujah, entirely alone in the American West, somehow bore a son and daughter who married each other and from whom "sprang the North American Indians, whose destiny it was to be conquered later by the white man from Europe."

Classmates, at around this time, noted in her autograph book: "A diamond is pure/so is a pearl/but the purest of all/is an innocent girl" and "May your future be crowned with success/Luck to our Future Authoress."

Henrietta was lithe and active and loved playing sports with the boys, when they would let her. Her childhood was spent outdoors, and like other wealthy Brooklyn kids, she got to spend a lot of time in the country, hiking, swimming, canoeing. At the end of a day of physical activity, a special treat was getting to sit on some mountainous vista, at sunset, reading and dreaming.

Adventurous episodes dominate her family's memories of her. Her younger sister Ruth remembers, at four, being thrown from a dock by Henrietta so that she'd learn to swim. (She did.) Once, in the dead of winter, Henrietta hitchhiked up Route 1 to Maine with her younger brother Sam, who was forever impressed with her courage. Indelible also in Sam's mind was the time Henrietta, in a sudden hailstorm at Schroon Lake, calmly navigated their canoe to shore. In her fourteenth year she hiked with ten-year-old Sam to the ranger tower at the top of Mt. Pharaoh in the Adirondacks. As they stood in breathless silence, glorying in the panoramic view, she declared,

"Sammy, I'm going to sleep here overnight. Can you imagine the sunrise!" Young Sam, usually adventuresome in his own right, beat a hasty, nervous retreat to the family's summer cottage at the base of the mountain, leaving Henrietta alone and defiant toward the onrushing darkness, with only the unseen ranger to protect her from all manner of nocturnal mountain evils. Sam barely slept that night with worry, and his mother may not have slept at all. When Henrietta marched back into camp next morning, she triumphantly tossed her knapsack onto the living room floor. "What a sunrise! What colors! Sammy, it's a shame you missed it."

But these remembered images of Henrietta shared equal space with two others: the intensely serious, book-loving, intellectually curious student and scholar; and the compassionate and responsible daughter, sister, and friend.

Henrietta was fifteen in 1924 when she graduated from Manual Training High School and entered college. New York City's accelerated progress system produced many particularly young graduates, but Henrietta was more precocious than most. Still, her older sister Belle wondered aloud at the time—and apparently resented throughout her own life—how Elias was willing to cover the substantial tuition fee for Henrietta at New York University, when Belle had been told, eight years earlier, that girls did not need a college education.

Henrietta looks frail next to her robust teammates in the picture of the NYU girls' field hockey team (on facing page). The team's captain, Edith Weil, remembered Henrietta vividly sixty-five years later, although more for her spunk and aggressiveness than for her skill. But the fact that a still-growing, barely-sixteen-year-old would take her place among the eleven women representing the university for the first time ever in organized field hockey was a notable reflection of Henrietta's characteristic boldness.

Some of her earliest college courses seemed to Henrietta an intrusion on her real passion, the reading of literature and philosophy. Sam remembers long discussions, often on hikes or in boats, where his older sister would regale him with tales of Arthurian deeds, Romantic poets, English moors, or Nietzschean ubermenschen. She got him to read Swift and Hardy, Schiller and Kant, Browning and Pound and Yeats. And she gave Sam an early taste of musical and

The Album

SCHMERLER   EDELSTEIN   KIRSCHENBLUTH   MCGARY   TAMOR   DISMEUKE
ROBBINS   WIMPIE   WEIL   ZINS   KENTFIELD

Girls' Field Hockey

EDITH WEIL . . . . { *Captain*
                                            { *Manager*
FRANCES FROATZ . . . . *Coach*

When the announcement was made that a Girls' Field Hockey team was being organized to represent the Violet for the first time, it evoked an enthusiastic response from the female athletes who flocked to the first practice in great numbers. Coach Froatz spent the first few weeks organizing the team and teaching the squad the rudiments of the game.

One contest for the fall term was arranged by acting-manager Edith Weil, this being a tussle with Oaksmere School at Mamaroneck. The Oaksmere aggregation was composed of many veterans, and their experience was enough to turn the tide. The Violet eleven was compelled to play a defensive game throughout, and succeeded in threatening its opponents' goal only once. Muriel Wimpie, Ann Haber, and Edith Weil flashed a fine defensive game and were instrumental in keeping the score down to 3-0. Stella Zins and Bernice Saul excelled on the offense for N.Y.U.

On the whole, the team showed continued improvement in the face of many handicaps and can be expected to give a good account of itself during the spring season. The opponents to be met during the second half of the year include Adelphi, Hunter, St. Joseph's, and there will also be a return game with Oaksmere.

Swimming

STELLA ZINS . . . . *Manager, 1923-24*
JOSEPHINE DEUTSCH . . . . *Manager, 1924-25*

Inasmuch as swimming is not a Varsity sport, all interest in Co-ed aquatic contests was drawn towards Interclass contests. Elsie Brinn, the mainstay of the Junior Class and a high individual scorer throughout the year, enabled '26 to maintain the lead during the 1923-24 season.

The 1924-25 season had a more auspicious start with Ethel McGary, a National and Olympic star, in our midst. The prestige of our Co-ed Swimming group was considerably increased and the prospects for swimming being recognized as a major activity are very promising.

In the Interclass meet, held on December 6th, the Frosh took first place with 14 points, leaving the Sophs and Juniors tied for second with 13 points apiece. The excellent swimming of Ethel McGary who, despite generous handicaps, took first place in all her entries and scored 10 points; Rejene Landsman who came second with 8; and Edna Jacobus with 6 points, was praiseworthy. Other outstanding stars were Muriel Wimpie and Mildred Simon.

Three Hundred Thirteen

1926

political consciousness when she took him to a Paul Robeson concert at the Brooklyn Academy of Music in 1926, before Robeson's fame became international.

Bertha Schmerler became ill in early 1927 with what was first misdiagnosed as diabetes and then discovered to be cancer. Her oldest son Fabe remembered hearing his mother singing to cover up the pain. Bertha was the glue that held together a family that was headed by a severe, isolated man and included six strong-willed children. But now, during a year of Bertha's progressively deteriorating health—and particularly an excruciating final two months—Henrietta bore the heaviest burden of buoying the family's spirits. Business setbacks had necessitated Elias's reducing the household staff, and the three older children, Belle, Tilly, and Fabe, were all living away from home. While carrying an especially heavy course load at NYU, where she had once again proved herself a serious, successful student, Henrietta watched over her dying mother, and looked out for her father, Sam, and young Ruth.

When Bertha died in 1928, Henrietta was nineteen years old and a senior in college, yet more and more her brooding father and her growing younger siblings counted on her for support and guidance. Elias wrote from a summer retreat, "The children are well and happy. They enjoy every minute of the day. Hen takes pretty good care of them, the household and everything is running pretty smoothly. She finds time for everything, also for making money and for enjoyment. May God bless her."

The loss of Bertha's kind, reassuring presence had, however, deeply affected them all. Many years later, her granddaughter Evelyn, who had never met her, was jolted when a tiny picture of Bertha fell suddenly from a decayed black leather address book which her daughter Henrietta had carried to Arizona and which was now among the long-forgotten exhibits from a 1931 murder trial.

In October, 1929 the stock market crashed, bringing with it the end to millions of American dreams and, more specifically, the beginning of the end to the modest fortune of Elias Schmerler. In one horrible week, his stock holdings became virtually worthless, and he was soon forced to close his one remaining factory. Within the year, he found himself in substantial debt. An intensely proud man felt helpless and lost. He wrote, "I am trying as hard as possible to stupefy my senses not to feel the seriousness of my deep wound, which fate has inflicted upon me."

Henrietta had, after her graduation from NYU in 1928, taken a poorly-paid but stimulating job as a researcher for the *New Jewish Encyclopedia*. Still nineteen, she was deferring the graduate work she knew she would eventually pursue, although she couldn't decide between English, philosophy, government, or—a later thought—anthropology. Her family needed her and, besides, she needed a break from school. Working among the scholars and intellectuals on the *Encyclopedia* staff, she again had the chance, at least for a while, to explore ideas for their own sake.

Henrietta was lively and outgoing, with a wide circle of friends, both women and men. No one can remember a particular man, or a special relationship, during these years, although she went out constantly with her friends. Her sister Ruth remembers a crush Henrietta had on a neighborhood boy "who later became a famous musician" (she wouldn't say who, out of respect for her sister's memory, but some evidence points to Tony Gallerini, a well-known accordionist and band leader of the '30s and '40s). Her brother Sam said that boyfriends were "singularly absent" in her life. She exuded a kind of fresh innocence, a non-sexual charm, in contrast to the sultry flappers of her era.

Henrietta's attention was increasingly drawn to the dramatic, pioneering work being done by hardy bands of young anthropologists, a large number of them women, a disproportionate number from Chicago and New York. They were feverishly studying the indigenous peoples of South America, the South Sea Islands, and the American West, trying to find commonalities and differences among races, the essence of what it is to be human. Margaret Mead was getting popular attention for her work in Samoa, Ruth Benedict was establishing a growing reputation as a poet/anthropologist, and the name of Franz Boas towered over all, as the "father of modern anthropology." They were all working out of Columbia University, a little more than a mile from the comfortable Central Park West apartment Henrietta's family had occupied since 1926.

Henrietta matriculated as a graduate student of anthropology at Columbia in February, 1930. Her first professors were Boas and Benedict. The air was alive with intellectual energy and unlimited possibilities. Henrietta was immediately taken with her new field and her new surroundings. These were—despite the Depression and its immediate toll on her father—exciting times for Henrietta.

By the end of her first semester, Henrietta had established herself within the department as a student of intense dedication and bright promise. She read everything she could get her hands on, she brought fresh perspectives to discussions, and she did not hesitate to challenge her famous professors when she heard an unsupported statement.

Henrietta had been painstakingly saving her money for two years for a trip to Europe she had planned to take in the summer of 1930. By April of that horrendous year, however, Elias had fallen behind by over three months' rent on the small apartment he now occupied, and the landlord was threatening eviction. The only person he had been able to bring himself to ask for help, as his fortunes worsened—and even then with great pain—was his son-in-law Irv Meller, Belle's lawyer husband. But now he was waiting for Irv's answer to an earlier proposal for a business investment, and he certainly couldn't bother him for rent money. He mentioned the problem casually, awkwardly to Henrietta, not looking at her. Without hesitating, she headed for the bank and withdrew the $400 earmarked for Europe—almost the exact amount of Elias' back rent. She never took that trip.

Instead she immersed herself in summer coursework. She was only able to schedule one anthropology course, since the anthropology department was traditionally depleted during the summers. Most of the faculty and advanced students were "in the field," studying the Mohawk or the Navajo or the Apache tribes, or, even more exotically, the Eskimo or Samoans or Balinese. Much of the excitement and gossip at Columbia that summer concerned the adventures of people 2000 to 8000 miles away. Henrietta never thought again about Europe that year. She was already avidly anticipating next summer's expedition to live and work among native peoples. Wherever it would be, she couldn't imagine anything more exciting.

Her second graduate year was a blur of heavy coursework and high-effort-low-pay research assistantships, which she now

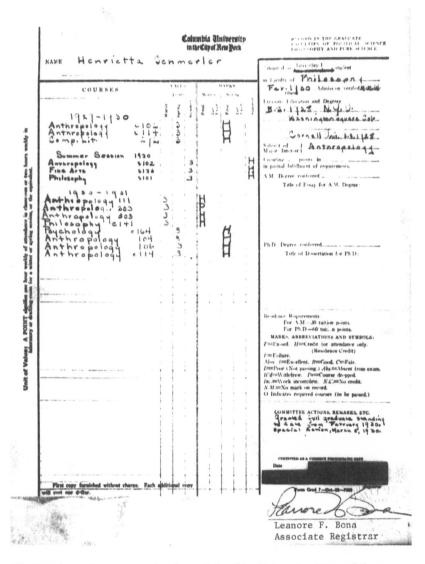

Henrietta's graduate transcript from Columbia University. Most of the courses she took were taught by Ruth Benedict or Franz Boas. The H is a desirable grade for a doctoral student.

desperately needed to cover her tuition. From the beginning of the year, too, there was angling among the graduate students for places in the big field trips the coming summer. Ruth Benedict's ethnographic expedition to the Mescalero reservation in New Mexico—she would go with six students from five different universities—would be a prize for anyone. Henrietta applied early.

Benedict, whose work on race and cultural patterns was beginning to command national attention, made it a point to call Henrietta to her office to personally give her the disappointing news. Students from Harvard, University of Wisconsin, Catholic University, and Chicago University would accompany her to New Mexico, and the only Columbia place was going to Jules Henry Blumensohn (who later, under the name Jules Henry, would achieve his own distinction in the field of ethnography). "I'm truly sorry you can't go with us," said Benedict, a tall, imposing woman in her late 40's, her hair already well on the way to silver gray. "But you shouldn't give up. I know Papa Franz"—as Boas was universally referred to within the department he chaired—"thinks highly of your work. I would think that, if you can make your case, he'll somehow find money for you to get into the field this summer."

Henrietta, now even more inspired by Benedict's personal attention, went directly to Boas with her plea. He reflected for a moment, then offered $500 from a special departmental fund for necessary research. "Think about the White Mountain Apache," he advised. "We can discuss other tribes, if you prefer, but we have had good projects at White Mountain in the past... and this year no one." Henrietta did not need to consider. She was enthralled with the idea of studying the Apache—even if it meant going alone.

Chapter Two

Budding Anthropologist

The Apache. Maybe the most ferocious of American Indian tribes, representing in one angry, scowling symbol all the horrible hazards borne by an earlier generation of Western pioneers. Sneak attacks, scalping, Geronimo. Anthropologists and other enlightened students of culture knew that by the 1930s the Apache had long since officially been "tamed," and were in fact fighting now only for assimilation, respectability, and survival. But the name could not help but send a slight chill through any who contemplated a real-life encounter. Henrietta was no exception.

Preparations for her trip dominated the rest of the spring of 1931. There were travel and living arrangements to be worked out, clothing and supplies to buy, and a lot to learn about her prospective hosts. There were worries about her father, still desperately seeking new business ventures; her sister Tilly, suffering from a recent stroke; and, of course, her younger siblings, Sam and Ruth, almost all grown up now but still missing the attentions of their mother.

Henrietta worried, among other things, that there was not sufficient time to learn the Apache language. Benedict told her that the best work in North American Indian linguistics was currently being done at the University of Chicago, which could be on her route to Arizona. Henrietta asked if she might be willing to arrange an appointment there for her, and Benedict agreed.

Potential problems of all sorts occupied her mind. She wrote to an old family friend at Washington University in St. Louis, a professor of ophthalmology, about the dangers of trachoma, an eye disease particularly prevalent among Indians of the Southwest. He sent a reprint of a recent review on the "etiology of trachoma" and reassurance that "ordinary hygienic care" would spare her the disease. He added in a postscript, however: "If you are worried about rubbing your eyes, wear a pair of automobile goggles while working among the Indians."

And she needed to make financial provisions for the fall term, if she hoped to continue studying. She filed scholarship application forms with both Columbia University and the Department of Anthropology, with the explanation that her family's finances had worsened in the past year. She applied to the Hattie M. Strong Foundation in Washington, D.C., requesting financial aid, and received a note that she could not get an answer until August, since current aid recipients got first priority. Meanwhile, Henrietta withdrew her remaining savings and turned them into traveler's checks, to supplement the $500 from Boas, which was already being eaten up by train tickets and special clothing for fieldwork. This trip was more important to Henrietta than financial security.

Her family barely saw Henrietta during that hectic time. Sam says he never knew that she would be going alone to the reservation until he got his first letter from Arizona in June. Ruth, then sixteen, only remembers being elated at the prospect of inheriting from Henrietta the job she had held the previous summer, reading to children at Madison Street Settlement House. Elias was uneasy at the thought of his dutiful daughter off among the natives, but, preoccupied with his imminent business deals, uttered not a word in opposition. A cousin, Gertrude, remembers her own father having said, "If Bertha had still been alive, Henrietta would never have been allowed to go."

Through all this, she faced the pressure of finishing the four important, advanced courses she was taking. Exams and final papers were on the immediate horizon. Two of the courses were given by Boas ("Anthropological Methods" and an independent study in "Anthropometry: Biometrical Methods") and one by Benedict ("Mythology of Primitive People"). Although both professors were involved in her trip preparations, and understood the time pressures she was under, she was especially anxious to do high-quality work for them, and so justify their faith in her. The fourth course was "Problems in Racial Psychology," taught by Otto Klineberg, who was also a fellow student of Henrietta's in Boas' seminar. Six decades later he clearly remembered Henrietta for her high intelligence and her congeniality. She managed to complete all her courses with the "H" grade Columbia awarded its resident graduate students when their work was moving them successfully toward an advanced degree.

And everything about the Apache needed yet to be learned. She checked out enough books from the Columbia library—including works on the Navajo and Pima, on rain-making rituals and working with string, as well as a six-volume set of anthropological papers on American Indians—to fill a large suitcase.

Meanwhile, there was the question of living arrangements. Benedict was making inquiries. She wrote to several prominent southwestern anthropologists about the most desirable arrangements for "a young female student to be working alone" among the Apache.

Harry Hoijer and Odd Halseth both warned that living with an Apache family would bring too many hardships to compensate for the increased accessibility. Hoijer, a professor at the University of New Mexico, cautioned that the "physical discomforts—such as flies, vermin, dirt, leaky roofs, dubious cooking, and howling infants— would seriously interfere with any attempts at securing information."

Halseth, the secretary of the Arizona Archaeological Commission, was even blunter. Families "will eat one out of house and home and equivalents. Besides, the Apache smells worse than any Pueblo could ever hope to." Both Halseth and Hoijer suggested that any visitors arriving alone should set up their own living quarters near the families. Halseth recommended that if Henrietta and another woman going independently to a different reservation could change their plans and go together, "with a double-walled tent and their own household, I think they would get on better."

Benedict had also indicated that Henrietta would have no car. "With proper previous arrangements," wrote Halseth, "one ought to be able to locate quite comfortably on the White River reservation, but a car should be part of one's field equipment."

"How will I ever afford a car?" asked Henrietta, when Benedict passed along Halseth's advice. "I don't even know how to drive." Like most children of New York City, rich or poor, she had not previously felt the need to drive. Benedict suggested she get a license before going, "just in case." Henrietta rushed to the Department of Motor Vehicles for her learner's permit.

She met one afternoon in June at Columbia with Benedict and Margaret Mead, who, at twenty-nine, had already achieved major literary success with her anthropological studies of Samoa and New Guinea. The conversation was relaxed and informal, a loosely-focused rehearsal of some of the interviews she might conduct and a preview of some of the experiences Henrietta might expect to encounter among the Apache. (Mead later wrote, in *Blackberry Winter* (1972), "The style, set early in the century, of giving a student a good theoretical orientation and sending him off to live among a primitive people with the expectation that he would work everything out for himself survives to this day.") They discussed the pros and cons of living with a family, the advantages and difficulties of working closely with the women, and the abundance of types of cultural information Henrietta could usefully collect. Henrietta left exhilarated by this stellar attention, but with her head swimming from the complexity of the task ahead.

Between her frenetic trip preparations and the immensity of the work challenge that faced her on the reservation, the trip itself loomed pleasantly as an oasis of relaxation. Henrietta was excited when she discovered that the best train route from Chicago to Arizona was via the Grand Canyon Limited. For an extra four dollars, she found, she could visit the Grand Canyon itself. She immediately planned an extra day to explore the Canyon, before heading to White Mountain.

She left from Grand Central Station on June 15, on the night train to Chicago. Her brother-in-law Irv, her sister Ruth, and her anxious father toasted her at a farewell dinner just before her departure. Ruth remembers a sudden frightened feeling when Irv joked about scalping and Henrietta laughed gaily. However, as she hugged Henrietta at the station, Ruth said nothing except, "Be careful."

Chicago was a heady experience. In her two days there, she managed extended sessions with both Fay Cooper Cole, the head

of the University of Chicago's richly-endowed anthropology department, and the renowned Edward Sapir, described breathlessly by
Henrietta as "*the* authority on linguistics in America." Sapir spent
several hours with Henrietta, "teaching me the phonetic system of
the Apache, or to be more exact, of their neighbors the Navajo," she
wrote her sister Belle. "You can just imagine how flattered I felt at that
alone, and then when he told me that he thought I had a good ear, I
was just sitting on top of the world."

Then on to Grand Canyon and a day astride a burro picking its
way down the Canyon trail to the bottom. "Boy, what a heart attack-y
trip!" she wrote her brother Sam on a June 23 postcard (below) with a
cover picture of an open-mouthed burro—the "Desert Nightingale"—
"laughing it over while waiting for a tenderfoot." She noted, "On the
last lap now—my bus leaves for the Apache in an hour."

Holbrook, Arizona, is ninety-six miles from Whiteriver. In
the early 1900s the stage coach to the reservation, through winding
mountain trails, took more than a day of rough riding. On June 23,
1931, the vehicle of transport was still called the "stage coach," but
it was now motorized and doubled as a mail truck, and the trip,
including a short lunch stop, took less than three hours. Henrietta,
sitting in the front seat of the van alongside the driver, had mixed
feelings. She was eager for the bumpy, dusty, sometimes reckless

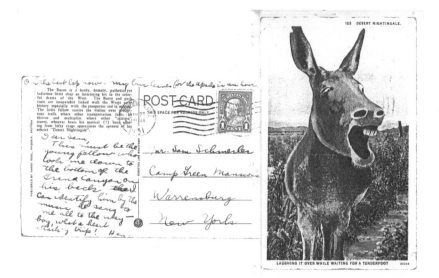

ride to come to an end; she also wished she had a little more time to compose her thoughts before confronting, head on, the adventure of her lifetime.

The driver, James McNeil, was not helping. He wanted Henrietta to know all about the shortcomings of the Apache: the drinking, the dirt, the sullenness toward outsiders, and a bit of treachery he had personally experienced. "I'm not worried," Henrietta replied quietly. "I've studied the Apache, and the record seems to show that if they're approached on a friendly basis, they can be as nice and hospitable as any other people on earth. I certainly plan to do just that."

White Mountain

The entrance to the reservation, when we first visited in 1987, was marked by a huge green and gold sign, "Welcome to the White Mountain Apache Indian Reservation." What Henrietta saw, as she crossed onto the reservation near the town of Hon Dah, was simply the countryside getting rougher and the vegetation growing wilder. Only the driver, McNeil, marked this passage with a gruff, "You're in Apache country now."

The White Mountain tribe was one of three main branches of the Western Apache, whose arrival in the southwest is dated to about 1400 and who survived primarily as buffalo hunters for several centuries. Under pressure from other tribes, they pushed southward and westward from New Mexico and Texas until finally settling in the White Mountain area of what later became Arizona.

The Apache were known more for their independence and self-sufficiency than for their aggressive instincts until well into the nineteenth century, when the continuing westward push of the white settlers left them no further room. Even into the 1860s, as civil war was about to explode in other parts of the country, the Apache tribes lived in harmony with each other and co-existed in relative peace with neighboring settlers.

By 1868 the social fabric had completely unraveled. There were raids in all directions—whites and Indians, raids and counter-raids. Fort Ord was established to bring order, but the raids only intensified. Apache attacks as far south as Mexico increased in ferocity. White vigilantes slaughtered defenseless Apache women and children at the Camp Grant massacre. Apaches turned against each other: Western Apache scouts were used by General Crook in his campaigns against the Tonto and Chiricua. In 1870 the War Department declared that the White Mountain homeland would become the restrictive reservation for all Apache of Arizona and New Mexico. The government's infamous "pacification policy" had begun.

Twenty more years of high tension—over-crowded reservations, inter-tribal friction, raiding parties escaping the reservation, Geronimo's depredations and surrender—were mostly over by 1890. Fort Ord had become Fort Apache, the reservation had been expanded and divided into White Mountain and San Carlos areas, Geronimo was touring as a side show with Buffalo Bill, the Apache had been "tamed." The Apache turned, reluctantly, to trying to make a living on partially arable land in wildly varying terrain and climate, with no buffalo and few reliable sources of meat and skins.

This history, freshly studied, resonated in Henrietta's mind as the stage rolled deeper into Apache territory. She also knew its legacy: there was a powerful accumulation of frustration and resentment on the part of a once-free and proud people forced to endure decades of virtual captivity and racial restrictions. There were poverty, debt, and high incidence of disease. There were internecine violence and the chronic, often public drunkenness. And there was a lasting tension between the pressure to assimilate, to become "good Americans," capable of sharing the riches of the American dream, and a strong need to retain their culture, their ancient identity, and their bitterly-won reputation as pre-eminent native warriors.

None of this was in evidence as the stage carried Henrietta toward Whiteriver. The grandeur of the mountains slowly yielded to the calm beauty of the valleys, streams, and fields. Junipers, cedars, and fir trees gave way to dramatic configurations of yucca, sage brush, cactus, and prickly pear. An occasional farmer or stock-tender looked up from their work and, although there were no waves of greeting, there was no apparent hostility. Wickiups and frame houses, in roughly equal numbers, became more visible. Elaborately garbed older women, carrying baskets, walked along the road, and several pickup trucks, containing bandanna-ed, t-shirted, young men, rattled by.

Henrietta, the anthropologist, noted this mix of cultures and generations and environments. Henrietta, the nervous, excited young student who had never before been west of Pennsylvania, held her breath in awe at this strange, beautiful new world.

The entrance to the town of Whiteriver was unmarked by any significant change from the preceding countryside, so Henrietta was startled when McNeil suddenly called out, "There's headquarters up there," and pointed to a small white frame building just ahead.

Chapter Three

On the Reservation

William Donner was known as one of the toughest old "Indian hands" around, crusty, cynical, and intensely proud of his ability to maintain order among the legendarily wild Apache. He had been superintendent of the White Mountain reservation since 1922, representing the full authority of the United States government and the Bureau of Indian Affairs. Nelson Lupe, tribal chairman between 1938 and 1962, remembered Donner as a stern, intimidating, white-haired man, "last of an old breed," who would harshly reprimand Indians for going too fast through town if their speed exceeded 25 mph, then himself come roaring back down the same street at a much higher speed, horn blaring, as a gratuitous reminder of his power.

He was not pleased, on the late afternoon of June 23, 1931, when a young white woman appeared in his office and announced that she was there for the summer. He was not prepared for her visit.

But Henrietta's plain looks, broad smile, and obvious excitement somehow reassured him on this day, and he did not give voice to his exasperation. His return greeting was cordial enough, if guarded. He knew well from long experience that any outside influence can at any time upset the delicate balance that goes into making a peaceful Apache reservation.

He himself had no official notice in advance of her arrival. He surmised, however, that someone in the office had had the details.

Donner did remember a brief discussion with Harry Hoijer about taking someone on for the summer, and he'd experienced the haste with which the big universities moved in the last few years to get their students out studying the Indians. Undoubtedly, the girl had been told by her professors that the reservation would be ready and waiting for her when she arrived.

"Columbia, eh? We've had a few people from there, and they've been okay." He paused. "But we've never had a girl alone, as young as you. Do you have a letter from them?"

"No, I don't," Henrietta responded. "But you can take a look at all these books I have from the Columbia library, if you need some proof." She gestured to the oversized, squarish suitcase, bursting at the sides, just outside his office door, and they both smiled. Formalities were dispensed with.

In his official report five weeks later, Donner wrote:

Miss Schmerler had no credentials or letter from the University and stated that she did not think that it was necessary for her to have a letter. She had with her, however, numerous library books, pamphlets, etc., from the library of the Columbia University; and as I saw no reason why she should not carry on her work here, no objection was made from this office.[1]

If no one had thought to notify Donner of arrangements for Henrietta, certainly there had been a lot of discussion—and debate—back in New York.

There were conflicting opinions about what aspects of Apache

---

[1] This quote, as much of the source material for this book, comes from the FBI file on Henrietta, "Murder on Government Reservation," totaling 455 pages and procured during a protracted two-year Freedom of Information Act (FOIA) battle. The FBI file, plus private family letters, extensive newspaper clippings, and files found at Vassar, the American Philosophical Society, Columbia, and the Arizona State Museum, among others, as well as through the American judicial system, provide the data on which this book is based. We have credited the speaker of a quote wherever it made sense, but do not generally provide the precise source or original location of the document in which it was found, believing this would unnecessarily burden the reader.

culture she should focus her study on, whom she should talk with, and who should accompany her in her work. No question brought forth more different opinions than that of where she should live on the reservation. Harry Hoijer and Odd Halseth had independently recommended against living with a family, the original plan at Columbia. Halseth suggested she live with another field worker in a double walled tent. Benedict and Mead then alternatively suggested she live in a wickiup in the midst of an encampment. Henrietta arrived in Whiteriver intending to follow Benedict's and Mead's recommendation, but Donner had yet another idea: she should "stay at the school for a while and work out from the school." ("The school" was the Theodore Roosevelt Indian School, a boarding school during the winter months primarily for young Navajos, using the barracks of the former Fort Apache.)

Henrietta did not like this suggestion. "Miss Schmerler stated that she did not feel she could do effective work if she lived among and with the whites; that her plan was to live in the Indian camps," wrote Donner. He relented, but insisted she should build her camp near the "government farmer," Chester Cummings, and his family. Donner would arrange for what he called "a reliable Indian" to assist her in building her brush camp, or wickiup.

In the meantime, he persuaded Henrietta to stay at government headquarters in Whiteriver, living among the employees, for what would ultimately amount to a six-day stay. In a June 28 letter to her brother Sam, she said of her temporary residence at government headquarters: "It's nothing more than an Indian reservation village, so it's been almost as good as being right with the Indians." She bragged to her sister Ruth, "I don't have to pay for my room at all— it's merely a matter of meals ($.50 per meal)."

But clearly her heart was set on getting away from the protected existence among the whites and out among the Apache. On June 25 she traveled around with Jack Keyes, looking to select the site for the tipi she would build. Keyes was what the Indian Office described as a "sub-chief," with responsibility for the Band B Apache in the East Fork area. He made it his business to be familiar with everyone and everything in East Fork and would, for a bit of compensation and the opportunity to be in the know, get Henrietta access to the people and resources she needed. By June 29, when she left her headquarters lodging, she had been convinced by Keyes to alter her plan yet again. She would move into a "little shack in the wilds near a settlement of Apache tipis," in East Fork, until the close of the rainy season, "as I understand that tipis are not exactly comfortable to live in at that particular time."

The shack turned out to be something less. She wrote her sister Til that, among her many trials and tribulations in finding a place to stay, were "having spent a number of nights sleeping in a chicken coop."

Once again the plan changed, as Henrietta continued to get new information. She wrote Boas: "Since these Apache are extremely nomadic (not at all by necessity, as I understand is the case among the Navajo, but by sheer whim and frequently a desire to be in on someone else's big tulapai party), it was difficult for me to decide where to settle. Besides, I was informed by one of their big headmen that if I should have a tipi built right in one of their settlements (my original plan after talking it over with Dr. Benedict) I might wake up one fine morning to find that because of my unwelcome intrusion the settlement had suddenly vanished, tipis and cradleboard and all, to paraphrase the old song."

The solution came in the form of a three-room cabin, recently vacated, in the midst of the scattered Apache settlement of East Fork. Small frame houses alternated with wickiups in this sparsely populated community, four miles from government headquarters in Whiteriver, three miles from Fort Apache, and, as Henrietta was pleased to point out, "about a mile from the nearest whites." Keyes brought her the news that Amos Massey's father, who had gone to the San Carlos reservation, was willing to rent her the cabin. Like many older Apache, he preferred to live in a wickiup than in the government-built houses. Henrietta was ecstatic to finally have a place of her own, and one that would allow her some independence from the local authorities. She informed Boas, two days after moving in, "From my short residence there, I think I have chosen wisely."

The cabin was not in the best of shape, nor even clean, when Henrietta moved in, but the advantages of having her own space made this a small price to pay. Old Massey used the back room as a rough storage area, and buckets of soil and hay combined with rusting farm implements to make the room virtually impossible to enter. Even in the second room, corn husks were strewn on the floor, with piles of old clothing. Henrietta simply set up her camp bed in the most available space, and kept her clothing in suitcases. She did not want to disturb a thing. In the front room there was a rough stove and a large work table and two chairs, and Henrietta had what she needed.

The porch was her heaven. It was covered and had another table for her writing and enough room for chairs. During daylight when she was home, her headquarters was here, the perfect place to receive guests. Best of all were the sunsets. "Every evening at sundown," she wrote her father, "I sit on my porch, which faces the west, and watch those glorious Arizona sunsets one reads so much about." She wrote her sister Til that "the place that I call home is a 3 room house with a delightful porch from which one can gaze at the mountains by which one is surrounded and which stretch away on all sides as far as the eye can reach. Last night I sat on my porch writing up a conversation I had had during the afternoon with a young Apache who had come to visit me, and at the same time I

Henrietta's cabin on the reservation

watched the most glorious sunset and listened to the rain pouring down around me. Curious, wasn't it?"

Professor Benedict had also urged that Henrietta hire a young Indian woman as companion and guide, and Donner echoed the suggestion when Henrietta arrived on the reservation. He told her he could find a "reliable Indian girl" to serve as an interpreter for her at fifteen dollars per month and board. Henrietta, again contrary to later stories of willful resistance to advice, readily agreed.

Henrietta spoke to two young women referred by Donner. The first told her that she would work for fifteen dollars for the month of July, but that she would be away for ten days during that time. Henrietta spoke to the second at length, found her agreeable, and asked her to begin the next day. She wrote to her friend Bertha that she was hiring a woman "with an illegitimate child as housekeeper and companion." However, the woman did not show up the following day, and Henrietta had second thoughts.

Donner's report on Henrietta's response to his recommendation does not directly mention either her subsequent hiring of the young woman, or the increasingly difficult issue of how she should spend the limited monetary resources she brought with her: "She first decided she would do this, but a few days later advised me that she did not think she would need to hire anyone—that she would be out for several days at a time and during that time would have no use for the girl." From Donner's partial accounting, it is easy to see how this could be interpreted by someone without the full story as just one more example of Henrietta's obstinacy.

The uncertainty of living arrangements did not deter Henrietta from plunging headlong into her work as soon as she arrived. She was determined to gather as much information as she could, from as many Apache as would talk to her, in the two months she was to spend on the reservation. She had no time to waste.

Donner had introduced her to Chester Cummings, the government farmer ("really the superintendent of that district," Henrietta explained), who could provide her both some measure of protection and entree to local Apache informants. Cummings, a genial sixty-three-year-old former Oklahoma wheat grower, would drive Henrietta around in his green Chevy for several days to meet potential sources, men and women, in the area. "He sure is a grand old fellow," she wrote of Cummings, and added, in one of many remarks which would become bitterly ironic in retrospect. "He assured me I won't feel the lack of a car the whole summer. Isn't that great?"

On her first morning on the reservation, Cummings had made it a point to bring Henrietta to a weathered shack just down the road from his own larger white clapboard house, which is where she first met Keyes, described to her as "the local guy you've got to know." Keyes agreed to help her build her camp and then, when that proved unfeasible, he later found her the cabin in East Fork that became her home. He introduced her to the Apache residents of East Fork, story tellers and interpreters. He recounted to her a great deal of Apache lore himself. Later he would introduce her to Golney Seymour.

Whomever Cummings or Keyes did not arrange for her to meet, Henrietta herself hailed with a cheery "Hello," as she walked through the village and, later, the camps. The response was not always what she hoped for. Many of the Apache men responded with a nod and a slight, diffident smile. If she was able to engage them in conversation, their faces brightened and they might even laugh. With the women, it was different. The nods were less perceptible and there were fewer smiles. Henrietta had been prepared for a certain shyness with outsiders on the part of Native American women—but from some she sensed hostility as well. By July 4 she would report in a letter to Boas: "Contrary to my expectations, I found it much easier to approach the men than the women. I have already made a number of 'friends' among the men, but have not yet been able to hold one real conversation with a woman." She would subsequently make it a point to try to receive introductions to the women with whom she wanted to talk, and in this way found a few willing sources.

Only with the children could she entirely relax. They, too, were shy at the overtures of the outgoing white woman, but she could see that their curiosity would allow her to overcome this. She wrote enthusiastically to Til on July 3:

> I got an interesting version of the tar baby story from a little boy who came to visit me this morning. He came with two other boys the other day (I didn't remember having seen them

before tho it's still hard for me to distinguish them one from another) and I gave them candy and they stayed for a while, tho they were so shy that they hardly spoke a word. I broke down their shyness a bit by starting to play string figures with them. After a while they left saying they'd be back soon. In a few minutes 2 of them returned and presented me with a bag of plums. Wasn't that cute?

This letter was interrupted by a sudden spurt of popularity on my part. I'm sitting in someone's car, and a whole bunch of kids who live up at East Fork (the part of the world I'm living in—about 4 miles from here) and whom I hadn't met yet but who evidently know me came clambering around the car. Of course, I cordially invited them to come and see me there. I believe that making a hit with the kids will be the nearest way of getting popular with the older folks. The kids are really awfully nice too and full of fun and pep.

Among those who conducted research on Native Americans in the frenetic years of the late 1920s and early '30s, it was not uncommon to aim to collect all the social and cultural data available from as many informants as possible, rather than limit the research to precise topics. Thus it was that Henrietta's field work would later be subject to many contradictory descriptions, and that Ruth Underhill, testifying at the trial of Golney Seymour, would say simply that Henrietta's task was to "study particularly the women of the Apache tribe."

Henrietta believed that her assignment was to find out everything she could about Apache culture, including kinship patterns, child-rearing practices, ceremonial behavior, spiritual ritual, and language usage. Benedict had told her that women would have special insight into many of these areas, and would in general be more accessible and probably safer to be with than the men—but she does not seem ever to have suggested she should interview women exclusively, or limit her study to their activities. Henrietta spoke to whoever would speak with her.

Once Henrietta had her own place, with a wide porch and some comfortable chairs, the conversations came easier. The word went out around East Fork that the "White Lady Who Stays Up All Night Writing" was eager to talk to any Apache with some good experiences and a good memory, and that she might even pay for them to tell stories to her. Visitors came on a regular basis to her cabin. And she listened carefully, writing all the time they spoke, and pausing only occasionally to prompt them with a question. It helped, of course, if they spoke English. But she was happy to hear good stories in Apache too, if she could get Silas Classey or one of her other neighbors to interpret for her.

Several younger Apache women who happened to be part Mexican spoke freely to Henrietta. Edith and Bessie Sanchez were regular visitors to her porch sessions, describing their complex family interrelationships and providing a wealth of information on domestic practices. Mary Velesques, the twenty-year-old daughter of a prominent Mexican rancher and an Apache mother, befriended Henrietta and described to her in some detail the social culture of the reservation.

Fifty-six years later, an aging Mary Velesques Riley, nearing the end of a venerable life which included a long term as the first woman member of the Apache Tribal Council, said tearfully to Henrietta's niece and nephew, with clear but understandable hyperbole, "She was my best friend."

But mainly it was men—old, young, and very young—who brought her the stories she needed for her research. There was Jack Perry, who lived in a wickiup behind his new, unused cabin just down the road from Henrietta and who told her stories of horse tending and stock herding and how the economy worked for a day laborer. Silas Classey brought a good working knowledge of both English and Apache and discussed phonetic differences in the two languages and the particular idioms of the Western Apache tribes. A number of the younger men—in their early twenties, Henrietta figured—liked to come around and talk about their work and their parties and their future plans. One of them, Peter Kessay, asked Henrietta several times to talk about New York.

Then there was fourteen-year-old George Wallen, who lived over at the Lutheran Mission and offered to tell stories for fifty cents. He turned out to be a prolific talker, telling her at length not only about life in a church home but about the social customs and mating behavior of adolescents on the reservation. To Henrietta, his intimations of his own sexual exploits sounded more like braggadocio, but she listened with interest and took careful notes.

Later in her stay the older men would begin to ask for more money than Henrietta was able to pay to tell their stories. "Somehow [the old men] got it into their heads that I was going to make a lot of money on them, and so they decided not to tell stories unless I paid more than I had offered them, and thus more than I could afford," she wrote. But they did appreciate a good audience and at the beginning were only too willing to talk.

The dances were a particularly rich source of material. There were social dances, with both whites and Indians in attendance, although mainly each group danced separately. In the public ceremonial dances, whites and Indians alike watched the theatrical Apache dancers. Finally, there were the ritual dances, customarily involving only the Apache themselves and scheduled at times and in places not conducive to spectators.

Henrietta wasted no time before getting to the dances. By June 28, only five days after her arrival, she wrote to her brother Sam that she had already been to two dances, both girls' adolescence ceremonials.

> The description of the ceremonies you'll see when I get home, but I must tell you about my personal end of it. They used to last all night (and sometimes still do), but now the first half takes place in the evening and the second half at dawn. The dance was held in a cottonwood grove across the creek (White River) from the govt. station. In the evening it was attended by a no. of whites so that I wasn't at all afraid. I stood there busily taking notes, and then at about 10:30 the whole thing broke up—that is, the dance broke up and the whites went home, but most of the Apache remained as they are camping there in temporary tipis (not that their permanent tipis are any better) until the big celebration they're going to hold over the 4th of July comes off. I went with the rest of the whites but was determined to see the sunrise ceremony.

Not knowing at exactly what time it started and not wishing to miss any of it, I got me out of bed about 2 o'clock in the morning and arrived at the creek at about 3:15. The world was in utter darkness and the only sounds I could hear from the other side of the creek were the occasional cries of a baby. This was my first experience with the Apache en masse. What to do? I sat there at the edge of the creek not daring to go over while the camp was utterly asleep and in horrible fear that a rattlesnake might like the particular spot on which I was sitting. At about 4 a.m. I heard the low beat of a tom-tom and breathlessly crossed the footbridge over the creek. Two Indians were coming out of the camp (evidently to perform certain necessary functions), and fearing to have them see me skulking around I spoke up and asked them when the dance would be held. They told me not for some time yet. I then advanced into the camp and quietly sat me down at the edge of it and waited, sitting crosslegged and as stolid (outwardly) as any old Indian for the subjects of my study to wake up. Pretty soon there were sounds of awakening in the camp, and boy! you never saw a more surprised bunch of Indians when each family group would wake up and some member would suddenly point in amazement to that white sitting there right in their camp! Did they stare! They were so amazed and amused that it was positively funny to sit there (and still taking notes, mind you) watching their expressions. After some time one man who spoke Eng. came over to me and asked where I came from and what I was doing there and as I answered each question he'd yell the answer back in Apache to the rest of the crew. Then another fellow wandered over and I talked to him for a while. They didn't seem to resent my presence and told me about the other dances taking place this week. When the ceremony (which was very interesting) was performed they gave me some of the corn pollen which figures prominently in the ceremony.

She found the experience exhilarating, and continued eagerly to haunt the dances. By July 4, she would write to Boas, "while sitting here waiting for some cowpunching events being staged in celebration of the Fourth of July for the Indians":

> All week long, at night and at sunrise, I have been watching performances of the girls' puberty ceremony, evidently their chief ceremony. They have gotten so accustomed to the sight of me with my notebooks in hand that last night two of the older men even invited me to dance with the rest. I can assure you that at that moment I felt prouder than upon the occasion of my first invitation to a dance in my adolescence.

The notebooks were filling quickly, and Henrietta began to store them in the black leather suitcase which still contained much of her clothing. She felt little danger of theft, but there was no point in tempting fate—or curious eyes—by leaving them out in plain view.

Henrietta's eagerness to get to know the Apache directly, and her frequent demurrals about having non-Apache assistance or accompaniment, ruffled a few feathers in the white community. Her separation from the whites was greatly exaggerated in later accounts, as in Donner's report to his home office in Washington, DC: "She paid very little attention to the white people on the reservation, associating almost entirely with Indians and to some extent with a few white men who were working as laborers at Theodore Roosevelt School, Ft. Apache."

In fact, mainly because of the continuing aloofness of the Apache, her most common social companions were still white. Beside Mr. and Mrs. Cummings, who had Henrietta over for several meals and continued to look out for her well-being, many of the white merchants and agency people in Whiteriver could be counted on for a pleasant greeting and, when she had time, a good conversation. They all thought she was "a very nice young woman," as Johnny Lee, son of W.A. Lee, proprietor of the general store, described her to us many years later. At the same time, several people took pause at what they saw as her unwillingness to distrust the Apache sufficiently, as they had advised. She told Cummings, for one, that she was "certain I'll be treated nicely, if I treat them with courtesy and respect. They're no different from other humans and they've endured some very bad treatment, historically."

Her most faithful follower, it turns out, was an itinerant white painter from Louisiana. Francis Warner lived in Whiteriver with his eleven-year-old son and worked under contract with the Navajo boarding school in Fort Apache. He was particularly solicitous of Henrietta, inquiring regularly about her safety and offering her whatever help she needed. She generally declined his assistance, preferring as always not to become too identified with the reservation's white people, but he was so courteous and concerned that she accepted his offers of rides on several occasions. She would undoubtedly have been surprised to hear Warner described in a later FBI report as having "been on drinking parties with the younger Indians and frequenting the sporting houses at McNary, Arizona," and hanging out with another Fort Apache employee known only as "Bruce," who was later ordered off the reservation for "immoral conduct."

She was in Warner's car on Sunday, July 12, the evening that her cabin was broken into. She had asked Warner for a ride after she had had, in the afternoon, "a couple of unwelcome Apache visitors." Peter Kessay, of whom she had specifically been warned to beware, dropped by, for the third time in three days, with a friend. They just stood around in Henrietta's yard, despite her telling them that she would not be able to talk with them. She finally, nervously, had to ask them directly to leave. They did, but with obvious annoyance.

She drove around with Warner for a while. They stopped and talked for several minutes with a couple of older Apache men, who were inspecting a field. Henrietta felt her good spirits returning, and asked to be brought home.

According to Warner, they were nearing Henrietta's home when they came upon a car containing Claude Gilbert and two other Indians blocking the road at a stock guard. Warner asked them to back up so he could pass, and they did. After dropping Henrietta off at her cabin, Warner apparently encountered the same roadblock on his return trip. This time he rushed out of his car clutching a jack handle, demanding to know "what the hell" they thought they were doing. Gilbert reversed his car again, and this time took off back toward East Fork.

Meanwhile, Henrietta had found the screen ripped out of her side window and her front door left ajar. She rushed in to find signs of upheaval in her cabin, her belongings—never neatly stored—now strewn totally haphazardly around the living area. Most conspicuously missing was the suitcase with two of Henrietta's notebooks and several items of clothing, and the three dollars in cash she had left on her table. She found a second window left open in the rear. Her heart sank. What had been a glorious adventure was becoming a difficult time. She locked the cabin as best she could, and walked the half mile to Cummings' place, where she spent the night. (If we are to believe Warner's account, in one of very many contradictory stories in this case, Claude Gilbert and the two drunken men in his car had walked Henrietta over to Cummings. Cummings—and Claude Gilbert—denied this completely.)

Warner also drove Henrietta into town and back on Wednesday, July 15, and asked when he would see her again. He said she told him it would not be before Sunday night, and "that her intentions were to have her an Indian dress made and she was going to be very busy and expected to sleep Thursday and Friday night as she was going to attend the dance at Canyon Day Saturday night." She wanted to go, she told him, with the Indians.

⊡ ⊡ ◉

The break-in had shaken Henrietta seriously. Her initial exhilaration upon arriving on the reservation, successfully making the contacts she would need for her work, hearing some wonderful stories and seeing some fascinating rituals from the inside, being treated as a serious scholar by the whole community—all this in the most spectacular natural setting she could imagine—had already begun to wear off. There were the continual admonitions by the whites to be cautious in her dealings with the Apache, and their impatience when she tried to deflect their concern good-naturedly. There was the stand-offishness of the Apache women. And there was the growing discomfort she felt at the attention of some of the younger Apache men.

At first, she was sure that the loneliness she was experiencing was natural for a young woman missing her family and friends in a faraway place. She mentioned the feeling of aloneness in almost every letter, but it was invariably subordinated to the good feelings—a perfunctory aside to let everyone know she missed them. "Please write some more letters—it's lonesome here," was the casual postscript on the early letter to Sam describing her breathtaking experience crashing the sunrise adolescence ceremony. She reassured her father in another letter that "I usually have visitors (mostly Apache) in the evening, and so I do not have much time to get lonesome." By July 18, she was writing, simply, "It gets awfully lonesome."

And she was beginning to worry about the quality of her research. Before her first week had ended, she wrote to Sam, "At times I get very discouraged." But she continued with the upbeat qualification that would mark all her letters until the very last: "But those who know the Apache say that I've really been making very good progress with them, because it's the hardest job to get them to open up at all." She wrote Boas a week later: "Even though at times I get frightfully discouraged, which I suppose one must expect on one's first field trip, I'm enjoying my work tremendously." A couple of weeks later, on July 16, her attempt to sound cheery to her father seemed quite strained:

> Even when I am discouraged out here—and there are occasions when I feel that way—I can console myself with the knowledge that things are going well at home... I'm getting along quite well out here. I've been told by several people and I've seen with my own eyes that I'm well liked by the Apache. If I weren't, my position here would be insufferable, as they are by no means a lovable people and would find it easy to make it unpleasant for me. However, I've been remarkably successful with them, according to the whites who know them best, even though in my eyes my success falls far short of my high hopes as budding anthropologist.

In her first days on the reservation, she had written that "the Apache look like a splendid lot" and "the Indians seem like a very nice bunch." Three and a half weeks later, in her last letter, she wrote her friends Anita Bell and Freda Fine:

The Apache are a peculiar lot. Their culture is still going strong, but it is a very poor culture as their main interest in life is tulapai, an intoxicating and awful tasting (I've had some) beverage. I am told by those who know them best here that I've made remarkable progress with them, yet I've been so discouraged a good bit of the time that I've felt like quitting and flying back to New York. The women are by far the worst and the most unfriendly of the lot. I have a good many men friends by now, but it seems impossible to get to know the women. As for test—baby or string figure or anything—it's absolutely impossible to do a thing. I'm having a hard enough time doing plain ethnology!

Chapter Four

The Ride to Canyon Day

The dance at Canyon Day excited Henrietta, beyond all else. Her greatest triumphs so far among the Apache—and maybe her most fun—had been at the dances. "I made a big hit with the Apache by dancing all night with them," she had written to her friends Freda and Anita about the July 4 dance. Now in her fourth week on the reservation, she was pretty well known. She could gather a great deal of information without interviewing, without having to work so damned hard to break down the reticence, the distrust. At the dances, the Indians let go. And she, for this evening at least, would be one of them. She would finally be wearing the buckskin dress that Mary Velesques promised to have finished for her, and maybe she could persuade Mary to lend her her beads. It was an appealing prospect.

Transportation to the dance was still an open question. She would be getting a horse, but not until the Monday following the dance, if Mr. Whipple's promise was to be believed. Twenty-five dollars would not have seemed like a lot to pay for a horse in New York—of course, why *would* she buy a horse in New York?—but here she was watching her precious funds dwindle rapidly. However, despite Cummings' assurance that she "wouldn't feel the lack of a car all summer," she was indeed feeling the lack. So she had arranged to buy a horse. In any event, she'd still need to find someone to take her to the Canyon Day dance Saturday night.

Warner and Cummings were her most common sources of transportation, but they were white men. Part of her problem in being accepted by the Apache, she believed, was her still-too-regular association with the white people. When she was alone, when the Indians—particularly the kids—visited on her porch, they were much more at ease and often talked freely. In the presence of other whites, they adopted a mask of stolidity, of taciturnity, even of incomprehension. In her new Indian dress, she should go to the dance in Apache company.

The Friday before the dance brought a stream of visitors, as was becoming the customary pattern at Henrietta's cabin. Bessie and Edith Sanchez came in late afternoon and sat for a while, talking about their family and trying to describe the kinship clans as Henrietta took notes. Peter Kessay came up to the porch, and the Sanchez girls quickly excused themselves and left. He came despite Henrietta's request the previous Sunday that he leave her yard, but now he was cordial and a little more humble. She spoke to him for about fifteen minutes, and then he left, too.

Shortly afterwards, Jack Keyes strolled over. Her closest neighbor and most regular visitor, Keyes was pleasant and garrulous, if not always believable. Henrietta would extend just the merest invitation, and he'd begin telling stories, of Apache life, history, customs. She'd write down all he said, then try to figure out later what was true.

Keyes had been talking only a short while, when a young Indian whom Henrietta had seen before, but never spoken to, stopped at the fence outside her yard. Keyes, in the middle of a sentence, called out to him in Apache. The man shrugged.

"I have asked him the name of that old Indian we were just talking about. He does not know," he explained to Henrietta in English.

Henrietta invited the visitor, a twenty-five-year-old garage worker named Claude Gilbert, to join them on the porch. The three discussed the meaning of various words for a while, writing some Apache and some English on pieces of paper. The sun was now beginning to disappear. Keyes got up to leave.

"I hear there's a dance over at Canyon Day tomorrow night," Henrietta said.

"That is what I hear," said Keyes.

"I see many Indians going down there," added Gilbert.

Henrietta told them she was having an Indian dress made, which would be finished tomorrow, but she hadn't figured out yet how she was getting to the dance. Gilbert said he'd be driving by way of East Fork and she could have a ride with him. Henrietta thanked him, pleased.

The way Gilbert told the story, in his statement to the FBI ten days later, he had said, "I may come here to East Fork tomorrow evening. If I do you might catch a ride with us." And Henrietta had told him, according to Gilbert, that she might catch a ride before that. "That is all," he said.[2]

In his first of many statements to the FBI, Keyes didn't mention having heard Gilbert offer the ride. He left before Gilbert did, he said, but not before warning Henrietta not to wear a dress such as Indian squaws wore. The government was attempting to educate the Indians out of their old mode of living and custom of dress; for a white woman to dress this way would create resentment and ridicule, he felt.

On the other hand, Keyes was reported to have told others that Gilbert was supposed to bring her to the dance. And Keyes privately told the investigators for weeks—even as he undoubtedly knew the correct identity of the murderer—that he suspected either Gilbert or a

---

[2] Did Henrietta wait until Friday to begin thinking about transportation to Canyon Day? No one on the reservation reported to the FBI having arranged to go with her. Even Mary Velesques, who on Saturday morning gave her the yellow fringed dress she had made, stated that Henrietta had offered to pay Claude Gilbert to drive her as well. *(In 1987 the elderly Mary Velesques Riley told us a different story: that she expected Henrietta to come to her house to travel with her family, and waited until after sundown before giving up and leaving.)*

Did Henrietta know Gilbert was married? Cummings says he chastised her on Saturday afternoon for not knowing, or not asking...or not caring. "My God, girl, that is the durndest reprobate on this reservation. I know he has one wife not more than 50 yards from Guy Sisson's garage and a bunch of kids."

Even more relevant, why did Gilbert offer her a ride when he had no car at his disposal? Gilbert's was "rented out to Father Augustine for ten days," he later told Agent Wren. And the ten days would not be up until the next Wednesday. Gilbert could only say, to the skeptical FBI man, that he had meant "*if* the car is back." (Wren later interviewed the garage mechanics—"white men"—who confirmed that Gilbert's car was in fact out of commission at the priest's home and not repaired until that Sunday afternoon.)

white man.

Five minutes after Keyes left, Henrietta began to gather up her books from the table on the porch and bring them inside the house. She came out with a handful of gingersnaps for Gilbert to eat on his way home, and he left.

Henrietta did not seem to doubt that she now had a ride to Canyon Day the next evening. Why else would she have turned down the chance to go with Mary Velesques, or told Cummings, whose daughter was being driven by Warner, that she had a ride? Where else would Keyes, who was right there, have gotten the impression she was going with Gilbert? And who else could she have had in mind when she wrote, in the unmailed letter found on her dining table after her disappearance, "I'm writing this while waiting for some Apache boy who's to take me in his car to a big Apache dance taking place some miles from here"?

When Gilbert got home at about 8:30 Friday evening, he later said, his wife asked him where he'd been. "I said, 'East Fork, and I stopped at the white woman's camp. We may go up tomorrow. If we do, she might catch a ride down with us.' My wife said, 'We have no car.' Then we went to bed." That, apparently, was the last thought Gilbert had about taking Henrietta to the dance.

At what point Henrietta began thinking about alternative transportation can only be conjectured. When Keyes passed her house at 7 o'clock on Saturday morning, she was already on her porch. She invited him up, but he was in a hurry to get on to his horse-hunting. When he saw her later, at about 5 p.m., he estimated, she had already picked up her dress from Mary Velesques and was still expecting Gilbert to bring her to the dance.

Mary had barely put the finishing touches on the dress when Henrietta arrived at the Velesques home at noon on Saturday. Henrietta and Mary, along with Cummings, had gone to get the material only on Thursday, and Henrietta expressed urgency that the dress be ready for the dance. Mary watched Henrietta try it on, exclaiming her delight, and then wrapped it neatly. Henrietta handed her three dollars, then listened for more than an hour as Mary related stories her great-grandmother had told her.

When Henrietta returned home from Mary's that afternoon,

she had time only for a little paperwork before beginning to prepare herself for the dance. She filed Mary's stories, along with those she had gotten the evening before from the Sanchez sisters, Jack Keyes, and the others. She was more careful with her notebooks now, since last Sunday's break-in. She wrote one letter, which she addressed to her friends Anita and Freda, apologizing for writing them together, but explaining that if she didn't, "neither of you would hear from me at all." She sealed the envelope and placed it in a conspicuous position on her dining table, so that she would remember to bring it to town for mailing on Monday. She didn't expect to be going anywhere on Sunday, since this evening's dance in Canyon Day was an "all night affair." From her July 4 experience she knew she'd want to be sleeping well into Sunday afternoon.

Cummings showed up around 4 p.m. to say hello, then to lecture her on her choice of Gilbert as an escort to the dance. Cummings had been kind to her throughout her time on the reservation, and it had been Cummings' house she had gone to for refuge the previous Sunday night, after she discovered that the intruder had visited her cabin. She had returned home Monday, feeling it important not to give in to the fear. But Cummings had warned her then, as he warned her now, to watch out that the Indians did not take advantage of her, that it would be easy for them—particularly the young men—to misunderstand her friendliness. Henrietta listened to him politely, and promised to be careful. She, too, felt some foreboding, and was no longer as confident as she had been at first that she could win the trust of the Apache. On the other hand, she was not ready to give up trying—especially not now, when she had experienced some little breakthroughs. It was particularly important that she remain open, friendly, trusting, if she wanted them to respond in kind.

Before Cummings left, she asked him to cash several travelers' checks for her in town. She needed the cash to pay for the horse, which would be ready for her on Monday or Tuesday. Cummings agreed to leave the money in his home, for her to pick up when she needed it.

Between 5:00 and 6:30 p.m. a procession of people passed her house heading in both directions. An older woman, whom she recognized as the wife of Samuel Seymour, came out of the Seymour camp about 200 yards up the road, along with a younger woman whom Henrietta could not identify with certainty but believed to be a relative. (This was Elizabeth Seymour, the family's twenty-year-old daughter-in-law, three months pregnant at the time.) They were traveling on horseback at a pretty rapid gait, heading for the Canyon Day dance. They didn't look at Henrietta, sitting on the porch as they passed her cabin, and she didn't call out to them.

A few moments later, the elder Seymour came out of the same gate and passed in front of Henrietta's cabin. He was known among the whites on the reservation as H-4, reflecting the sporadically followed tradition dating back to the government "pacification" policy of numbering, rather than naming, Indians. Often the older Indians were referred to by the numbers—usually far easier for the whites to pronounce than the Apache names—and the younger ones by their given names, now invariably common English names. Henrietta, of course, thought of her neighbor as Samuel, also the name of her own younger brother. Yet Seymour, who spoke no English, never seemed interested in conversation with Henrietta, and solemnly went his own way. This day, when Henrietta called out "Hello" to him as he passed, he waved, and went on.

According to Seymour's later testimony, Henrietta was at that time—which he placed at 5:30—still dressed in the clothing she'd brought with her from New York, and not her new Indian dress.

A while later, John Doane came out of the Seymour camp, where he says he had spent a good part of the afternoon. He stopped in front of Henrietta's cabin. She was sitting on the porch, writing in her notebook. He called out a greeting. She walked out to the fence to speak to him. He introduced himself, in English, and told her that Keyes had said she might be interested in his doing some interpreting work for her.

"Oh, yes," said Henrietta, "I know your name. Mr. Keyes has told me that John Doane is a good interpreter of Apache into English. Why don't you come by on Monday? It's very possible I will have some interpreting work for you, maybe even for a few days."

Doane, who was twenty-nine-years old, thanked her, said he

would come back, and left.[3]

Then, four men came through in fairly rapid succession. It is likely that Henrietta spoke to three of them, and the fourth waited across the road as she spoke briefly to the third.

Jack Perry, a cousin of Keyes who had earlier met and joined him while horse hunting, rode on ahead of Keyes just prior to coming to Henrietta's cabin. She was on her porch, writing. Next to her on the table was a large ladle which she used for dipping water from the stream that ran one hundred yards behind her house. Perry called out to Henrietta, asking if she could give him a drink of water. She grabbed the empty ladle and quickly came down to the fence where Perry sat on his horse.

"I'm sorry," she said. "I just finished the last bit a few minutes ago." She held the ladle sideways to show him there was no more. It always made her feel bad to disappoint an Apache when they asked a simple favor. Perry nodded, said, "Okay," then urged his horse to move on.

As Perry trotted away, her old friend Keyes rode up. "Hello, Mr. Keyes," she greeted him. "Did you find a lot of horses today?" Keyes smiled and nodded. "Easy. About ten horses were together near a cliff in Seven Mile Canyon." He did not address her by name. He didn't know what to call her and, anyway, no one could pronounce her name.

"Did you happen to see Claude Gilbert today, Mr. Keyes?"

---

[3] We know of this dialogue from John Doane's own account to Agent Street. Yet we are less certain of the true actions—and character—of Doane than of almost any other player in this drama. Incredibly, Doane was reported by Gatewood as having confessed to him, days after the murder, that he had stolen Henrietta's suitcase containing papers and "other articles" (primarily clothing, according to her report), from her cabin. He had thrown the papers into the brush somewhere in East Fork.

Even more incredibly, Doane was reported by a "squaw named Dora" as having told some people in Forestdale, Arizona, where he had moved almost immediately after Henrietta was reported missing, that he had "witnessed the murder of the white girl and saw her running through the brush from Seymour and also screaming for help." Dora did tell Street that Doane had said this while drinking; furthermore, when Doane later emphatically denied to him ever making such a statement or seeing any such thing, Street reported that Doane was "about half drunk on tulapai."

Curiously, after his denial, Doane was not prosecuted, nor ever again questioned by the FBI.

Henrietta asked, a bit anxiously. The sun was lower over the White Mountains. "He's supposed to drive by to bring me to the dance."

Keyes snorted and shook his head several times. "Claude Gilbert! His wife would not let him come with you, I bet. Where is he? You are crazy if you think he will come. He is not a good boy."

Henrietta began to feel distress. Cummings had told her virtually the same thing a few hours earlier, and it was now getting late.

Keyes watched her. "Ask Max Seymour." He gestured behind him. "I know he is going to Canyon Day."

Henrietta looked up the road just a short distance to where Keyes had pointed. Two young men were ambling slowly on horseback toward her, watching with interest her conversation with Keyes. She had seen them both before, but had spoken to neither. The more familiar one was larger, more solidly built, with a dark complexion; she recognized him as the son of Samuel Seymour. She remembered that his name was Golney—the name had interested her and she meant to ask about it—but he was called Max. She thought he lived with his father, her neighbor, but the living pattern of extended Apache families was often complex, and he had never done more than stare and nod at her when he passed. She was not sure whether it was antagonism or shyness which motivated such greetings, but she was careful not to press.

This time she waved, and the two men continued toward her. The smaller man, whom she thought to be another member of the Seymour clan (Robert Gatewood was in fact the husband of Samuel Seymour's daughter Bessie), veered off to cross the road—he was heading for the gate to the Seymour camp. Golney Seymour rode up to the point where she stood with Keyes.

"Hello. Mr. Keyes says you are going to the dance at Canyon Day." She spoke in English, slowly and distinctly, not certain how much of the language Golney understood. In all but a few cases, the Apache people she had met spoke at the least more English than she did Apache.

"Yes," said Golney, after a moment's pause.

"Do you have another horse?" She held up two fingers to reinforce the point.

"One horse," he replied and pointed to his horse. He looked at her quizzically.

She was uncertain of his meaning. Was he suggesting she ride with him? She thought of the many warnings she had received in the past three weeks about over-familiarity with the young Apache braves.

"I am waiting for Claude Gilbert. Thank you," she said.

Golney shrugged and turned his horse toward his father's camp. He gave a half-smile and trotted over to where Gatewood waited. The two went through the gate and up the path.

Henrietta, perplexed, waved good-bye to Keyes, who had edged away during her conversation with Golney, and went back into her cabin.

It was now after 6:30, there was as yet no word from Gilbert, and there seemed to be no good alternative transportation to the dance available to her. She dressed anyway, determined to find a way to get to the dance. Gilbert would yet show up, or *someone* would come along to help her.

Henrietta put on her new fringed dress and her borrowed necklace. She went back out to her porch to wait.

⊟ ◧ ◎

To this point, the story of Henrietta's afternoon has been reconstructed from the statements of Keyes, Perry, Cummings, Jesus and Mary Velesques, Samuel Seymour, Doane, and Gatewood, as well as Henrietta's letter of that day to Anita and Freda. It was Golney Seymour, of course, who provided what was ultimately the publicly accepted version of the murder, most of it coming from his formal confession and trial testimony.

Here, as signed by Golney Seymour on November 1, 1931, witnessed by FBI Special Agent J. A. Street and five other members of the law enforcement community or reservation bureaucracy, and interpreted by Thomas Dosela, is what Golney had to say about the events of that afternoon:

Before going into my father's camp I had a conversation with the white girl and she said that she desired to borrow a horse from me to ride to the Canyon Day dance. I told her I had only the one horse, but she could ride with me to the dance if she desired to do so. Later on Robert Gatewood and myself left my father's camp, passed out of the gate, Gatewood going down the road and I stopping at the white girl's house. We remained there a short time and we left, the white girl and I both riding the same horse, she riding in front in the saddle and I was riding behind.

Down the road a short ways from the white girl's camp I saw Robert Gatewood off to the side of the road as he was going toward his camp. We went down the road further. It was getting dusk and we met Simon Wycliffe who passed us going up the road in the direction that we were coming from. I recognized him but wondered if Simon recognized me. We went on past the seven-mile canyon and we turned off on the trail that leads in south of the old Fort Apache cemetery and goes south of the Fort Apache town.

By all accounts, Golney and Gatewood had remained at the Seymour camp only a little more than half an hour before they came back out, with Golney stopping at Henrietta's cabin and Gatewood heading toward his own home. The "short time" that Golney remained at Henrietta's cabin before they left together for the dance would seem to be just moments, in which they exchanged conversation or she went inside to get her bag. This would correspond with his statement that they were still in sight of Gatewood, who was traveling "off to the side of the road," as they began the ride to the dance. Gatewood in his statement described even more explicitly the moments after he and Golney arrived at Henrietta's house:

Golney Seymour got off his horse and opened the gate and I rode through and started on west down toward my camp, and a short way I looked back and he was still wiring the gate. I rode a short distance further and looked back and I saw Golney Seymour's horse tied to the fence in front of the white girl's house. I also saw Golney Seymour and the white girl (Henrietta Schmerler) standing on her front porch, as though they were talking. I continued on down the road, west, then turning to the south and going on top of a little hill, and it was then beginning to get dusk. At that time I saw Golney Seymour and the white girl (Henrietta Schmerler) riding on the same horse, the girl was riding in front in the saddle, and Golney Seymour was riding behind. I could see that she had on an Indian dress.

Although Seymour's later courtroom version of the events leading up to the ride differed dramatically from his signed confession, the jury would choose to take the original story at face value. His contention that Henrietta gradually overcame his reluctance to riding with a single woman by plying him with alcohol was not believed.

Rather, we imagine Henrietta waiting, unhappily, in her new fringed dress, despairing finally of Claude Gilbert showing up, furious with herself for the rides she had earlier refused, and now desperate for another way to get to the dance. We can imagine a little tremor of excitement when Golney Seymour returned, to her surprise, apparently willing to have her ride with him. On the other hand, we can envision the alarms this triggered within her: the awareness of what can happen when men and women are alone, the memory of the warnings she'd been given, a natural cultural wariness. Still, there was her fervent desire to believe that the Apache people would respond positively to her own goodness, there was the urgent need to get to the dance, and, finally, there may have been an impulsive willingness to take this one little chance. She had seen Apache men and women riding together on the same horse: husbands and wives, fathers and daughters, boys and girls. The Canyon Day dance was an opportunity she would bitterly regret missing.

When Henrietta began the ride toward her death, we imagine that she felt an unusual nervousness, beyond even the vague anxiety she had increasingly felt in the previous week. This young Apache was brusque, a little too self-assured, and maybe a bit tipsy. Certainly there was a whiff of tulapai in the air. She didn't know him or his family as well as she would have wanted, and she was well aware that everyone would tell her she was a fool for accepting a ride with an Indian man, alone. If the ride turned out badly, she would face a contemptuous chorus of "I told you so's." Maybe that's why, finally, she said yes. Too many people, too self-righteously, possibly with too much prejudice, telling her how not to deal with the Apache. Well, she'd done pretty well so far, thank you, doing things her way, treating them openly and without fear. Yes, there was some fear—more in recent days than earlier —but she would not let them see it.

Golney signaled for her to get up in front of him. She wondered about this—didn't second horseback riders ride behind the horseman?— and hesitated for a moment. Then, with another shrug of resignation, she swung her leg over the horse and settled into the saddle. The horse wheeled quickly and headed in the direction of Canyon Day.

Interchapter

At the Dance[4]

Elizabeth Cummings rode to the Canyon Day dance in the back seat of Francis Warner's car with her two brothers and two sisters and Warner's eleven-year-old son; Warner and an "old white man" sat in front. Just outside East Fork, they picked up Peter Kessay and Fred Banashlay, who rode on the running boards on each side of the car. This was just past 6 p.m., and there was still some sunlight left.

Marcus Altaha drove in from Springerville in his Essex with his brother, picking up Addie DeClay in Whiteriver. When they reached the dance, however, Addie got out to spend the evening at her mother's place nearby.

Claude Gilbert and his wife and two other couples and some children drove to the dance in a borrowed Dodge truck. When they arrived—it was late and the dance was in full swing—they sat in the car and watched for almost an hour. Only Claude got out, to reclaim the lantern he had lent Harvey James to use as a headlight on his way to the dance, and to dance by himself near the truck.

Mary Velesques arived around 8:30 p.m., along with her sister, her aunt, her mother, four little children, and two Mexican boys and an old man. She began immediately to look around for Henrietta,

---

[4] Most of the details of this interchapter are taken directly from Agent J.K. Wren's FBI report of August 6, 1931.

to see how she looked in her buckskin dress. She saw Gilbert, who Henrietta said was bringing her to the dance, but she did not ask him about her.

Elizabeth Seymour had arrived at the dance on horseback accompanied by her mother-in-law, and was annoyed that her husband Golney did not show up for several hours.

Claude Gilbert thought everyone might want watermelon and talked Marcus Altaha into driving back down with him to Mr. Sisson's garage at Fort Apache Junction, where they picked up five melons. They sold them for ten cents a slice, and were quickly sold out. Mary Velesques heard he was selling beer, too, but he never said anything about that in his FBI interview. Gilbert joined in with the singers for a few songs, stayed for a while to cheer them on, and then "danced with a woman, just once," he reported.

Margaret Gilbert said, in her interview, that her husband Claude "danced all night with the night watchman's wife." When he rejoined the family, it was sun-up and time to leave.

Golney Seymour arrived after eleven, conspicuously under the influence of tulapai, and quickly found himself a comfortable spot near the woodpile to curl up in.

Several other people wondered where the young white woman was. She had promised a dance to Francis Warner. Peter Kessay had been told by friends that she was coming dressed as a squaw and wanted to see how she looked. Elizabeth Cummings had been specifically told by her father, the government farmer, to keep an eye on her. But, as Gilbert said, it was crowded, people came and went, the drink flowed, and there was just too much going on to keep track of anyone else.

Chapter Five

The Search for Henrietta

Jack Keyes, who liked to keep an eye on everything in his neighborhood, was the first to worry on Sunday, July 19. His cabin was across the road and just a short distance from Henrietta's. He often passed by her house three or four times on a normal day, and this Sunday he was particularly anxious to hear about her experiences at the Canyon Day dance.

Keyes usually saw her on her porch, writing by herself or interviewing Indians when she could persuade them to stop by. She had an insatiable appetite for the stories they told, and scribbled furiously while they talked, interrupting only occasionally to prompt them with a question. Now it was late afternoon and the cabin was still silent. Even if she had returned very late from Canyon Day—the dances usually lasted until after sun-up—and allowed herself a healthy sleep, she would be up by now. Keyes knew that, as recently as Saturday evening, there was still a great deal of uncertainty about how she would get to the dance, and his concern grew.

Keyes spoke to several people in East Fork who had been to the dance. No one had seen the white girl there.

On Sunday evening her cabin remained dark. Keyes knocked on the front door, then again on the back door, and shouted for her. There was no answer. He thought of the possibilities and was now deeply troubled.

There were no new signs of life Monday morning. Keyes walked rapidly to the home of Chester Cummings, a quarter mile away, to report his fears about the girl. He was sure something had happened to her, he told Cummings, who had himself worried about her safety. Cummings, however, smiled at Keyes' agitation and offered reassurance.

"Oh, Jack, she is around some of the Indian camps—she will show up," Cummings said to him, according to Keyes' later statement to the FBI.

Nevertheless, that very afternoon Cummings paid a visit to reservation superintendent Donner to report that Henrietta had disappeared.

Donner had worried a lot about Henrietta's security from the moment she had first walked into his office four weeks earlier. Her reluctance to follow his advice on where to live had troubled him at first. But he generally found it best not to argue with a determined woman.

When Donner met Henrietta on the morning of July 5, after she had spent the night in the midst of a secret ceremonial dance, he warned her more forcefully to beware of socializing with the young Apache men. She told him that she was getting along quite well, thanks, and was making many friends. He later said that she seemed to consider his warning a joke. A week or so later, he felt impelled to repeat his warning to her, mentioning particularly the danger of the young men under the influence of tulapai, or in a social situation where there was drinking.

"The only thing I'm afraid of here is the rattlesnakes," he said she responded.

Now it was hard not to let his imagination run wild. There had been at least eight murders on the reservation in the last three years alone, and he couldn't begin to count the number of attacks on women that had been reported to him—let alone those in which the victims suffered in silence, or let members of their clan extract private revenge. He knew there was a certain protection afforded by white skin. But this Columbia girl seemed to be pushing the limits, and he had felt that way increasingly each time he'd seen her or heard about some of her adventures.

"Well, nothing I can do about it tonight," he thought. "Let's just hope she'll turn up tomorrow."

Meanwhile, Jack Keyes had become seriously agitated. All his questions about Henrietta's whereabouts were met with puzzlement, amusement, or silence. He went again to Chester Cummings' house, and convinced Cummings and Francis Warner, who happened to be at the house at that time, to accompany him to report Henrietta's disappearance to Jesus Velesques.

Velesques was a stock rancher of some influence in the community. A Mexican, he had married an Apache woman and had been living on the White Mountain reservation for over forty years. He was a large man, spoke three languages well, and was often consulted by the Apache for his wisdom and understanding. When Keyes, Cummings, and Warner showed up at his door, around sundown, he had just returned from a long, hard day up in the mountains working on horseback with his cattle, and was now relaxing with his son, George, and daughter, Mary.

Velesques listened to the story of Keyes' fruitless search for information about Henrietta and shook his head in concern. Cummings and Warner filled in some details. Warner motioned toward Velesques's daughter.

"Mary, didn't you make a dress for her to use at the dance?"

Mary nodded. "Yes, she picked it up here Saturday afternoon. She tried it on. And she borrowed some beads from me too."

"She didn't show up at the dance, you know," said Warner.

"I know," said Mary. "I looked for her." Mary told them that Henrietta had offered to get her a ride to the dance with Claude Gilbert, who would be taking her. Mary said she already had a ride. Henrietta had then said, "You must hunt me up." "All right," Mary said she had told her.

But at the dance she saw Claude Gilbert selling watermelons and maybe also selling beer, but not a trace of Henrietta. She did not ask Claude if he had brought the white girl with him; for some reason, she had decided that Henrietta had changed her mind.

Velesques told them he thought this should be reported

immediately to Superintendent Donner—but that he himself was just too tired to make the trip that evening. He hoped they would. But the three men decided instead to adjourn to Cummings' house. Cummings did not mention that he had already spoken privately to Donner that afternoon.

On Tuesday morning, Velesques, Keyes, and Cummings rode together into Whiteriver to make their report to Donner. Velesques said later that Donner "did not take the matter very seriously." Keyes and Cummings said he told them not to worry, she was certainly around somewhere, probably interviewing out in the camps. She had, in fact, let it be known that she may be away for a day or two at a time, doing research in remote parts of the reservation. But they were also aware that she had as of yet neither car nor horse. They left Donner's office, not entirely comfortable with his seemingly casual reassurances. But it was clear from the subsequent actions of Donner and almost everyone else on the reservation that, from this point on, the situation would be treated as serious indeed.

Donner called several of his sub-agents around the 1.6 million acre reservation to find out if anyone had seen the woman, and spoke to a few trusted Apache informants as well. No luck anywhere, although each of them kept him on the line to tell him about some place or another they'd run into her in the previous weeks. She'd been at the July 4 dance at Whiteriver and she'd been over at the Indian school in Fort Apache and she'd been down at old W.A. Lee's general store. Donner knew all that. Where was she *now*?

Several people, on their own, began to search the nearby trails for her. Dan Cooley, operator of the Fort Apache gas station, heard from Keyes on Monday that Henrietta was missing, and headed out immediately to look for her. His first stop was a trail, visible from his pumping station and used occasionally by intoxicated Indians trying to escape the notice of the officers in Fort Apache. This trail passed southeast of the old military cemetery, and had served the same purpose in the 1870s for Apache trying to avoid being seen by the fort sentries. It served as a shortcut from East Fork to Canyon Day. Monday night he drove his car close to the old cemetery and walked up the draw there and traversed part of the trail. The next day he drove to the west side of White River to check out some high cliffs near to where Claude Gilbert lived. Keyes told him that Gilbert had arranged to take Henrietta to the dance, and Cooley wanted to check in case Gilbert had thrown her body over the cliff. Cooley was only part Apache, with a white wife, and, like most others on the reservation who were not full-blooded Apache, was ready to think the worst of the young Apache men. He found no trace of Henrietta.

Jesus Velesques, who had been a young Army scout before he came to White Mountain, tried a few trails leading away from Henrietta's East Fork home, and he too found nothing.

From the beginning, some things about the appearance of Henrietta's cabin made Keyes uneasy: the side window was broken, not far from the porch table where she usually worked; and the door handle sat at an odd angle, as if it had been forced. But he knew he should not approach too close to the house, lest he be caught and accused of having something to do with her disappearance. On Tuesday he persuaded Jesus Velesques to take a look at the house with him, but the doors were still locked and Velesques too was wary of breaking in. They peered through the broken window and could see a number of dresses hanging behind the stove, Henrietta's hat resting on a cot, and little else. Velesques rode quickly over to Cummings', a quarter of a mile away, only to be told by Mrs. Cummings that her husband was in town at that very moment, talking to Donner. Entering Henrietta's house would have to wait until Wednesday.

Meanwhile, Cummings drove rapidly up to the squat, stucco headquarters building on Whiteriver's main street. He held an envelope aloft as he slammed into the superintendent's office.

"I didn't want to open this without you, Bill," he told Donner, "but I think this should tell us something. It was sitting right on top of her writing desk, just like this."

Donner called in his secretary, Gertrude Cobb, as an additional witness, then carefully unsealed the envelope. The three-paged hand-written letter was addressed to "Dear Anita and Freda." Donner read it first, his lips moving over the words.

"Jesus, I guess we should have gone inside two days ago. She was on her way to the dance Saturday with an Indian," he said. "She's got to be dead." It was the first time Donner had given voice to a feeling that had been nagging at him since Monday. It was now Wednesday, and that meant that four days had passed since anything had been heard from Henrietta.

"I'm writing this while waiting for some Apache boy who's to take me in his car to a big Apache dance some miles from here," the letter began.

Donner spent the remaining late afternoon hours huddled with his office staff and top Apache advisors, planning strategy for an all-out search the next day. He thought for a moment about wiring his boss, C.J. Rhoads, United States Commissioner of Indian Affairs, notifying him of Henrietta's disappearance (and, for that matter, of her *existence*) for the first time. Rhoads' first question, he well knew, would be "Why did you wait this long to tell me there was a problem?" Donner decided to wait one more day before contacting him.

His aides were instructed to speak only on a confidential basis with trusted people who might help with the search, and to avoid the press or public officials. This would indeed be an explosive story.

Search parties were organized for Thursday, with local peace officers and Indian Affairs staff taking the lead. Some Apache tribesmen joined in the search, but most ignored the calls for volunteers which went out to the different clans and tribal regions. Individuals and small groups began to comb the wooded trails and scour the hills. The reservation was now buzzing with news of the missing white woman. There was wide expectation of big trouble ahead.

The Apache in the letter, everyone knew by now, was Claude Gilbert. Everyone was also saying that Gilbert had been at the dance all night Saturday with his wife; there were people ready to come forward to say he'd sold them watermelon or beer. Nevertheless, Donner wanted Gilbert for questioning, and he also wanted to be able to show a quick arrest. He had Gilbert brought in on charges of selling beer.

One of his first calls was to the Navajo County sheriff's office. He spoke to his old friend, Sheriff L.D. Divelbess, who dispatched his deputy, George Woolford, to take charge of the investigation. Woolford rounded up a few officers and was soon heading for Whiteriver, seventy-five miles to the south.

It was Woolford, or one of his men, who happened to mention

the assignment to an Associated Press stringer assigned to the sheriff's office. This story would appear in Friday's *New York Times*, and in dozens of papers around the country, under an AP tag and July 23 dateline, from Holbrook, Arizona:

> Indian guides of the Apache country trailed through the mountainous White River region today searching for Henrietta Schmeler [sic], Columbia University research worker, who has been missing since Saturday.

> Claude Gilbert, an Apache, 25 years old, was arrested at the White River Reservation for investigation.

> Friends of Miss Schmeler at White River said she had intended to go to a dance with Gilbert at Fort Apache.
> Gilbert asserted she did not go with him. He said he had not seen her since Saturday afternoon, and denied all knowledge of her whereabouts.

> Assigned to Arizona by the university to study Indians and their mode of life, Miss Schmeler had been living in a cabin at Eastfork, four miles from the reservation at White River.

The headline read, "GIRL STUDYING INDIANS VANISHES IN ARIZONA; APACHES SEARCH FOR COLUMBIA RESEARCH WORKER OVER MOUNTAIN TRAILS."

The length of time it took to launch an all-out search for Henrietta did not go unnoticed. Ben Wetherill, the son of a well-known archaeologist, wrote on July 25, the day after the body was found:

> She was to have received a horse she had bargained for Monday.... This evidently brought the fact that she was gone before the people in the neighborhood. A little investigating was done Tuesday. Wensday [sic] a few employees went around asking questions. Thursday was wasted in the same

way. Friday a few men were put out and some preparations for a searching party were made. The deputy sheriff from Showlow was called down Friday morning late. As far as I can find out a message to this Deputy was the first word to get out. Evidently no messages were allowed to go out. From what we found out at McNary our messages were the first ones out. Whiteriver called an hour or so before we wired to find out if any messages had gone out.

As far as we can find no volunteers were called for and offers were ignored...

P.S. One report is that they had a man watching her (the Agency) and that they missed her Sunday. If so that wasted a lot of time. What we were hollering about is that they would not get out while there was still hope.[5]

The White Mountain Apache Reservation spreads out over a large chunk of east central Arizona; it is roughly seventy-five miles from west to east and forty-five from north to south, and covers more than 1.6 million acres. By Friday morning there were searchers in every quadrant of the reservation, looking for signs of a young white woman whom few of them had met. Bureau of Indian Affairs agents knocked on the doors of cabins and shouted into wickiups, inquiring if anyone within had come across a white woman visiting the camps.

In Fort Apache, where most of the people seemed to have met or seen Henrietta during the previous month, there was a sudden frenzy of activity, now that the nervous rumors of the past few days had become official: the white girl had disappeared without a trace.

George Woolford, deputy sheriff of Navajo County, brought seven men with him from Holbrook to interview merchants and ranchers in the Fort Apache vicinity. Donner's team of BIA personnel questioned their key Apache informants. And independent trackers and investigators, white men and Indians alike, rode and walked

---

[5] This letter appeared, with no additional context provided, in the file we obtained at Columbia University.

the trails and hidden areas near Henrietta's cabin and reservation headquarters. A rumor spread quickly that there would be a cash reward for finding the woman, and searchers proliferated.

Jesus Velesques was up before dawn on Friday, determined to work the back trails all the way to Canyon Day, if necessary. He had not stopped searching Henrietta's neighborhood until well after sundown the previous night. Now he was eager to continue following what his instincts so powerfully told him: Henrietta had run into trouble between her home and the Canyon Day dance. His daughter Mary swore that nothing—short of violence—could have kept Henrietta from the dance. He had been willing to listen to Donner and the others for a couple of days: the young anthropologist was headstrong and independent and thus unpredictable, and had most likely gone off somewhere without telling anyone. It was a big reservation. But now it was Friday and he was pretty sure he was looking for a body.

Today he thought he'd follow the Indian trail that followed the river just off the highway and wound past the old military cemetery, although Dan Cooley told him he'd already taken a look a couple of days ago and he'd seen others on the road as well. Velesques would keep his eyes glued tightly to the trail, and maybe his old scout training would help him see something others had missed.

Velesques began the trail only several hundred yards from Henrietta's cabin and worked his way methodically forward for almost three hours. There were plenty of things to notice—horse tracks, horse droppings, mud slips from a recent rain, even car tracks that looked new—but nothing that struck his imagination. The sun was high in the sky. He was dimly aware that he had just passed the cemetery when his eye was caught by something metallic just off the trail. He scurried over and pulled from its nesting place behind a chokeberry plant a large silver flashlight—showing signs of recent rusting and, he noticed with a slight exhalation of breath, visibly dented.

He gently replaced the flashlight, hurriedly tied his horse, and began to pace the immediate area, peering intently at the ground.

Moments later, his eye was caught by the reflection of colored beads, barely concealed by the hanging branch of a cottonwood tree. It was a beaded leather purse, half submerged in the clay. Velesques studied the purse for a moment, then dropped it where he found it. He surveyed the area as he knelt, and noticed that the vegetation had an unsettled quality, twigs inclined askew and leaves damaged, as if some animal—or animals—had thrashed about. The woman's body is nearby, he thought, even before he first noticed the buzzards circling in the ravine below.

He mounted his horse and turned away from the ominous birds, back toward Fort Apache and help. He had found the woman, he told himself; let someone else be with him to face the body. Dan Cooley would be at the garage, within shouting distance of the trail. He'd want to be part of this.

Fifteen minutes later, Velesques and Cooley were on their way back to the trail from which Velesques had just come. Just as they were about to leave the Fort Apache road toward Seven Mile Canyon, the familiar black Chevrolet of Superintendent Donner sped into view up ahead. Velesques waved for him to stop.

"You better come with us," he said. "I think I know where the girl is."

Donner was motionless for a second, then nodded. He followed slowly in his car as Velesques and Cooley on horseback turned off the road. Their horses trotted quickly along the narrow trail, with Donner's car moving cautiously behind, at least fifty feet back.

At the spot where he had made his discoveries, Velesques dismounted and motioned for Donner. He pointed to the flashlight, then to the purse, then to the buzzards, who continued to hover above. Donner shook his head sadly. Then the three began to work their way down the side of the draw, toward the birds.

Only a few steps over the edge, Velesques was first to spot the body toward the bottom of the shallow ravine, bare legs first. The others stopped at his shout and stood still for several long seconds, holding onto the nearest branches and staring at the scene below. Then they clambered the final seventy-five feet down the side of the ravine onto the dried out stream bed and stood without speaking over the body of Henrietta Schmerler.

She wore a fringed yellow buckskin dress, now torn, rain-soaked and clay-smeared and bunched up above her waist. With a start, Velesques recognized this instantly as the garment his daughter sewed in their living room the week before. Her right arm reached straight upwards above her head; her left arm was bent awkwardly with the hand resting against her hip. Her legs were drawn up underneath her, a large, ugly bruise covering the front part of her thigh. Her underclothing was torn.

Her face stared upwards. Her nose was mashed, her jaw badly distorted and missing several teeth, her hair matted and tangled and mixed with the red clay from the wash. There was a large, deep gash covering most of the right side of her neck, beginning under the ear, with a few remaining traces of caked blood. Donner tried reflexively to read from her face her feelings upon dying, then realized quickly that a week of rain, mud, and possibly animals would have transformed the expression dramatically. He, and the others, averted their gaze.

Stunned as they were, the significance of the scene was not lost on any of the men. Donner, in particular, felt the full weight of the moment. A white woman visitor to the White Mountain Apache Reservation had been brutally murdered. The wrath of the outside world would descend. Life on the reservation would never be the same.

The superintendent took charge. Donner instructed Velesques and Cooley to remain with the body, to touch nothing, to allow nothing and no one to interfere until he returned. He would go to summon the doctor and report the death to the law. The sixty-six-year old scrambled up the side of the ravine, and the Chevrolet backed hurriedly toward Fort Apache.

While Donner was gone, Velesques and Cooley took turns watching the body while the other did reconnaissance in the area. They had both experienced enough death to know that their perceptions and findings now would later count for something. Cooley paced off the distance from the body to the top of the draw, where the first struggle had apparently taken place: 101 steps. Not far from where the purse was still lying, he found a fountain pen crushed by what appeared to have been a horse's hoof. He carefully studied the clay on the banks and the clay that rested on Henrietta's body and clothing. He concluded that she had lain in this spot since before the rains began on Monday, and most likely had been attacked and murdered on this spot. There also seemed to have been a struggle up at the top of the draw, and he figured she had run down here before she was finally caught.

⊞ ⊡ ◎

It was noon when Henrietta was found, and by 2:15 p.m. more than a dozen people were clustered around the body, which remained in its original position, virtually undisturbed. Two doctors, Dr. John C. Hupp of Whiteriver and Dr. Ray Ferguson of the Theodore Roosevelt Indian School in Fort Apache, had completed their examinations and were finishing up their notes and waiting for permission to leave. George Woolford, Deputy Sheriff of Navajo County, had taken charge of the site and was making detailed notes of his own. Chester Cummings, Henrietta's neighbor and frequent patron, had been called to provide formal identification. Willard Whipple, justice of the peace in Whiteriver and "Acting Coroner," was overseeing a coroner's jury of seven citizens: Herbert Cooper, Earl E. Karr, T.E. Shipley, Eugene L. Mentor, C.G. Montgomery, J.L. White, and himself, They declared the cause of death to be "wounds inflicted on her head and body by some sharp instrument in the hands of someone unknown person or persons." Mr. Calvert, a Whiteriver merchant, bustled around the scene taking photographs from every angle with his Kodak, capturing not only the body but all features of the scene, every spot where the evidence was found, and even, secretly, the people who huddled over the body.

Both doctors agreed that the body was in a state of decomposition, indicating that she had died more than five days previously, congruent with the assumption that she was murdered on the night of the dance. They observed knife wounds above her right eye and on her right hand, but concluded that the deep knife wound on her neck—two and a half to four inches long and one and a half to two inches deep—was the probable cause of her death. They each noted that the severe damage to her face, including the broken nose and missing teeth, was undoubtedly caused by a blunt instrument or object. Dr. Hupp concluded she had died within twenty minutes from the time the wounds were inflicted. Dr. Hupp also believed, based on the position of her body and condition of her clothing, that she was "ravished." Dr. Ferguson, on the other hand, did not feel that the position of the body told anything about whether the victim was raped or not, and would not venture an opinion.

The formalities took most of the afternoon before Henrietta was finally wrapped in a blanket and carried on horseback, for the last time, out of the ravine.

COLLECTION OF RICHARD S. MICKLE

Ravine at the bottom of which Henrietta's body was found.

Chapter Six

Response to the News

Sam Schmerler strolled from his bunk toward the mess hall, wondering if he'd have any time today to write a couple of letters. Maybe this afternoon, after riflery and before he had to report back to the waterfront. The cook strode excitedly across the lawn toward him, waving a newspaper. "Anyone you know, Sammy?" he shouted. As soon as Sam was close enough to make out the headline—GIRL STUDENT SLAIN IN ARIZONA CANYON—he felt a deep, searing pain. The subhead on the *Times* article confirmed the worst: "Searchers Find Body of Henrietta Schmerler of Columbia University—Signs of Struggle."

◫

By the time the newspaper had reached her brother Sam at Green Mansions Summer Camp, on Tripp Lake in the Adirondacks, Henrietta's body was in the Winslow Mortuary, just north of the White Mountain Apache Reservation, in the final stages of preparation for return transport to New York City. Undertaker Drum had, with practiced fingers, pressed the nose back as close as he could get it to normal position, although it remained flat and slightly tilted to the left. Her mouth was pulled closed; however, because of the missing teeth in the bottom row, the expression was queer. The abrasions were covered with powder. The deep slash in the neck was covered with the high collar of the dress the coroner supplied to replace the torn buckskin in which she had died.

▣

Moments after Velesques made his discovery, word raced rapidly throughout the 3,300 square miles of the reservation that the worst had happened. A white person was dead, almost certainly murdered, probably by an Apache. Since the Indian wars of the 1870s and 1880s, when last Geronimo had led outlaw bands in raids on white soldiers and settlers, there had been only a few such incidents to mar the overall tranquility. There would be trouble ahead. The men out searching for the body returned to their cabins and their wickiups to await the next blow.

▣

The telegraph office in McNary, ordinarily a sleepy outpost but already roused to hectic activity in the past two days by reports of Henrietta's disappearance, became a madhouse after the body was discovered. Telegrams shot back and forth to New York, New Mexico, Phoenix, Washington, and even Europe, announcing the news to relatives, officials, and anthropologists. The press materialized instantly; stories were fired off not only to New York newspapers but quickly to almost every metropolitan area large enough to support a daily paper. The Associated Press made sure everyone else heard the news.

◎

Freda Fine, a college friend of Henrietta's in New York City, was shocked to receive a telegram from Arizona asking her what to do with the body. The letter found lying on Henrietta's kitchen table, written on July 18 and addressed to Freda and Anita Bell, had provided authorities with their initial clue to Henrietta's disappearance and now the name of someone who might help them with their immediate problem of the disposal of the remains. Freda, in panic, called the Schmerler home and found they had received the same request.

▣

Two reservation lawmen hurried to Henrietta's cabin and sealed off the different rooms, marking the locations of her books, clothes, and other possessions, and the condition of her bedding. Gingerly, they picked up several soiled paper towels and tissues from the floor and behind her bed, and deposited them in a cardboard box labeled "specimens." (A few weeks later, a Chicago laboratory, after some confusion, would report the presence of "sperm heads" on the towels.)

Speculation proliferated on the motive for the murder. "Jealous squaws" were the subject of early headlines, allegedly having resented the attention Henrietta received from their men. Henrietta had uncovered secret ceremonies and had to be killed, went another line of thinking. The Apache simply resented the intrusion of the white woman and did away with her, others said. After Henrietta was found, and the condition of her body and clothing was made known, speculation focused more conventionally on a "crime of passion."

◙

Dixie Miller read about Henrietta's death in the papers of Leo, Georgia, and wrote immediately to the President of Columbia University that she supposed they would "soon send someone to fill the young woman's place" and wished herself "to make application for the work." Others were not as understanding. Mrs. Minnie Grimstead Himes, Director of Social Morality for the Nebraska Woman's Christian Temperance Union, wrote furiously to Columbia that "the Apaches alone did not kill her, you people partly did it in allowing her to go by herself. No young woman is safe in the hands of vicious men and especially when these men are not far removed from savagery." A letter from Tulsa, Oklahoma, signed "Disgusted," began, "Of all fools, you Columbia people must be the limit!" An otherwise unidentified writer named "Maverick" sent a post card saying simply: "You know in Arizona alleged 'research work' does not carry the privilege of other people's husbands—moscow ideas don't go there."

◙

Elias Schmerler was totally distraught over this latest, and most horrible, blow, and could barely speak to the relatives and friends who came to comfort him. Neither Bertha's death nor the loss of his fortune had prepared him for the shock of the brutal, obscene murder of his daughter. To several people, he mentioned that life was not worth living. To Ruth, his youngest child, he wrote, "Fate has inflicted on me the most cruel blow which has destroyed my life forever." He would shortly be intimating to Columbia University that he was preparing to sue them for negligence, in improperly supervising his daughter's dangerous work.

❖

Reporters were firing out stories as quickly as they could get access to the teletype machines, often before they could get their facts straight. Henrietta, who would have turned twenty-three on October 23, was described variously as twenty-one, twenty-two, twenty-three, twenty-five, and thirty, in accounts put out by the AP and UPI alone. She was spending the summer in Whiteriver to work on a master's degree with a Columbia grant, some said; she was financing a year in Arizona with her own money to work on a doctorate, others maintained. Fifty-two Indians were arrested following the discovery of the body; or, according to other accounts, the number was seven.

❖

Each official who came in contact with the murder recognized quickly the potential magnitude of the case and wanted to share the responsibility with higher-ups. Reservation Superintendent Donner called John Gung'l, United States Attorney for Arizona, minutes after the body was discovered, and asked for help. Gung'l wired R.H. Colvin, special agent in charge of the Bureau of Investigation's El Paso office, then headed for the reservation. Colvin knew well his first responsibility and instantly wired the Bureau of Investigation's young but already powerful director, John Edgar Hoover: "Am pulling Wren off Reynolds case for few days to work on urgent murder investigation Fort Apache Military Reservation." Hoover immediately recognized the savage murder of a white woman as the number one news of its day, and cabled back instructions to Colvin to keep him personally and frequently informed of all developments. Then he contacted Vice President Charles Curtis.

Donner was already in touch with his own boss, Commissioner of Indian Affairs C.J. Rhoads, who had been contacted by Arizona Governor George W.P. Hunt when he received an urgent plea from Columbia to search for the missing Henrietta. Rhoads cabled Donner to "make sure Indian gets square deal in Schmeler [sic] case," anticipating the public outcry against the "savages" under the care of the Bureau of Indian Affairs. Donner was quickly beginning to feel overwhelmed by the rush of the numerous government agencies to the reservation. He turned down Rhoads' request that he call in (former) Governor H.J. Hagerman, then a special commissioner of the U.S. Indian Service (Hagerman later came anyway), denying there was "any trouble between Indians and whites" on the reservation.

With Claude Gilbert already in jail but vehemently denying having even seen Henrietta on Saturday, Superintendent Donner sent reservation officer William ("Tulapai Bill") Maupin to bring in Peter Kessay and Frances Warner. According to one widely circulated AP story, an Indian deaf mute reported he had seen Warner on the night of July 18 placing the inert form of a young woman in his car, but this story was totally unsubstantiated and quickly dismissed. Warner argued that he had not seen Henrietta at any time in the week before her murder. Warner, Kessay, and five other Apache men were arrested by Maupin on a variety of charges. Twenty-five to thirty others were brought in for questioning. The tiny sheriff's office with the little jail back by the kitchen filled up quickly.

Chapter Seven

The Anthropologists

Columbia University in 1931 was the home of an anthropology department with few equivalents historically among academic departments in terms of influence, celebrity, and sheer output. American cultural anthropology is widely considered to have been born there, and the achievements of those early Columbia anthropologists still largely define the terms of anthropological study today. Franz Boas came to Columbia in 1899 and within a short time had assembled a department including such luminaries as Margaret Mead, Ruth Benedict, Alfred Kroeber, and Gladys Reichard. Their pioneering works—Boas' *Race and Culture*, Mead's *Coming of Age in Samoa*, and Benedict's *Patterns of Culture*—are still commonly studied in introductory anthropology courses, and the methods they devised in the '20s and '30s are in many ways those employed today.

Anthropology brought an important degree of enlightenment not only to our knowledge of other cultures, but to our total understanding of the nature of being human. The early Columbia anthropologists have stood in the liberal public perception for the highest human ideals: racial understanding, human equality, truth over superstition, the value of freedom. Their work led the way for the decades of social science which provided a foundation for the end of legal segregation in this country, produced some of the basic intellectual rationale for opposition to Nazism, and, informed by the extensive field research they sponsored, instructed us of our mistreatment of Native Americans.

Boas, Mead, and Benedict are universally accorded places in the pantheon of American social scientific scholarship. Their names are associated not only with their intellectual pre-eminence, but with a profound dedication to truth, and to a heightened sensitivity to the human condition.

In their private responses to the Henrietta Schmerler tragedy, however, they showed us a very different side of themselves.

The Schmerler family first heard from the anthropologists soon after the murder through a series of condolence notes, which were polite and appropriately sympathetic. Benedict wrote from the Mescalero Apache reservation in New Mexico, where she was heading her study group of six—the main southwestern group from which Henrietta was working independently. Boas wrote from Europe.

Mead's note followed a little later, written to Henrietta's sister Belle:

> May I extend to you my deepest sympathy at your sister's tragic death—a shocking penalty to have paid for too great enthusiasm and ambition to do notable work... All of us are most horribly shocked.

Actually, Mead had responded to Henrietta's death much earlier. As an emerging international celebrity, the author of two important books, she had been sought out by the press in her American Museum of Natural History offices for reaction. She told the New York World Telegram on July 28:

> The killing of Miss Schmerler may have been a pathological one, such as cannot be guarded against even in civilized communities. Or the girl may have failed to have trusted sufficiently to the protection of the Apache women, in whose friendship her safety lay.

The headline read, MISS SCHMERLER'S DEATH SHOULDN'T

HALT EXPLORING, ASSERTS MARGARET MEAD.

Privately, the anthropologists were even more critical. "Both Ruth [Benedict] and I spent hours advising her and she disregarded every bit of the advice," Mead reported to Boas on August 14. Ruth Underhill, another Columbia anthropologist then in the field in Sells, Arizona, wrote Benedict that "The white people of the district concur in the statement that Henrietta was utterly indiscreet, refused all help and advice, and finally offended everybody, Indians and whites alike."

It is not surprising that anthropologists would be deeply concerned by the brutal murder of a student doing field work, not just as a reminder of their own vulnerability, but also as a threat to the always-delicate privilege of studying another culture. Those working with American Indians would be particularly troubled. And those from Columbia University would be, understandably, the most worried of all.

One would expect, furthermore, irritation at the source of this trauma: a young woman who, despite her obvious qualifications and potential, seemed to have been excessively independent, even headstrong—and careless.

The publicity would be even worse. The nation's press was still yellow enough to cluck with delight at the specter of "wild redmen" and "savages" confirming old stereotypes. It would not, however, be especially sympathetic to a woman venturing alone into man's territory—particularly an intellectual young New York woman— probably Jewish. The newspapers ran what appeared to be a doctored photo of Henrietta with a shortened nose, narrowed mouth, and intelligent beauty. It was a sensational story.

Meanwhile, the sensitive working relationship with the Indians, in this particular case the Apache, so assiduously developed in recent years, would be jeopardized. The bureaucrats and the old Indian hands of the Bureau of Indian Affairs, always suspicious of anthropologists, would now have cause to begin closing some doors.

This new "science," developed in Europe and given its most comprehensive and successful expression under these very Columbia professors, would again be subject to a mass of contemptuous public and academic opinion.

No wonder they were angry at Henrietta.

Franz Boas was in Europe—ill—when the murder occurred, and thus at a distance from the instantly developing controversy. He had obviously known and liked Henrietta, who had been his student in several courses and had worked with him. His tone appeared genuinely sorrowful and respectful. He wrote to Donner on the reservation that Henrietta "was a very faithful student and appeared sensible in every way and I have the greatest respect for her character." But there was reproach as well:

> Unfortunately Miss Schmerler did not follow the advice we gave her in regard to procedure. We wanted her to stay with an Indian family, or if that was impossible to engage a mature Indian girl to stay with her the entire time. I do not doubt from what I know of her character that the only reason she proceeded in this way was an excess of eagerness to bring home good results from her trip... In this respect I see a certain unmistakeable guilt on her part, that does not by any means do her dishonor.

Benedict had reviewed for Boas the instructions given to Henrietta:

> I talked over with Miss Schmerler a number of times the arrangements which she should make when she reached Whiteriver. I told her there were two possibilities: either she might live with a friendly Apache family where she trusted the middle-aged mother of the family who would look out for her and know where she was, or she might live by herself with a woman servant and companion.

Benedict did not explain, however, how Henrietta might find a family to fit this description immediately upon arrival on the reservation. She concluded:

> I believe that Miss Schmerler decided to make her own plans which differed from these instructions in a number of ways. The tragedy that occured [sic] was out of all proportion to

the error of judgment that I believe she made, and I have not spoken of my instructions to her except in this letter, feeling that it would be unnecessarily cruel for this comment to come to her family and friends.

In truth, Benedict—and the other Columbia anthropologists— were making it *widely* known that Henrietta had disregarded their instructions. But they were not willing—or able—to specify in public exactly what these instructions had been, or to produce anything in writing about them. The Bureau of Indian Affairs began asking Columbia immediately following the murder for the University's policy on fieldworkers and for the specific instructions given to Henrietta. The request of Frank Fackenthal, Secretary of Columbia University, to Boas or Benedict for these instructions went unanswered for a considerable time.

One reason for the vagueness was that the instructions were actually not so clear-cut. There were no written guidelines at all. Columbia, according to students of the period, commonly gave its fieldworkers a great deal of discretion in methodology, and not very much direction.

Despite the extensive exchange of letters the previous spring with southwestern anthropologists, and the numerous discussions about their varying suggestions, Henrietta had still arrived in Whiteriver on June 23 without any arrangements having been made for lodging, transportation, or companionship. She came with what appears to have been no more than informal, spoken advice, general and in some ways conflicting. The reservation superintendent had been surprised by her arrival, and complained that she had brought "no credentials or letter from the university." None of this was atypical of Columbia's approach to the field; instead, it reflected their sense of urgency to take advantage of all research opportunities while they still existed.

What *was* of great concern to Benedict, Underhill, Reichard, and others in the field that summer were the repercussions of the murder, the ensuing manhunt, and the prospective trial.

Naturally, those who were working daily with Indians on the reservations of the Southwest would think first, after the initial feelings of horror and sympathy, of the murder's effect on their own situations. Headlines in newspapers across the country like "BELIEVE INDIAN SLEW COLUMBIA GIRL WITH KNIFE," "SEIZE FIVE INDIANS IN SLAYING OF GIRL," "COLUMBIA GIRL FOUND SLAIN IN APACHE WILDS," "GIRL STUDYING INDIANS VANISHES IN ARIZONA," and "APACHES VEIL CO-ED KILLING" were not likely to increase the rapport between the anthropologists and their hosts.

Henrietta's tragedy would not be allowed by the determined Columbia scholars to interfere with their summer's fieldwork. "I have been anxious not to be too closely identified with the investigations at White River on account of the possibility of involving the group here, so I have heard nothing directly," wrote Benedict on July 28. "Fortunately, all this group here (Mescalero) are very much liked and working smoothly and quietly and I think our work will not be interrupted by this tragedy," she wrote on July 29. And, on the same day: "It has made much less stir here than I could have hoped. Unless some Indian is convicted and held, it seems unlikely there will be any feelings roused among them that will hinder our work. Most of them know nothing about it." Ruth Underhill, working with the Papago in nearby Sells, wrote, "My white people have been very nice about it and haven't made me pay any penalty at all. The snippy agent, though he thinks anthropologists are 'unconstructive' nevertheless has behaved like a gentleman. In fact, everything is going gloriously with me."

The anthropologists in Sells, Ganado, and Mescalero would, in fact, finish out their summer's fieldwork without major interruption. Benedict would ultimately concede that her party did not get out to live with families as much as she'd planned. "Henrietta's death made us observe some circumspection that was only to avoid any appearance of isolation," she would write Boas on August 24. She was forced to deny permission to one of her researchers to visit Silas John, notorious leader of an Apache religious cult, in Whiteriver.

Despite the bravado and their apparently successful tight-rope walk through the late summer of 1931, the anthropologists were deeply worried about the future of their fieldwork among the Indians. "Henrietta is still a nightmare and I dread the consequences," wrote Boas to Benedict on September 8.

In fact, Donner had informed the Secretary of Columbia University as early as July 31 that "under no consideration would I again permit a woman of her age to take up the branch of ethnology she was working on while here." The Bureau of Indian Affairs was already putting heavy pressure on Columbia to be more specific and more restrictive in its guidelines for fieldworkers, and beginning to design some new ones of its own.

Part Two:

THE HUNT FOR THE KILLER(S)

Chapter Eight

The Hunt Begins

*White River Apache Reservation, Ariz., July 27 (AP)—
The Spartanlike Apache, nearly as silent as the
pine-clad White Mountains among which the body of
Henrietta Schmerler was found, continued today to
mystify officers seeking a solution of the killing
of the 22-year-old Columbia University anthropology
student.*

It was not until Monday, July 27, three days after Henrietta's body was discovered, that the Justice Department arrived on the reservation and the search for the killer—or killers—began in earnest.

Everyone had known instantly, of course, that there was a murderer on the loose—and that it was highly likely that the murderer remained among them. With the exception of a band of Navajo who had been moving on and off the reservation as cow-herding needs dictated during the summer, there were few transients in the area. And there were no obvious suspects, no one known to have hated the white girl or who had reason to bother her, let alone kill her. True, some of the women may have resented the attention Henrietta had received from the men, and many had looked suspiciously at her free, confident movement about the reservation. But she was trying to be friendly, and a few of the younger women—like Mary Velesques and Edith and Bessie Sanchez—had tried to be helpful. Some of the white people, too, were skeptical of her work, especially those who knew she was critical of the way the Apache were treated by the whites. But none of this would have been a reason for murder.

The word went out quickly that this was most likely a sexual crime, and few on the reservation were shocked. White women had been attacked before, and young Apache women knew they were at risk from some of the younger Apache men. Agent Street later reported that Jesus Velesques told him, when Street first joined the case: "No white girl as well as no Indian girl is safe in living alone among the Apache Indians, as they have attempted to assault several white women in that vicinity in the last few years, and he (Velesques) knows it to be a fact that these young Indians are assaulting the Indian girls of that vicinity, and through fear the girls are not letting it be known." For them, it was a reality to be lived with.

There were immediate things to be taken care of before mobilizing a full-fledged search for the murderer. The body had to be cared for and returned to the east. Henrietta's personal effects needed sorting, separating those required in the search for the killer and as evidence for a future trial from those which could be returned to her family. Everyone needed to be notified; masses of letters and telegrams were sent because it could not be assumed that those concerned would hear the news on their own. Columbia University, the Schmerler family, the Bureau of Indian Affairs, the Justice Department, Congress, the Vice President of the United States—and the press—had to be kept fully informed. Superintendent Donner alone wrote dozens of letters, dictated to his secretary, Gertrude Cobb.

Much of Donner's energies were directed toward keeping things calm on the reservation—and convincing his correspondents that things were, in fact, very much under control. He wired his boss, John (C.J.) Rhoads, Commissioner of Indian Affairs, "Any reports of trouble between Indians and Whites entirely false. Whiteriver about coolest and quietest place in west. Unfortunate press is so exaggerating the case." Nevertheless, he privately wrote to the BIA asking that the superintendent of the San Carlos Apache reservation, who was experienced with tribal crises, be sent to Whiteriver immediately "to help us straighten out some trouble with some of our Indians." He would want to lock up some suspects in the case, to let everyone know that there would be a response. But he was pretty sure he'd have to wait until the federal investigators arrived before he'd get any meaningful information.

Over the weekend, two spontaneous encounters would take place that later took on greater significance:

An ad hoc investigating party consisting of Jesus Velesques, Chester Cummings, Dan Cooley, William Moffitt, and one or two others convened Sunday in East Fork. They met not far from Henrietta's cabin and the beginnings of the trail which they presumed she had been traveling before she was killed. As both Velesques and Cooley later told Agent Street in their first interviews with him, the group was sitting down and speculating about who might have seen Henrietta en route to the dance, if that indeed was where she had been heading, and what her exact route might have been that would have taken her to the bottom of that lonely canyon. Then Jack Keyes, who rarely missed a gathering but had not been seen much since the discovery of the body forty-eight hours earlier, rode up on horseback. After exchanging a few quick pleasantries, Cummings had said to Keyes: "Jack, this is a horrible crime and the Indians and the whites must join together and bring to justice the parties who were responsible for the murder of this girl." Keyes became very nervous, according to Cooley's statement, and after about a moment's hesitation pointed his finger at Cummings and Moffitt, the only two white men in the group, and said "You and you meet me at this place tomorrow morning and I will give you some information that will possibly solve this matter." Both Cooley and Velesques later independently told Street that it was their understanding that Cummings and Moffitt had returned the next morning but that Keyes did not show up. FBI records, however, do not show that Cummings, Moffitt, or Keyes was ever subsequently questioned about this incident.

At roughly the same time, Dr. Ray Ferguson was being visited in his Fort Apache office by a young Apache man who he later came to understand was Golney Seymour. As Ferguson was dressing the raw wound on his hand, the young man asked, "I wonder have they found out who murdered the white girl?" When told they had not, the young man said, "Maybe so it was a Navajo, a Negro, or a White Man."[6]

Early on Monday, United States Attorney John C. Gung'l and Special Agent John K. Wren of the Bureau of Investigation met up in Holbrook, Arizona, and headed south together the ninety-plus miles to Fort Apache.

Gung'l was in close touch with the reservation from his Tucson headquarters within minutes of the body's discovery the previous Friday. He asked Special Agent in Charge R.H. Colvin in El Paso to send the best man he had. Colvin quickly decided to send Wren, a longtime peace officer who had done considerable work with the Indian tribes and lived among them in Oklahoma and in Mexico, even though he knew Wren was working simultaneously on another case and would need to return in a "few days." (Wren had played a prominent role in solving the Osage Indian Murders of 1925; prior to that he had been a Texas Ranger during their controversial and violent involvement in the Mexican Revolution, 1918-19.)

By mid-day Monday, Wren and Gung'l had arrived in town, spoken at length to Donner, visited the spot where the body had been found, and set up a "court of inquiry" at the Whiteriver agency. Townsfolk milled curiously around, as they observed the beginnings of a long parade of interviewees summoned one at a time through the oak doors. None appeared more interested than Keyes and Samuel Seymour, identified in the FBI report as "Indian H. Fore" (aka "H-4"). Velesques, waiting for his own interview, observed Keyes and Seymour whispering together and was suspicious enough to walk by in an attempt to overhear their conversation. He heard enough to report later to Agent Street that Seymour had told Keyes, in Apache, to "Not tell them anything—to keep them thrown off the track." Whether Velesques reported this conversation to Wren that day is not recorded, but as a respected citizen and sometime confidant of Donner, it is unlikely he sat on this information—and

---

[6] Seymour is not the only one to have made such a suggestion. In a handwritten response found at the bottom of a sympathy letter from the superintendent of the Santa Fe Indian School, C.E. Faris, to Commissioner C.J. Rhoads immediately after Henrietta's body was discovered: "CJR" had written, "Thanks for this. But I am not prepared to admit an Indian did it. It may have been a white man, a Mexican, a negro, etc."

his suspicions—for too long.

After being briefed on Henrietta's stay on the reservation by Donner and Cummings, and getting eyewitness accounts from the two doctors who had viewed the body, Wren immediately focused his interviews on the Canyon Day dance. He wanted to hear all he could about Henrietta's actions just prior to the dance and the whereabouts of anyone who may have come into contact with her or been at Canyon Day that evening. Much of the earliest interview material established a vivid all-night scene at Canyon Day of casual comings and goings, singing and dancing, and a great deal of drinking. Missing from these descriptions is anything untoward or even particularly noteworthy—and any notice of Henrietta. Even young Mary Velesques [*who, as a tribal elder over half a century later, told us she had looked everywhere for Henrietta at the dance*] did not mention to Wren any attempt to locate Henrietta or any concern for her absence at the dance.

The questioning intensifies

The only interview to be transcribed verbatim, and sworn and witnessed, was that of Claude Gilbert, who was detained on August 1 as the "principal suspect." He described in careful detail his one encounter with Henrietta—on Friday evening—and his various activities on the Saturday of the dance. On Henrietta's porch Friday they had talked about some words and names, along with Keyes, and Gilbert said that he had left five minutes after Keyes had, carrying some gingersnaps Henrietta had given him. He added that he had mentioned, unasked, that he might drive by on his way to the dance. He said Henrietta had told him "she might catch a ride before that. That is all," Gilbert said.[7]

---

[7] This interview shed more light on Henrietta's own interview techniques than it did on the FBI's techniques or Henrietta's fate. Wren honed in on a piece of paper that had been found in Gilbert's trousers pocket when he had been arrested.

"Where did you get that paper from?"
"The white woman wanted to find out different things."
"When?'
"Friday night."
"And you put it in your pocket to take down to the dance? When did you put it in your

Gilbert and his wife were, it turned out, driven to the dance by friends whose car he helped fix. He said further that he had come home from the dance at sunup and had never thought about Henrietta that night.

---

pocket?"

"Saturday night when I changed my clothes to go down to the dance."

"Is that your writing?"

"My writing."

"Where did you write that?"

"At the woman's house. Out on the porch."

"When?"

"Friday."

"What pen did you use?"

"Fountain pen."

"Where did you get that pen?"

"She had it."

"Is all this writing in your handwriting?"

"No."

"What word is in your handwriting?"

"This." (the word "*anthropolar*")

"You state that word is not in your handwriting. I will ask you to write this word on this piece of paper. Now I'll ask you to look at the word 'anthropolar' as written on the piece of paper and the word 'anthropolar' as you have written it and see if they are not exactly the same."

"No, not the same."

"Now as a matter of fact, you wrote that word on that piece of paper. You wrote it on that other piece, too."

"No."

"It is the same writing, same slope, same curves, same "R," same "H.""

"No. I make a "P" different. I make an "R" different."

"Then you say you didn't write the word?"

"No, I didn't."

"Who did?"

"I don't know."

"Did the white woman write that word?"

"I don't know whether she did."

"Was it on that paper when you left the house?"

"I didn't look at it. I don't know just what was on it."

"Why did she give you that paper?"

"She wants to find out different meaning of Indian words."

"You already told her the different meanings of these words. Why didn't you leave this paper with her?"

"I just talked what it meant."

"That was for her. She should have kept this."

"She didn't want it. She just wanted the meaning."

"When you got down to the dance, did you look for this white girl?" Wren asked.

"I didn't look for anybody," answered Gilbert.

"Why didn't you look for this girl? You knew she was coming to the dance, didn't you? Why didn't you look for her?"

"You couldn't see anybody there. There was just crowds of people all around."

Wren then turned to the issue of why Gilbert would have led Henrietta to believe he might come by to drive her to the dance when, in fact, his car had been loaned out (to Father Augustine, no less) for ten days. "I said *if* my car was brought back," said Gilbert. And he continued to maintain, as Wren questioned this over and over again, that he was only thinking of giving Henrietta a ride *if* his car was somehow returned. Wren gave up and ended the interview.

Keyes was from all appearances an eager informant. He had had significant conversations with Henrietta the Friday night before her death, again on Saturday morning, and once more early Saturday evening, not long before she began the ride to Canyon Day. He took pains to point out that when he had left her home Friday evening, Gilbert had still been on her porch. Keyes said that he had spoken to Henrietta very early on Saturday from his pony as he took off for a long day of "hunting" his horses. On his return—at what he first estimated to be about 5:00 p.m., but then amended in later testimony to about 6:30, based on his revised thinking about the daylight—he had had a more extended conversation with her. She told him about her purchase of the Indian dress from Mary Velesques and her plans to wear it to the dance that night, and her expectation that Gilbert would be driving her to the dance.

Keyes's comments, as recorded by Wren from their July 27 interview, are, in hindsight, very explicit in many areas and noticeably vague in others. He is quoted as saying that, when he visited Henrietta that Saturday afternoon, Jack Perry was with him "and another man on the road behind." While he went in, said Keyes, "Perry and the other man went on." Later, Keyes stated to Wren that "he left her house about 5 o'clock and went home and did not see her again and did not see any automobile go to her house that afternoon, nor did he see any White man or Indian go there on a horse. *Said he did see two boys down on the road below* (emphasis added)."

It is not clear from the report whether Wren asked the identity of the "other man" or the two boys, or had any concern about this part of Keyes's story. What is virtually certain from subsequent events, including the murder confession and Keyes's later statement, is that the other man would have been Golney Seymour, and that the "two boys" were Golney and his brother-in-law Robert Gatewood.[8]

Immediately after Keyes spoke to Wren, Samuel Seymour, "H-4," was questioned through an interpreter. Keyes had mentioned that he had seen H-4, who lived with his wife 300 yards from Henrietta's cabin, "down the road towards Fort Apache" on Saturday evening. The elder Seymour told Wren that on Friday and Saturday he was cultivating his garden just across the road from Henrietta's house and periodically saw her sitting on her porch. He did not mention having seen anybody at the house other than Keyes, whom he said he passed on the road. He said that he had not seen Claude Gilbert at the house, but that he had seen him at the dance early Sunday morning.

Wren somehow "ascertained from the investigation and by interview" that "evidently Miss Schmerler's house was robbed after the murder and there were missing from her place a large, black suitcase, containing evidently some of her clothing, a diamond ring, worth about $300, and some of her notes taken from the Indians, as well as a book of ABA checks." Which of these items was missing from the break-in of July 12, which Henrietta had reported, and which from the break-in after her murder—if it occurred—remains unclear. Her extensive field notes were in the possession of the Justice Department for the duration of the trial. Most of the travelers' checks were later accounted for. As far as the "$300 diamond ring" was concerned, none of her family or friends had ever heard of, or even imagined, her having such a ring.

---

[8] In the margin of our original FBI report of Wren's interviews, next to Keyes's mention of the "other man," we had written, "Golney! (realized 8/90)." Our delayed understanding—two years after having first read the document—may have mirrored Wren's failure to take notice of the omission.

Looking outside the reservation for leads

U.S. Attorney Gung'l wired the El Paso office to ask that they take up with the New York Bureau office "the matter of interviewing a girl connected with the Anthropology Department of Columbia University whose first name was Bertha and whose last name began with the letter "C" with reference to a letter she had received from the deceased to ascertain if Miss Schmerler had mentioned the names of any Indians whom she feared or who might have threatened her." Bertha Cohen, an employee of the department and a friend of Henrietta's, responded to the investigators that she had "received one letter from the deceased shortly after her arrival in Whiteriver in which she expressed fright at the general conditions but mentioned no particular person or thing and gave no names of persons of whom she might be afraid."

Interviewed by the authors over 55 years later, Bertha Cohen tried with difficulty to remember any of the details of a traumatic episode she had long since attempted to forget. She professed shock at hearing from us that Henrietta had been sexually assaulted—"I just thought it was a regular murder" —and did not remember anyone trying to blame Benedict or Mead for faulty supervision. She thought she remembered Henrietta as a "very hard-working girl...."

Wren's lengthy report summarizing his six days on the reservation produced very detailed portraits of the festivities at the Canyon Day dance, the search for Henrietta, and the discovery of her body. It provides a sketchier picture of Henrietta's activities during her three and a half weeks on the reservation, focusing mainly on the warnings that those who were her hosts and guides say they gave her about living arrangements and dealings with the Apache people. Even less complete were the attempts to trace the comings and goings of individuals who might have passed her house on Saturday night or could give any clues as to who might have killed her. With Gilbert finally released, no active suspects remained.

Wren left the White Mountain Apache Reservation August 2 to resume his on-going work on the "Reynolds case." His departure, although anticipated, was not happy news for those on the reservation increasingly desperate to find the killer.

Why nearly three weeks passed between Wren's departure

and Street's arrival on the reservation remains a mystery. The gap is even more puzzling when it becomes clear, in retrospect, that in his first day on the reservation Wren was literally within inches of knowledge of the killer's identity—or at least face-to-face with one person who knew the murderer quite well. Donner tried to put the best face on the lost time when he wrote his boss on August 22, soon after Street appeared in Whiteriver: "To date we have been unable to find a definite clue leading to parties implicated in this murder. We have been letting the matter rest for a few days thinking that some of the Indians might gradually give out some information, which might give a working clue, but to date they either are very close mouthed or a very few of them know who committed the murder." He added: "Mr. Spear [he meant *Street*] of the Justice Department is with us this week and we are doing our best to find some evidence in this case."

Having quite clearly failed in their initial effort to penetrate what they assumed to be the unwillingness of the Apache to inform on any of their own, the lawmen continued dutifully to plod along other avenues. A voluminous correspondence between FBI offices and bank officials around the country to find the missing travelers' checks led nowhere. (It turned out that, of the $300 in checks originally drawn from the Corn Exchange Bank in New York City, thirteen of the $10 checks turned out to have been cashed by Henrietta, and the single $100 check was used by Henrietta's father, Elias, to pay his landlord, the Hotel Newton, on Broadway. The remaining seven checks were never found. One Corn Exchange executive, sounding bemused, suggested to the FBI that they forget this line of investigation since "experience had taught him that such checks are rarely ever presented at a bank for payment by the person who stole them.")

The FBI also persisted in attempting to track down Henrietta's friends in New York City—and, in one case, Cincinnati—to see if any of the letters they received may have contained clues to the killer. Freda Fine and Anita Bell, the intended recipients of the unsent letter found on Henrietta's writing table, expressed complete bafflement, since the first they had heard about Henrietta spending the summer doing fieldwork in Arizona was in a telegram from Donner asking what to do with the body. Bertha Cohen was interviewed at some length by Agent Connelly of the New York City office, but could remember in the letter she had received nothing beyond Henrietta's general concern over the conditions she faced. She added a strong endorsement of Henrietta's character, stating that "she had known her since 1929; that she was very studious and a girl of exemplary conduct; that she did not drink and was not the type of girl who would carouse in parties." The friend in Cincinnati had not heard at all from Henrietta.[9]

Others were not quite as calm about the lack of progress as the federal agents appeared to be. The Schmerler family could not understand why the murderer had not been caught. Henrietta's lawyer brother-in-law, Irv Meller, wrote repeatedly and increasingly urgently—to the reservation, to the Bureau of Indian Affairs, to Columbia University, and, finally, to the FBI—describing the agitation and impatience of Henrietta's father, Elias, and of other family members with the slow progress of the case. Frank Fackenthal, secretary of Columbia University, wrote: "The family of Miss Schmerler is quite naturally much stirred up over the loss of their daughter and are bringing pressure to bear on us for a thorough investigation."

Questions about Henrietta's character

Elias had become enraged when he saw Donner's lengthy July 27 report to the commissioner concluding that Henrietta was "extremely careless in her actions." He wrote to Assistant Commissioner C. Norris Millington: "Practically every cultured person is interested in a case of this kind, except Mr. Donner, to my great sorrow. I believe that I will be able to convince your Department in due time that Mr. Donner has been trying right from the start to prevaricate the true facts, and that in his report … he was trying to create an impression reflecting upon the conduct of the girl by various incorrect statements." In a report of his own August visit to New York City, Millington said that Elias Schmerler "is apparently quite determined that the Office of Indian Affairs was lax in regard to protection for his daughter and by our delay in starting an investigation. He feels that we have been unduly

---

[9] The name of the Cincinnati friend is one of the few excised in the FBI file that were not eventually revealed through my FOIA suit.

diligent in protecting the Indians and have not been on our toes in seeing that the guilty one or ones are brought to justice." Millington also mentioned that Elias had, in fact, repeatedly expressed the belief that the murder was a "tribal matter" which Donner was denying to keep from "reflecting on his own administration."

The family did not know about uglier suspicions that were already circulating about Henrietta's "indiscreet" behavior on the reservation, nor, for that matter, about the hunt for evidence of her sexual activity that began even before the search for the murderer got formally underway.

The siblings and friends of Henrietta who were still alive when our own investigation began almost sixty years later all professed shock and—for those with the energy for it—outrage at the suggestion of any inappropriate sexual behavior on Henrietta's part.

John Edgar Hoover was in his eighth year as director of the Bureau of Investigation when Henrietta was murdered in 1931. (It would officially become the United States Bureau of Investigation the following year and, finally, the Federal Bureau of Investigation in 1935.) He was notified by telegram the day after the body was found and would maintain a close personal interest in the case for the next several years. He inserted himself directly into the proceedings via a telegram on July 28, the day after his agent had arrived on the reservation: WIRE BRIEF SUMMARY NIGHT LETTER PROGRESS AGENT WREN INVESTIGATION INDIAN CASE ARRANGE SUBMIT FREQUENT REPORTS BIA.

Chapter Nine

Outsiders and More False Starts

Commissioner Rhoads's first telegram to Donner after the discovery of the body had been announced (sent from Bryn Mawr, Pennsylvania, on July 26) established his own priorities: MAKE SURE THAT INDIAN GETS SQUARE DEAL IN SCHMELER [SIC] CASE. CALL ON HAGERMAN AND FARIS FOR ASSISTANCE. DO YOU NEED LAWYER OR OTHER ADVISER. WIRE ANSWER.

Donner was quick to respond to the second suggestion: HAGERMAN OR FARIS COULD NOT BE OF ASSISTANCE.

Donner had good reason for his response. H.J. Hagerman had a long and controversial career as a diplomat, former governor of New Mexico, and official BIA appointee to "represent Indian interests." Under his current title, Special Commissioner to Negotiate with Indians, he had become a roving troubleshooter to the various reservations of the Southwest—and reservation superintendents had come increasingly to view him as an unwelcome meddler.

In 1906 Hagerman had been appointed by President Theodore Roosevelt as "reform governor" of New Mexico, and was fired by Roosevelt seventeen months later. Later in 1931, while the killer of Henrietta Schmerler was still being sought, he would achieve some notoriety for a less-than-thorough investigation of sexual misconduct charges against the superintendent of the Ute Reservation in Colorado.

Hagerman had already gotten his teeth into the Schmerler case, however. Rhoads had cabled him on July 26 to request, as he had of Donner, that Hagerman "help to see that Indians get a fair deal in Schmerler case." Although Hagerman was temporarily dissuaded by Donner's rejection of his offer to come to the reservation immediately, by August 9 he had made it to Whiteriver, along with Senator Carl Hayden (then serving the first of six legendary terms). Hagerman remained for two days, speaking at length to Donner and other white men on the reservation. Donner was at this point much disturbed both by Wren's departure when there had been little progress in solving the murder and by the lack of an immediate replacement; he was happy to have someone else to whom he could vent his increasing frustrations. Not least among those was his growing anger at Henrietta for what he was now portraying as gross indiscretions.

The hopes among the BIA and other government officials that the killer may not have been an Apache were clearly beginning to fade. Wren had left without having identified a suspect, but the talk around the reservation was that numerous members of the tribe knew who had committed the crime and were eager to keep this knowledge from the authorities. Hagerman's report of August 13 reflected this. After dutifully voicing some suspicions about the behavior of several white men on the reservation, he concluded: "It looks as if the crime was perpetrated by bad Indians." In what would soon become a torrent of recrimination from him, Hagerman then indicted Henrietta: "I don't believe tho' that even the worst of them would ever have done it unless she had—consciously or unconsciously—provoked them to excess."

The crime had not been solved after dozens of interviews, at the least, and there was no longer a federal investigator on the reservation. But, if his letters to Rhoads are an indication, this was of less moment to Hagerman than what he thought he had learned about Henrietta's character. "The U.S. Attorney has taken the case in charge—but Donner is watching and working every day to get clews and check up the various possible suspects. I believe they will get the truth in time," is all he said about the search for the killer.

But Hagerman had plenty to say about Henrietta.

"The woman...was not only indiscreet but—no doubt—much more than that," Hagerman wrote to Rhoads in the August 13 report, his ire building.

> The girl was most frightfully indiscreet—provocative would put it plainer—to the Indians, and what happened in her cabin prior to her murder is scarcely a matter of conjecture. She openly danced with the Indians all night—rode on the same ponies with them—and what she did at her cabin— seems, according to Donner's investigations not uncertain. Horrible—horrible—and these awfully dirty Indians! *[This may have been a particularly ironic comment, coming from a man whose title at the time was Special Commissioner to Negotiate with Indians.]* Her cabin when they found it was a filthy place. When she came in there Donner warned her in as plain language as he felt he could against too great familiarity. She wrote back to her friends in N.Y. saying that she had been warned to be careful or she might be raped and they found a letter from one of these girl friends of hers in reply—jocularly congratulating her—and saying that there were 1,400 old maids and young women there waiting to be raped. She told Donner that she was there to study the Indians' 'sex life.'

"Can you imagine such a rotten business—in the name of science and ethnology and apparently backed by a great university?" he concluded.

Hagerman's outrage was not solely the product of his own active imagination. Donner, who had been cordial to Henrietta during her stay and said she "seemed to get along very well" with the Apache, was feeling increasingly beleaguered and blamed. His reports of her actions—from her defiance of his and others' advice as to how to comport herself among the Apache to the by-then-current speculation that her transgressions may have included regular sexual activity—grew ever more critical in the weeks following.

Immediately following the discovery of the body, Dr. Hupp had taken vaginal smears using cotton swabs to check for the presence of sperm, a routine procedure for exploring the possibility of rape in homicide cases. The next day, lawmen investigating her cabin made the decision to collect several paper towels and tissues that appeared to have been thrown behind Henrietta's bed. According to Donner, who accompanied them, "I am frank to state that I had not thought of sending them to the laboratory had not these men suggested it, as at that time I personally did not suspicion the girl of any immoral actions."

Donner later explained to Ludvig Hektoen of the John McCormick Institute for Infectious Diseases in Chicago, whose lab examined the specimens and who had expressed mystification about the reason the paper towels had been sent: "The cotton swabs were for the purpose of determining whether Miss Schmerler had been raped, and the paper napkins were for information that might lead up not only to the motive for the murder but the probable guilty parties who had been at her home on various occasions immediately previous to the murder." *(In retrospect, the implicit assumption that 1931 forensics could assist in the identification of a rapist by examination of sperm cells is somewhat stupefying.)*

The laboratory, as anticipated, found the presence of spermatozoa on one of the cotton swabs "said to carry vaginal smears." The finding on the paper towels was only slightly less definitive: "While complete spermatozoa have not been found, due, I think, to the softness of the texture of the paper, there is no doubt but that heads of spermatozoa are present."

For U.S. Attorney Gung'l, who had originally ordered the smears to be taken, the evidence of sperm was an important development in the search for the killer, indicating that "the squaws [the focus of many early theories of Henrietta's murder] can be eliminated from further suspicion." But he took an additional leap when he asserted, upon hearing that "sperm heads" were found on the paper towels, that this was "in my mind conclusive evidence that she had been carrying on illicit relations with these young Indian men."

Gladys Reichard comes to help

Gladys Reichard was an assistant professor of anthropology at Barnard who had taught Henrietta the previous fall in Anthropology 203: Research Work in Anthropology. She also happened to be spending her summer—one of many there in a long and illustrious career—with the Hubbell family at what later would become famous as the "Hubbell Trading Post," long a center of Navajo culture and ethnologic study and now a national historic site, 130 miles away in Ganado, Arizona. Her *Social Life of the Navajo Indians* (1928) had already won her some recognition in the field; her masterwork, *Spider Woman: A Story of Navajo Weavers and Chanters*, would be published in 1934.

As the closest Columbia anthropologist to the scene, Reichard reacted quickly. She cabled Donner on July 26: I AM INSTRUCTOR HENRIETTA SCHMERLER AT GANADO ARIZONA. CAN I HELP YOU ANY? IF SO I WILL COME. AM WILLING TO DO ALL I CAN.

Donner responded with his reflexive NOTHING YOU CAN DO HERE AT PRESENT. But he followed with: WILL BE GLAD TO HAVE YOU COME HERE SOME TIME AT YOUR CONVENIENCE AND PERSONALLY HEAR FACTS OF CASE.

Reichard paid her visit to the Apache reservation little more than a week later, accompanied by "young Mrs. (Dorothy) Hubbell." Reichard set about immediately to convince a wary Donner that she was quite different from the youthful and inexperienced Henrietta. (She had turned thirty-eight the day before Henrietta was killed.) Apparently she succeeded, since, as Hagerman reported, "Donner seemed to think very well of her—that she is an entirely different sort from the murdered girl—much saner, sounder et cetera."

It did not hurt that she brought stories providing some validation for the changing picture of Henrietta's probity. Hagerman reported: "She told Donner that the Schmerler girl had never had any attention from men in N.Y.—was crazy and indiscreet and all that sort of stuff—that her friends in N.Y. knew it and that no doubt this job with its particular sex angle wasn't suited to her, women who understood it better (like herself, I suppose) should have been sent—or stuff to that effect. Can you imagine? Messy beyond words!"

And Donner himself heard from Reichard what he needed for his own purposes. "She did not condemn the local administration, but rather condemned her own administrative office in sending this inexperienced woman to the Fort Apache Reservation, especially in view of the fact that they knew considerable about the woman before they sent her out."

A challenge to fieldwork

Reichard may have intuitively sensed, in separating herself from Henrietta, what she could not at the time have fully known: that the BIA and all others concerned with tribal matters in the Southwest were already in heated discussion about how completely—and how quickly—to remove fieldworkers from reservations. Reichard herself was the object of immediate discussion. Secretary Fackenthal of Columbia University tried to assure Assistant BIA Commissioner Millington that Reichard was "a girl of experience in the field of research work and was apparently doing a very satisfactory job from the standpoint of the university."

Millington noted in his subsequent report to his boss: "In view of the fact that the reports which we have in the Office concerning this person say that she seems to show a considerable degree of ability and tack [sic], I did not even suggest to him that she be withdrawn at this time." He went on: "I did, however, suggest to him that he take up with Professor Boaz [sic], immediately upon his return from Europe, the question of sending young single women, inexperienced, out to do this type of work in the future. I also mentioned that it had been suggested by Mr. Rhoads that we might refuse permits and letters of introduction to single women for research work on reservations in the future."

Hagerman, of course, was not buying. He did not get to meet Reichard himself, but noted, "However, I heard enough about her at Gallup from three different sources, to warrant me in believing that, while she is, no doubt, a much more sophisticated person than the poor murdered girl—and, no doubt, a clever ethnologist, whatever that may mean—she has the same trend. I am sure that—with this Apache horror in mind—she would be much better off away from the Navajo reservation altogether."

Hagerman wanted action. He wrote to Rhoads: "It seems to me that if you or Sec'y Wilbur could personally get in touch with Nicolas Murray Butler or some one else high in authority at Columbia and have her [Reichard] quietly withdrawn, it would be much the best method, don't you? And if there are any other young women from this or any other institution on Indian Reservations, delving, under the guise of science, into this sort of stuff, by all means we should get them to quit and prohibit further analyses of such sort."

Hagerman's particular fulminations were dismissed by the authorities, but the notion of imposing tough new restrictions on fieldwork caught on quickly. Later that year, under pressure from the BIA, Ruth Benedict would draft a new, greatly toughened set of guidelines for fieldworkers, which was then submitted over Franz Boas's signature.

Enter Agent Street

With the second FBI agent, J. A. Street, finally in place on August 21, reservation officials were forced to face once again the fact that a murderer was still free. It was evident from Street's initial orientation conversation with Superintendent Donner that little progress had been made in the nineteen days since Wren had departed, and some on the reservation still clung to the hope that the murder may not have been committed by an Apache. In fact, Donner reported to Street soon after they met "his belief that possibly some of the white men at Ft. Apache might have something to do with the murder of the deceased." However, he immediately undermined that belief by reporting that the whereabouts of one of the two men he suspected, Francis Warner, was accounted for on the night of the murder, and that the other man (someone he knew only as Bruce) had not been shown to have even been acquainted with Henrietta. When pushed by Street, Donner conceded that, in any event, "his only suspicion relative to these two parties is that they may have influenced some of these young Indian bucks to have murdered the white girl."

What became abundantly clear to Street, almost immediately after arriving in Whiteriver, was that Keyes might well be crucial to identifying the killer. Indeed, Keyes was, in the minds of many of the professional and amateur investigators, quite clearly someone who knew a lot more than he was telling. W. A. Lee, owner of the town's general store, was blunt in his assessment of Keyes. During his interview on that first day, Lee told Street that "If Jack Keys [sic]...would do so, he could put his finger on the one who murdered the girl, but doubted him doing so through fear and also that Keys wanted to be a leader of the tribe and might think that would cause him trouble in that way." Lee further stated that he, Lee, had known Keys in his school days; that at the time he was principal of the Indian School, Keys was one of his pupils and one occasion he found that Keys was attempting to make the younger Indians believe that he was a medicine man; that he had a group of younger Indian boys before whom he was pretending to perform miracles, leading them to believe that he was something superior; that he found this out and gave Keys a good trouncing and that stopped his career at that time; that Keys is not a Catholic but is a leader of some other religious organization; and while he paid his debts and is considered honest, he is a *very treacherous Indian and an agitator* [italics in original FBI report], and would probably promote and protect a crime of this kind; that it might be possible that he could be induced to tell what he knows relative to this matter for a small sum of money."

Dan Cooley, described in the FBI report as a "half-breed Apache Indian" and operator of the pumping station at Fort Apache, told Street about the incident in town, two days after discovery of the body, when Keyes had excitedly said to Cummings and Moffitt that he would give them some information which could help the solve the case the next day and then didn't show. "Mr. Cooley is strong in his belief that Keyes *and Apache Indian H-4* [have] information as to who the parties are who murdered this girl."[10]

Finally, Jesus Velesques also told Street about the Sunday gathering where Keyes suggested that he had information about the crime and told the two white men in the group, Cummings and Moffitt, to meet him the next day. Moreover, he told Street about the "whispering conversation" he overheard between Keyes and "Indian H. Fore" the following day, where, as he walked by, he heard Keyes tell H-4 in the Apache language to "Not tell them anything—to keep them thrown off the track."

When he finally spoke to Keyes, Street was armed with these suspicions. He interviewed him for more than two hours. He

---

[10] The FBI report was actually typed this way: "… in his belief that Jack Keys, an (sic?) Apache Indian H4, has information…" It appears that the typist—whom we know from Street's own less-literate handwritten notes was someone other than Street—thought H-4 was just a further description of Keyes instead of the designation of a separate man, Samuel Seymour. Whether this delayed further investigation of Seymour is unclear.

reported: "He talked fair English and understands more than he will admit, and when he does not care to answer a question he pretends not to understand. Agent handled him in a very careful manner."

Street led Keyes through the various (and numerous) connections that Keyes had had to Henrietta during her weeks on the reservation, and focused particularly on the events of the final two days of her life, Keyes's subsequent realization that she was missing, and the search. Street does not give any indication in his report of having caught an important contradiction in Keyes telling him that, other than Jack Perry, he had seen no one in the vicinity of Henrietta's house in the late afternoon of July 18. (As noted earlier, Keyes had told Agent Wren weeks before that there was "another man on the road behind" Perry, who went on when Perry went into Henrietta's yard. Keyes had also mentioned in that earlier interview that later he had seen "two boys on the road below" as he left Henrietta's house, and that he had also seen H-4 at that time going down the road to Fort Apache.) Nor did Street ask Keyes about the statements by those who said that they had heard Keyes promise some information which could solve the murder, nor did he ask about the "whispering conversation" with H-4 nor, in fact, about *any* connection Keyes might have had with H-4.

The "careful handling" of Keyes was more than likely motivated by a desire not to frighten or antagonize someone he believed could solve the crime for him. He appealed instead to Keyes's sense of tribal loyalty, his pride as a leader, and his self-interest, though not necessarily in that order. Street reported that he

> insisted to Mr. Keys that, he being the leader of the Indians, that this would be a great reflection on the Apache Tribe if the murderer of this white girl was not found and punished according to law. Mr. Keys became nervous and stated that it was possible that he could later obtain information as to who the party or parties were, and if possible, he would do so and so inform the authorities. Agent then asked Keys if in his opinion a little money might be of assistance in getting information as to who the guilty parties were, and Mr. Keys stated that he believed it would; that if he had a few dollars he

believed he could get information that would assist in solving this murder.

As with so many other aspects of this Depression Era case, the "little money" that Keyes suggested might buy some information proved harder to pry out of the Justice Department than it might in other times have been. Street had Colvin cable a request to J. Edgar Hoover for "a reasonable amount of money, say $50 to $75," which would be supplemented by some money from Superintendent Donner. "I am confident that Keys knows to a reasonable degree of certainty who committed this crime but, like most Apaches, aside from his native reluctance to give information against a tribesman he is also avaricious," Street wrote. Hoover ultimately approved the request, but only "for a reasonable sum not to exceed $50."

It is one of the remarkable sidelights of a search which ultimately lasted over three months that Street left the reservation after his initial eight-day visit without having penetrated further into the secrets to which Keyes—as virtually everyone (including Street) believed—was apparently privy. During his first visit, Street spoke formally to Keyes only once, and he did not speak to H-4 (Samuel Seymour) at all. He concluded his report with a short section entitled "Undeveloped Leads," where he stated:

> At the proper time, will again interview Jack Keys and Indian H. Fore, as it is believed they can give valuable information in solving this matter, if they can be induced to do so.

The reservation is left on its own once again

When Street left the reservation August 29 to testify in an ongoing case in Santa Fe, the BIA people were frantic at being left once again without federal help in tracking the murderer. Donner and Rhoads wired Colvin repeatedly about getting Street back, and ultimately Senator Hayden, Assistant Attorney General Nugent Dodds, and Hoover himself were barraged with requests for Street's speedy return. In the first of several formal explanations, Colvin wrote Donner September 17: "I received a long distance telephone call from Washington this morning to the effect that you were somewhat perturbed at the recall of Agent J. A. Street."

Colvin explained that Street's mandatory court appearance had not been concluded until September 3, after which Street had to conduct "urgent business" in Roswell and Carlsbad, NM, on the way back to Texas. Street arrived in El Paso (his home and Colvin's regional FBI headquarters) on September 5, "having taken ill on the road," and, even after a week of sick leave, said Colvin,

> is still in very bad condition. Agent Street advised me today that the doctor stated that he might be able to go to work in a few days, but I am afraid that his condition is worse than he suspects and that it may be a week or ten days before he is able to proceed to Whiteriver. My opinion coincides with yours in that Agent Street is the logical man to conclude the investigation and it would be a mistake to send a different agent on this job, and I wish to assure you that Agent Street will resume the investigation at the earliest possible date and will not be recalled (emergencies excepted) as long as he appears to be accomplishing anything toward the solution of this crime.

Colvin's resolve to send Street back to the reservation was not his alone. Hoover had been following events carefully from Washington, getting reports from the Attorney General's office as well as from his men in the field. Colvin understood that the Bureau of Investigation now considered bringing Henrietta's murderer to justice to be a top priority, and that Street was their best hope for doing that. Meanwhile, in Street's absence, Hoover offered his reassurance to the BIA that Colvin "has been instructed to give the case appropriate attention."

As was the case when the reservation was previously left without an FBI man on site, however, attention turned again to New York City and the search for information from Henrietta's friends. They had already reported that her letters gave no indication of specific problems that Henrietta was having or of people she felt threatened by, but the FBI continued to pursue that line of inquiry. Frank Fackenthal and Bertha Cohen were both interviewed again, this time by an Agent Carver; they repeated that they had heard nothing further.

Carver did, however, speak to someone at Columbia who reported that "they had also given her instruction ... as to the manner of dress which she should adopt, pointing out to her that knickerbockers and puttees were particularly offensive to Indian women and that she should avoid appearing in such dress, but that from the information reaching them it appeared she had adopted her own ideas which were contrary to their own suggestions." This informant also stated that "in this connection that she felt that Columbia University did not deserve the blame for having sent the victim out as ninety-one other young ladies in the past several years have undertaken similar work among the Indians under customary instructions, without untoward incident."

This informant's name—one of only three remaining in contention after two years of a FOIA suit—remained blacked out in the final version of the FBI documents we received, despite a ruling from U.S. District Judge Gerhard Gesell in 1988 that we were entitled to know all the names in the file. We believe that this informant was almost certainly Ruth Benedict or Margaret Mead, since they and Franz Boas were the only people known to have given Henrietta guidance on her fieldwork, the information came from a Columbia employee, and the pronoun in this case was "she."[11]

Echoing a theme that had already been frequently introduced by the Columbia anthropologists and was later offered by the defense at the trial, this informant also made the "general observation that the victim had failed to observe the instructions issued to her by the University; that she was warned of the danger of living alone and admonished that she should preferably live with an Indian family where there were young girls, who should accompany her in her work; that she was assigned to investigate the Indian children and that

---

[11] The Second Circuit Court of Appeals reversed Gesell's decision in Schmerler v. FBI, 1990. This decision was effectively overturned by the Supreme Court's later Landano v. U.S. ruling (1993), which effectively gave us the right to the small amount of material remaining in contention. The government acknowledged this legal obligation, but the bureaucratic obstacles proved larger than the anticipated pay-off (we had the information we needed), and we abandoned the pursuit. Ironically, and bitterly for us, during the three years between the Court of Appeals and Supreme Court decisions, Schmerler v. FBI was used as precedent *against* the claims of Freedom of Information Act requesters.

such an assignment did not necessitate her contacts and association with the mature male residents of the Reservation." *It should be noted that the planned subject of Henrietta's research had been more often described, previously, as family or social mores or the role of women than as "the Indian children."*

It may be understandable that local BIA and law enforcement officials would be reluctant to pursue active leads to the uncaught murderer(s) on their own, without an FBI man present. Nevertheless, the continuing delay—and the repetitive, seemingly unnecessary interviews with New York informants—loomed even larger with Street's own conclusion, in his August 31 report upon leaving the reservation, that "information was obtained that some of the Apache leaders do know the guilty parties." That report even described the context of the murder exactly as it later turned out to be: "Indications are that deceased was lured to this isolated spot by some person or persons on horseback under the pretext that this trail was a near way from her house to Canyon Day where the Indian dance which she was supposed to attend on the night of July 18, was to take place."

Chapter Ten

The FBI Gets Serious

Street finally returned to the reservation on October 3, five weeks after he had left, but he was not happy to be back. Whatever had disturbed his stomach in September was still not totally gone from his system. In fact, he needed to be admonished to remain until the case was solved. On October 17, Colvin wrote:

> I note what you say about wanting to get away from there, and I know it is not very pleasant perhaps to eat the "grub" they have there. However, since it is such a hard place to get to, I want you to stay there as long as you can possibly do any good. The Bureau is very anxious to solve this murder and we must leave no possible stone unturned. I do not like the idea of you coming out of there and then having to go back again and, therefore, want you to continue your efforts just as long as there is a possible lead which has not been thoroughly run down.

It was in that same October 17 letter that the earliest reference to Golney Seymour appears in the FBI file. Colvin refers to Street's note of "the 15th instant": "I think you have a good lead in regard to Seymour and Gatewood and want you to do your best to break it." There is no exact record of when the two men first came to Street's

attention. However, H-4's son
and son-in-law became prime
suspects sometime after Street
wrote on August 31 that "some
of the Apache leaders do know
the guilty parties," identifying
Keyes and H-4 as possessing
important information, and
before he wrote to Colvin on
October 15.

FBI Agent J. A. Street

Two more weeks would
go by before Street first directly
approached Gatewood or
Golney Seymour.

Street's activities during those weeks back on the reservation
remain shrouded in some mystery. Part of what makes it difficult to
get at the truth of his investigation is the selectivity of the information
the Bureau released to—and withheld from—the press after the
arrest several weeks later. In those early days following the arrest,
Street was under clear instructions not to talk with the media. He
reassured Hoover in an early report that, beyond confirming that
Golney Seymour was in custody, he gave nothing to the multitude
of reporters from all around the country who were "annoying" him
constantly for information.

Most of the stories describing Street's work maintained that
he operated incognito among the Apache. The Associated Press,
normally more sober and accurate than its overheated journalistic
rivals in reporting on the case, said that Street "disguised himself as an
Apache brave." One of the many detective or "men's" magazines that
carried articles about the case quoted a purported "extract from the
confidential report of Detective Street," in which Street supposedly
said, "I've been on this murder case now for six months. I've lived with
the Indians, hunted with them, eaten and slept with them, and I'm
sure nobody knows I'm a white man."[12] And a Memphis newspaper

---

[12] We never saw any such report and believe *Illustrated Detective Magazine* fabricated
the quote.

reported that Street "disappeared into the Apache country, lived and spoke as an Apache… and finally returned to his headquarters with a solution and a confession."

What's more, there was little heard from Street himself during that time. He returned with the confession in hand "just as department officials were beginning to worry over his long absence. They had not heard from him for several weeks," reported the AP. This was a distinct exaggeration, but it was true that neither the home office nor Donner at reservation headquarters heard from him nearly as often as before.

As he had promised five weeks earlier, Street now focused from the outset on the belief that Jack Keyes and Samuel Seymour could identify the killer. In fact, the two sources he most trusted, Jesus Velesques and Dan Cooley, both told him clearly on his first day back that they were convinced that "it was some of the near relatives or friends" of Keyes or Seymour who had murdered the white girl. Cooley, in private conferences on various occasions, insisted to him that, "while he did not have specific information… he believed beyond a doubt" that Golney Seymour or Robert Gatewood, or both, were responsible for the murder.

Street continued to use Velesques and Cooley throughout the month as "confidential informants," in his words. He described Cooley as a "half-breed Apache… married to a white woman," who had an "excellent reputation." Velesques, according to Street, was an American-born Mexican who married an Apache "Indian squaw," had been a "government scout," and had "rendered valuable assistance in the apprehension of the famous Apache Indian Geronimo." *[This last assertion would appear unlikely, since Geronimo's final surrender took place in 1886, forty-five years earlier; Velesques would have had to have been a boy then, at most.]* Strangely, given what appears to be Velesques's generally good standing with the Apache tribespeople, Street mentions parenthetically in his report that "Mr. Velesques refers to the Apache Indians as savages."

It was Keyes who drew most of Street's attention. Street reported that, during this time, he was "continually contacting and having interviews" with Keyes, who he was sure could give him the name of the murderer. "Agent used every means possible to get Keyes to divulge some information regarding the matter, never meeting Keyes without making a date with him and having him come to agent's room where agent would interview him for hours at a time, often bringing the Chief to the point where it looked like he was going to divulge something, but would never give any information, always stating that he believed it was the white man, Warner, or Claude Gilbert, the Apache San Carlos Indian, who was guilty of the murder."

Street began to shadow Keyes. He had been told by Velesques that Keyes and Samuel Seymour had never been close before the murder but had become inseparable since. Street noticed on several occasions that Keyes, after leaving an interview with him, would meet up with Seymour on his way back to camp or just outside of town. Seymour, on the other hand, was rarely spotted near the Agency.

In a crucial interview on October 10, Silas Classey, an Apache interpreter, said that toward sundown on the day of the dance, he and Paul Johnson were "working on an old Ford car" up the road which led from Henrietta's house to Canyon Day. He saw Samuel Seymour's wife and daughter pass on horseback in the direction of Canyon Day, and soon after that Golney Seymour and Robert Gatewood came from the opposite direction, stopped briefly to talk, and then headed toward Seymour's camp "and the white girl's house." Jesus Velesques told Street that, from his own inquiries, he gathered that Golney was telling other Apaches that he had accompanied his mother and sister to the dance. However, it was clear that he had not been with them.

Meanwhile, Street was hearing Golney Seymour's and Robert Gatewood's names mentioned through another line of inquiry. "Knowing the disposition of the Indian as agent does—that after an Indian has participated in some crime he usually will flee from the place where the crime was committed, stay away for a few days, and then probably return," Street elicited a list of "five or six Indians" who had been away from the vicinity during the July 18–24 period when it was realized that Henrietta was missing and the search for her had begun. Golney Seymour, Robert Gatewood, Jack Perry, and Amos Massey stood out as men who did not normally work much with cattle, but were nevertheless said to be off in the cattle camps during most of that time.

Street now saw that many of the Apache were spread out around the reservation, coming in and out of the towns and spending much of their time in the hills. Donner had just negotiated a major cattle deal with some California ranchers, who would expect the cows to be turned over to them around October 20. Because work was so hard to come by at that time, most of the men were eager to be out participating in the cattle roundups. The streets of Whiteriver and Fort Apache were often all but deserted.

Street headed out to the camps himself, looking for leads. He "began to visit the different round-ups, obtaining any conveyance possible, where the roads were passable, using an automobile, but mostly using a horse, going to the different round-up camps, interviewing the stockmen in charge of the round-ups, who were usually white men, but using Indian cowboys." He shadowed some of the Indians and picked up "a number of leads," but usually discovered them to be of no value.

As he pursued his investigation, Street took special interest in Samuel and Golney Seymour and Robert Gatewood. He noticed that if they were present, whenever he "would approach a bunch of Indians at any gathering, at cattle round-ups, while shipping cattle from McNary, and at the Indian Fair which was held at Whiteriver, these parties [the Seymours and Gatewood] would usually sneak away, seemingly not wanting to be in agent's presence."

On Sunday, October 24, five days before making an arrest, Street went to Keyes' camp to pay him a rare visit, as he had been unable to get in touch with him "for a day or two." He found Samuel and Golney Seymour, Robert Gatewood, and Edward Jennings with Keyes, and all of them appeared to him unusually nervous. To respect Keyes' need to keep his "confidential informant" status private, Street made up a story about being sent by Superintendent Donner to get them all to come to a cattle weigh-in that Tuesday.

As he left that gathering, Street whispered to Keyes, out of the sight of the others, to come talk to him the next day. Keyes showed up dutifully at Street's room the next morning and, in response to Street's increasingly insistent questions, continued to deny any further knowledge of the murderer. Street told him, forcefully, that he was sure Keyes knew who the murderer was and that he was demanding the truth. At this point, according to Street, "the Chief cried." He swore he would bring back some valuable information from the cattle roundup he was on his way to in McNary, if Street would let him go there. Street assented, then followed him there at a distance. About a mile and a half from McNary, Street watched as the two Seymours and Gatewood joined Keyes.

Tuesday, at the weigh-in at McNary, Street watched the Seymours and Gatewood disappear into the large crowd upon his approach. Soon afterward, he ran into Velesques, who provided the final exclamation point to Street's new certainty about the killers. Velesques said he had obtained information from a "squaw known as B-6" that she had been told by Golney Seymour's mother that Golney, Robert Gatewood, and Jack Perry "were seen sitting on their horses talking to the white girl in front of her house, at which time she had given them a drink of water." (Street says he later spoke to B-6, who denied having made that statement, but concluded "from her actions that she was denying this through fear.") Velesques said it was now "his belief beyond a doubt that Golney Seymour and Robert Gatewood were the murderers of the white girl."

Despite the extensive—and often imaginative—press accounts, Street had never pretended to be an Indian. In one of the first news stories to get closer to the truth, a week after the arrests, Street "laughed over the suggestion he had disguised himself as an Indian. As a matter of fact, he had posed originally as a cattle buyer and, later, had declared himself a detective seeking the killer of the white woman."

Closing in

With signs pointing increasingly to three suspects, Street decided finally to take action. On October 29 he asked Donner to have Golney Seymour, Robert Gatewood, and Jack Perry (who had been seen with the other two in Henrietta's yard on July 18) brought in for questioning. "Tulapai Bill" Maupin, a white officer in the BIA police force, brought in Seymour and Gatewood the next day, "keeping them separated," as instructed by Street. (Perry was apparently off in some remote part of the reservation on a hunting trip.)

What actually happened during the interviews leading to the confession is, again, clouded by some confusion, mainly because our primary supplementary sources, beyond the FBI reports, are the various dramatizations in detective and adventure magazines and some colorful newspaper stories. Some of these accounts clearly had the backing of the FBI publicity machine, and some details, when examined against the original documentation of events, have the ring of authenticity. Others are blatantly fictionalized. (An example: "J-39, with a Few

Drops of 'Water,' Traps Apache Murderer," from the New York World Telegram, *January 31, 1933.)*

Even before giving the order to bring in the three suspects, Street had made a call to his friend Ted Shipley, of the San Carlos Apache reservation police, asking him to bring Tom Dosela—"who is the official Apache Court Interpreter at Globe, Arizona, and who has interpreted for agent in several murder cases on the San Carlos Apache Indian Reservation, and who agent knows to be an honest and reliable Indian"—to Whiteriver. Street reported that he "was strong in his belief that the Whiteriver interpreters would not interpret correctly if they were used when Seymour and Gatewood were interviewed." "This may have been a misapprehension on the part of agent," he noted, "but he desired to take no chances." He also pointed out that he noticed a "look of disgust on their [the two interpreters in the Whiteriver office] faces at the appearance of Dosela." In fact, he kept Dosela "under cover" until Saturday morning, when the suspects were first questioned.

Golney Seymour was the first to be interviewed, and he vehemently denied any knowledge of the murder. He told Street he had never met Henrietta, although he had seen her on numerous occasions. He repeatedly stated, through interpreter Dosela, that he had never once spoken to her. He also told Street that he had gone to the Canyon Day dance on July 18 with his mother and sister. Street did not directly contest Golney's story in that initial interview, although he sometimes asked the same question again and again. But despite Golney's simple, consistent, and adamant responses, Street was confirmed in feeling that "subject's actions proved his guilt." Specifically, Street had already learned from several other informants that Alva Seymour and Bessie Gatewood (Golney's mother and sister) were seen en route to the dance… alone.

In Street's two reports of this interview, its length was described variously as "more than two hours" (November 4 case report) and "about four hours" (November 9 letter to J. Edgar Hoover). As far as we can tell, these are the only accounts of Golney's first examination ever provided. Despite the inconsistencies in the two reports (Street also contradicts himself on the days of the week on which the interviews took place, the dates, and how long it took the police to bring in the suspects, among other things), we have chosen to accept his general account of this particular interview. Overall, it is clear that Golney offered him no new information on his relationship to the murder—and gave Street only one new item to work with: his declaration that he went to the dance with his mother and sister. What we will never know, of course, is the amount of duress applied to Seymour during this meeting and subsequent ones. It is clear that, in this first interview, he stuck to his story of complete innocence.

Before Gatewood was brought into the interrogation room (actually a small anteroom just off the main reception area), Street took pains to see that Golney was safely back in one of the two cells in the rear of the building. He wanted no contact of any sort—even eye contact—between the two brothers-in-law.

From the outset of his interview, Gatewood denied having any information about the murder. He made it very clear that he had never met Henrietta and certainly had never spoken to her. He said that he had not gone to the Canyon Day Dance, and, in fact, had gone to sleep early that night in his own camp. But he did provide significant new information on his and Golney's movements throughout the afternoon before the dance.

Gatewood told Street that they had ridden their horses past Henrietta's house sometime after 5 p.m. and saw her give Jack Perry, sitting on his horse, a cup of water. Gatewood said he opened the gate to Samuel Seymour's camp across the road, then waited as Golney went over briefly to speak with Perry and the girl. He said he did not know what they had said to each other, and did not ask. After a minute or two, Golney rejoined him and they continued into his father-in-law's camp. No one was there, he said, which meant presumably that Samuel Seymour, his wife, and his daughter (Gatewood's wife) had already left for the dance. Gatewood said he then returned to his own camp, leaving Golney behind, and "knew nothing about what happened later."

As the questioning continued ("until about dark," reported Street), Gatewood became increasingly reticent, refusing to answer many of Street's questions, and was visibly quite nervous. Street knew "from his actions that he was not telling the truth and was holding something back through fear or from some other cause." He saw Gatewood glancing repeatedly at the interpreter, Dosela.

At this point, Street arranged to have Golney Seymour transported from the Whiteriver headquarters to the McNary, Arizona, jail twenty-two miles away, to spend the night separated from Gatewood. Donner approved the plan, and Officer Maupin led Golney away.

Meanwhile, Street dismissed Dosela for the day, and asked Velesques to bring Gatewood to the Whiteriver jail, with specific instructions that no other Indian was allowed near the jail. He told Velesques ("in Spanish, there being no one present who understood Spanish") to speak to Gatewood in Apache and try to find out why he was so nervous and would not talk. He told Velesques he would wait for him at the little café just up the street from headquarters, where they would have a late supper together.

When Velesques did not return within half an hour, Street wandered toward the jail. From a distance he could see Velesques and Gatewood, in front of the jail door, in animated conversation. He turned quickly and returned to the headquarters office.

Shortly after, Velesques returned with the news that Gatewood "desired to tell the truth in the whole matter." The problem was that the interpreter was Apache and that "if he [Gatewood] divulged what he knew in the presence of the interpreter, he being an Indian, he would tell the other Indians, and he believed they would murder him if they ever had the opportunity, for divulging what he knew." Velesques reported that Gatewood was willing to tell the story—but in the presence of Velesques, Street, and Donner only, and only on the condition that it be kept secret. Street asked Velesques if he would be willing to remain in Whiteriver overnight, as his ranch was five miles away, and Velesques agreed.

Saturday, October 31, was also the night of the Halloween dance in Whiteriver. This was, understandably, a dance primarily for the whites of the reservation, most of whom seemed to attend. Only a few Apache were there. Nevertheless, Street waited until after midnight, when almost everyone but a few inexhaustible dancers had gone to bed, before asking Velesques to bring Gatewood, without anyone seeing, to his (Street's) room.

Gatewood gives his statement

Gatewood's signed statement is presented in full below. According to Street's November 4 report, it was "taken in long hand" by Street and read back to Gatewood that night in both English (by Street) and Apache (by Velesques), in the presence of Superintendent Donner, who had been wakened for that purpose. Before signing the document, Gatewood was "advised by Mr. Donner and Mr. Velesques that the Government did not want him to tell anything but the truth and if he told the truth it would be kept a secret from the Indians in as much as possible; that he would probably have to testify in Court but before and after doing so he would have the protection of Mr. Donner and the agency, as well as other government officials."

Before he signed the statement, Gatewood made sure to tell the assembled group that "he had always intended, if approached by some white man, to tell the truth regarding the matter, and that the reason for his not telling the truth about the matter when questioned by agent in the presence of the interpreter was that he was afraid that the interpreter would divulge what he had told to the Indians, and that he believed that Samuel Seymour, or Seymour's squaw, would murder him if it was found out that he had told; that Seymour's squaw was one of the most desperate, and the meanest squaw on the Apache reservation."

The longhand statement was typed up the next morning by Gertrude Cobb, Donner's secretary. It was again read to Gatewood in Apache and English, this time in front of a larger group, and Gatewood signed it again. In addition to Street, Donner, and Velesques, the witnesses included T.E. Shipley, of the San Carlos Reservation; Gertrude Cobb, stenographer; George Woolford, sheriff in Showlow, Arizona; and Officer William Maupin.

Missing from all of the accounts of Gatewood's interrogation and statement, quite naturally, is any mention of what led Gatewood to believe he needed to offer the damning testimony he did. Was there simply an appeal to conscience? Was it just logical persuasion? Were there threats? Was there physical coercion involved? We will never know the answers.

Here is Gatewood's statement, which, although the transcript was dated October 31, was actually given early Sunday morning, November 1:

Whiteriver, Arizona, October 31, 1931

Reference the murder of Henrietta Schmerler
near Fort Apache, Arizona, on the Apache
Indian Reservation, July 18, 1931.

I, Robert Gatewood, after being warned of my
constitutional rights that anything I might say
with reference to the case now under investigation
(Murder of Henrietta Schmerler) could and
would be used against me in the prosecution of
this matter; after being so informed, it is my
desire to make a statement and tell the truth,
as I best remember regarding this matter:

My name is Robert Gatewood. My age is 22 years.
I am an Apache Indian residing on East Fork on
the Apache Reservation near Fort Apache, Arizona.
I am the son-in-law of H-4 (Samuel Seymour),
and the brother-in-law of Golney Seymour, who

is the son of H-4 (Samuel Seymour), who also
lives on East Fork near the Lutheran Mission.

On Saturday, the 18th of July, 1931, the day that
there was a dance at Canyon Day, at night Golney
Seymour, (who is also known as Max Seymour), came to
my wood camp, which is about ½ mile south and west
of the camp of H-4 (Samuel Seymour), which camp is
also near the house where Henrietta Schmerler (the
white girl) lived. He arrived at my camp about five
p.m. He asked me to cut his hair, stating that he
wanted to go to the dance at Canyon Day that night.
I told him I had nothing to cut his hair with, that
my razor had gotten wet and rusty and I could not
use it. I took the razor out of a paper which it
was wrapped up in and showed it to him. It was now
getting late in the evening and Golney Seymour and I
then left my camp on horseback—I was riding bareback
and he had a saddle. We started to go back to the
camp of H-4 (Samuel Seymour). When we got near the
camp, at the gate which goes into H-4's camp, we
came to the house of Henrietta Schmerler (the white
girl) which is just across the road and opposite
the gate that goes into H-4's camp. On our arrival
there we saw Jack Perry sitting on his horse outside
of the white girl's gate, and the white girl was
standing on the ground talking to Jack Perry and
gave him a drink of water from a cup which she had
in her hand. On our arrival there I rode over to the
gate and opened the gate while sitting on my horse.
Jack Perry left and went up the road which is east—
what we call, "going up East Fork." Golney Seymour
had a short conversation with Henrietta Schmerler
(the white girl) and then came on to the gate and he
and I rode over to the H-4 (Samuel Seymour's) camp.

When we arrived at the camp there was no one there,
but I saw my wife and little boy down in the field,

and they later left, walking, going back toward my
camp. Golney Seymour and I remained at the H-4 camp
for about 30 minutes and while we were there we were
looking at a newspaper. We then got on our horses
and came out to the gate which is just north and
in front of the white girl's house. Golney Seymour
got off his horse and opened the gate and I rode
through and started on down west toward my camp, and
a short way I looked back and he was still wiring
the gate. I rode a short distance further and looked
back and I saw Golney Seymour's horse tied to the
fence in front of the white girl's house. I also
saw Golney Seymour and the white girl (Henrietta
Schmerler) standing on her front porch, as though
they were talking. I continued on down the road,
west, then turning to the south and going on top
of a little hill, and it was then beginning to get
dusk. At that time I saw Golney Seymour and the
white girl (Henrietta Schmerler) riding on the same
horse, the girl was riding in front in the saddle,
and Colney [sic] Seymour was riding behind. I could
see that she had on an Indian dress. I could tell
that the dress came down low and covered a good
part of the horse's shoulders, and the dress was
yellow with some white in it. At that time they
were traveling the road which leads south and west
in the direction of Fort Apache and Canyon Day. I
then went on to my camp and my wife and little girl
arrived there just after I did, they walking.

That night after I had been in bed sometime, I do
not know the exact time, as I had been asleep, I
heard someone call me. I answered, getting up and
putting on my clothes. I went out and it was Golney
Seymour. I talked to him for quite a little while.
He told me he had killed the white girl (Henrietta
Schmerler) in a canyon down below Fort Apache, at
that time saying to me that "I know you saw me with

this girl and I came back here to tell you if you
ever tell it I would kill you". "I have bought a gun
and have it hid up on the mesa and if you report me
I will get it and kill you and your wife", (which
is his sister.) While talking to him I noticed blood
on both of his arms, on his shirt, the most being
on the right sleeve. He told me at that time that
when they arrived at this canyon (he did not tell
me which one) that he insisted on having sexual
relations with the white girl and she refused, and
they became involved in a fight. That the white girl
got a knife out of her beaded purse and attempted
to cut him with it; that he took the knife away from
her and cut her on the head and finally succeeded
in raping her, but did not tell me how many times.
That he later cut the white girl around the head,
also cutting her neck, and when he left her she
was dead. He later went into my camp and got some
water and washed the blood off of his sleeves and
hands and related part of the conversation he
had had to me in the presence of my wife, again
telling us that if we reported him he would kill
us. After he had washed the blood off of his
sleeve and his hands he got on his horse and left,
saying that he was going to the Canyon Day dance.

While I was talking to him I could not see any
blood on his pants, as they were dark, and if there
had been blood on them I probably would not have
seen it. On Sunday morning, the next day after the
Canyon Day dance, I went over to H-4's camp and
there I saw Golney Seymour laying down and noticed
that he had on a different shirt from the one he
was wearing the night before. At that time he was
lying down and as I walked by him he repeated to
me again, "If you tell anyone or report me for
killing the white girl I will kill you sure."

My wife nor I have not talked to Golney
Seymour since that time regarding this
matter, as we were afraid of him and have
avoided him as much as possible.
I do not believe that my wife would tell of this
matter as she is a sister of Golney Seymour, and
also the daughter of H-4 (Samuel Seymour), also the
daughter of Alva Seymour, who is the wife of H-4
(Samuel Seymour), who is the toughest and meanest
Indian woman on the Apache Reservation, and that
my wife, if she desired to tell anyone, would be
afraid of her mother, as well as her father.

I further want to state, referring back to the
time we came to the camp of H-4, when we saw
Jack Perry talking to the white girl and she
gave him a drink of water, at which time we went
into H-4's camp, that H-4's wife and H-4 had
already left their camp and gone to the Canyon
Day dance, and that there was no one with Golney
Seymour and the white girl when I saw them going
toward the Canyon Day dance on the horse.

I further want to state that when talking to
Golney Seymour that night after he had come to
my camp and woke me up, in that conversation he
stated that there was no one with him at the time
he murdered and raped the white girl and the only
person that he saw on the road while with this girl
was an Indian that they passed on the road, whom
he believed was Simon Wycliffe, but it was his
belief that this party did not know who they were.

I further want to state that it has been my
intentions, if ever questioned by the proper
authorities, that I would tell the truth about this
matter, but when questioned on this day and in the
presence of an Indian Interpreter I evaded telling

the truth to him as I did not want the Indians to
know that I had told this and was afraid that this
Indian might tell the other Indians what I had told.

I further want to state that with reference to the
sore hand of Golney Seymour I did not notice his
hand being tied up or being sore on Saturday when
he came to my camp to see about having his hair
cut. The first time that I saw his hand being tied
up was along about the first of the week, probably
Monday or Tuesday, after the Canyon Day dance.

That the above statement has been read to me
in the Apache language by Jesus Velesques,
and in English by J. A. Street, Special Agent
of the Bureau of Investigation, and was also
read to me and interpreted in the presence of
Wm. Donner, Superintendent of the Fort Apache
Indian Agency at Whiteriver, Arizona.

(Signed) Robert Gatewood.

Witnesses:
Jesus Velesques, Ft. Apache, Ariz.
J. A. Street, Spl. Agt., Bureau of Investigation,
Dept. of Justice, El Paso, Tex.
Wm. Donner, Whiteriver, Ariz.
T. E. Shipley, San Carlos, Ariz.
Gertrude Cobb, Steno., Whiteriver, Ariz.
George Woolford, Sholo, Ariz.
Wm. Maupin, Whiteriver, Ariz.

It was still early Sunday morning when Golney Seymour was
brought back to Whiteriver from the McNary jail, 22 miles away.
Just before he was brought into Street's makeshift office, he asked
Interpreter Dosela where Gatewood was, and was told he was in jail.
Seymour asked if he had been interviewed any further before he left

the headquarters. Dosela said no—"which was the truth, as far as Dosela knew," according to Street's report of the incident. Dosela went on to tell Seymour that Gatewood was being held for refusing to talk, and pointedly reminded Seymour that he, too, was being held for refusing to tell the truth.

What happened next was either a prime example of what made the FBI in the coming decades an exemplar of tough, smart police work—or Exhibit A in the process by which the FBI created its own mythology. Either way, it opens a window into the vaunted FBI public relations machinery as practiced in 1931.

Apart from various creative accounts that appeared in detective and adventure magazines through the 1960's, the only formal description of what happened during Golney Seymour's interrogation comes in two reports by Street. The first, in Street's official case report of November 4, tells us extremely little. He devotes only one paragraph to introducing Seymour's confession:

> The next morning, which was October 31, 1931 [sic: *it was, in fact, November 1*], subject was returned from McNary, Ariz., which is only 22 miles away, and interviewed by agent. After confronting the subject with some of the facts which were obtained through Gatewood, but not divulging to subject the source of the information, subject stated that it was his desire to tell the truth about the entire matter, and a statement was taken from him, same being taken on a typewriter by Mrs. Gertrude Cobb, stenographer, in which subject admitted assaulting and murdering the white girl (Henrietta Schmerler).

It was undoubtedly the words "but not divulging to subject the source of the information" that attracted the immediate attention of J. Edgar Hoover and Assistant FBI Director Harold Nathan, who called Street on November 9 asking for elaboration. This occasioned Street's more thorough report of that same date, addressed directly to Hoover.

Ironically, during FOIA proceedings fifty-eight years later, which ultimately resulted in the release of virtually the entire FBI file, the first

half of that controversial sentence—"but not divulging to subject"—
was originally excised in the documents released to us, the niece and
nephew of the murdered woman—as if in 1989 the FBI was just as
concerned with the public getting a glimpse of a dubious 1931 crime-
solving technique as the FBI was in 1931. The full wording of this
document—as later revealed by court order—also showed that the
FBI's "privacy" and "confidentiality" rationales for withholding that
part of it did not in fact apply.

Street wrote Hoover on November 9 that there were "a number of minor details which agent omitted in the report on this matter, owing to the fact that he believed that they would [not?] be of any assistance in the prosecution of the matter and would only make a voluminous report."

Remarkably, the paragraph which lays out the manner in which Street obtained Golney Seymour's confession begins with a parenthesized sentence: "(This is prejudiced.)"

The meaning of this sentence, and at what stage in the process and by whom it was added, are all unclear. What *is* clear is that the FBI was aware from the beginning of the sensitivity of the unorthodox method in which this confession was obtained.

Here is the explanation Street provided in that report:

(This is prejudiced.) The first thing that agent said to Seymour upon this interview was, "I talked to the white girl last night— you didn't know that I could do that—have you ever heard of spiritualists?" Seymour replied that he had not. Agent then said to him, "I am going to tell you what she told me and I want you to tell me whether it is true or not," at which time subject as well as the interpreter each laughed. Agent told Seymour that the white girl said "On Saturday evening you and Robert Gatewood came by her house and she asked to borrow a horse from you, and that you told her that you had only one horse, but if she desired she could ride with you on that horse to the Canyon Day dance, which she accepted." On relating this much of the purported conversation between the white girl and agent, subject became very nervous, his eyes glaring, as well as that of the interpreters. Agent continued to tell Seymour what the white girl had said in this spiritual interview, and finally subject became so nervous he could not sit still, at which time he turned to the Interpreter and said in the Apache language, "I guess I had as well tell the truth about the matter, as she has told him all," to which the Interpreter replied in Apache, "You might as well, as he seems to know just what happened." At this time subject related the entire story, in the Apache language, which is set out in his signed statement in report of this agent.

On November 10, when he transmitted Street's report to Hoover, L. C. Taylor, acting special agent in charge, took pains to note: "I do not believe it to be in the best interest of the Government's case at this time to offer to the press any information concerning the manner in which Mr. Street first gained the confession—that is, his assumption of the role of a medium." Hoover responded November 19, in what appears to be at least partial disagreement: "I believe it would be well to exercise every precaution to see that the United States Attorney responsible for prosecution is acquainted with all the facts in connection with this incident, in order that the trial of the case may not be jeopardized by the raising of any issues in Court which may surprise the United States Attorney and thus prove prejudicial to the judicial arbitrament of the case in question."

Golney Seymour never discussed the interrogation during the trial, in any statements he made about the crime while he was inside the justice system, or in any of a large quantity of letters written by him in prison that we have obtained. Thus, Street's version of what happened that morning stands as the final, official word on a particularly murky chapter of this story.

Early on the morning of November 1, Golney Seymour signed his own confession describing his murder of Henrietta Schmerler during a fight following "sexual relations." The confession included details of his actions prior to beginning his ride with Henrietta, an extended description of the "fight" at the scene of the murder, and a brief account of his subsequent encounter with Gatewood. This confession (see page 199) was later the source of significant controversy during the trial, and was only admitted into evidence after a protracted legal battle. Once it was written out by Secretary Cobb, Golney Seymour was re-read the written confession by interpreter Dosela—and signed it without further question in the presence of six additional witnesses.

Part Three:

FACING THE TRIAL

COURT PONDERS ON EVIDENCE IN APACHE'S TRIAL FOR MURDER

Globe, Ariz., March 20 (Æ).—A stolid Apache cowpuncher's denial that he slew a Columbia University co-ed, and the assertion of a Department of Justice agent that the Indian had confessed the crime, will be pondered tomorrow by a Federal Court jury.

Testimony was completed yesterday in the trial of Mac (Golney) Seymour, the Redman, accused of fatally stabbing Henrietta Schmerler, 25-year-old anthropology student.

Neither the Government nor the defense used all the witnesses that had been summoned. United States Attorney John C. Gung'l did not bring to the witness chair any witnesses in rebuttal after Seymour asserted from the stand that "I did not kill her."

The Apache admitted during his direct testimony that he had fought with the anthropology student in a ravine on the night of last July 18, as he was escorting her to a dance. He declared, however, that he did not intend to kill her.

Under raking cross-examination by Gung'l, Seymour aroused from his stoical impassivity and declared

Golney (Mac) Seymour

she was searching for a knife to stab him when he got on his hoi and "made horse go fast aw from there."

Previously the Indian told of alleged intimacies with the g carried out after she gave h whisky and encouraged his : vances.

The Government entered into record a purported confess made to J. N. Street, Departm of Justice agent who arrested S mour: The Apache was quoted admitting he killed the white with a knife, stabbing her in neck as she lay before him on ground.

(Other pictures on page 21)

Chapter Eleven

Each Side Struggles to Frame its Case

Within hours of the time Golney Seymour signed the confession—even before the AP and UPI were putting out fevered stories about "GOSSIP OF INDIANS LEADS TO SLAYER" and "BELIEVE INDIAN SLEW COLUMBIA GIRL WITH KNIFE"—the big trial questions were being framed:

Should the death penalty be sought? (The FBI, prosecutors, and a large chunk of the press would answer with an emphatic yes; BIA officials and anthropologists would say no.)

Would issues of Henrietta's purported character—her naïveté, her foolhardiness, and, as her harshest critics would have it, her promiscuity—be introduced in the courtroom?

Would Golney's confession stand?

Meanwhile, other, more conventional trial issues were soon being thrashed out: Where would the trial be held? How soon? Who would be called to testify? How much information could be released to the press without prejudicing the case, and who would control the release?

An ugly rift between the two branches of government most involved with the case, Indian Affairs and Justice, opened almost instantly. The collaboration between Donner and Street—from all outward appearances quite harmonious until the capture of Golney Seymour—turned out to have been built on a foundation of distrust, jealousy, and territoriality.

Two days after Golney's confession, Donner would complain to his boss that "Considerable fuss is being made about the capture of this boy by public officials...If the apprehension and capture of this boy is a great feat, then the capture of a tame kitten is an equally great feat."

Soon afterward, the FBI's Colvin would alert Hoover to the "more or less pernicious activity of William Donner, Superintendent of the Whiteriver Indian Reservation, whose attitude is one which, to my mind, should not be tolerated and which, in my opinion, should result in his removal from the Indian Service..."

Colvin later warned, "From what I have heard, I consider Mr. Donner to be a serious menace to the proper arbitrament of this case and, if possible, some means should be taken immediately to eliminate him from any further activity in favor of the defendant Golney Seymour."

The tensions may have originated in Donner's initial unwillingness to concede that the murder had likely been committed by an Apache, and his continued insistence, even after a second FBI agent arrived on the reservation, upon promoting various white men as suspects. At that time, Street had felt, if not overt resistance, at least a lack of enthusiasm on Donner's part for pursuing the most obvious leads among the Apache.

Now, with Golney in jail and an explicit confession of a brutal sex crime in hand, Donner went immediately to work to prevent imposition of the death penalty.

He would not argue for total leniency, however. In a November 3 letter to BIA Commissioner Rhoads, Donner advocated taking the middle road in prosecuting Seymour:

> It is rather a complex case in that to fight the boy's battle and get him off with a light sentence will be a very bad influence on the Indians of this reservation, as we now have four or five Apaches on the reservation who have willfully murdered other members of the tribe, some being acquitted and others serving only a few years in the penitentiary. It gives the Indians the impression that a cold-blooded murder is

anything but a serious matter. In a sense it jeopardizes the life of employees who work with them, as there are, especially in the Eastfork district, a large number of Indians more or less of the renegade type. In fact, it has been their history from the beginning, and as a moral lesson to this type of Indian, parties committing murders, whether it be within their own people, or otherwise, should be more severely punished. In this case, however, I am not in favor of the maximum penalty; namely, hanging. Any suggestions from you in this case will be appreciated. In the meantime, newspaper stories and other wild statements made should be taken lightly. Our own Department of Justice, while diligently prosecuting the case, can conscientiously conserve some of their energy for the conviction of criminals of the type of Capone.

Rhoads wrote back immediately, affirming that the course of action suggested by Donner ("to see that this young man is punished but...[to] also do everything in your power to see that the maximum penalty is not imposed") "meets with the approval of this office."

Meanwhile, Boas and the other Columbia anthropologists were weighing in, unsurprisingly, against the death penalty. Political, philosophical, and professional convictions would all dictate compassion for a young, oppressed, and "primitive" offender. But there was also more than a tinge of recrimination for Henrietta in their appeals on behalf of Seymour.

Boas wrote to Donner:

I cannot make myself think that an Indian who had his family and his whole life at stake would, under these circumstances, commit a wilful murder. I do hope and pray that a most lenient attitude will be taken towards him, which I think is imperative, not only on account of the specific conditions that prevail but also on account of the difficulties of the cultural conditions of the Indians in our communities.

FBI Agent Shivers reported Boas's elaboration in an interview conducted in New York City in January:

He stated that in his opinion the death penalty would be too severe in this case. He likewise stated that this defendant should not be judged by "our" standards, and felt that Miss Schmerler's conduct may have given the Indians a wrong impression, and in this particular case her actions probably aroused uncontrollable emotions at the time of her murder, which to his mind could not be construed as a premeditated murder. Extenuating testimony is to be expected from [Boas] if he is ever called as a witness in this case.

Benedict was even more emphatic in the case she made for a lighter penalty. She told Agent Shivers that she

did not believe that in passing judgment on the above subject for this offense he should be judged by the same standards she would apply to herself or this agent; that *she felt the Indians were children mentally* [emphasis added] and did not believe that under all of the circumstances the death penalty should be sought. She seemed to feel that the unconscious and unintentional acts of Miss Schmerler in her contacts with the Indians may have given them the wrong impression of her, and in the case at point such should serve as circumstances which would mitigate the offense.

While it might not be unexpected that the Columbia anthropologists would argue for the social if not legal "innocence" of the young Apache murderer—and that they would be opposed to the death penalty in general—Elias Schmerler's response in that regard was surprising. Henrietta's father was known as a stern, not-easily-forgiving man; the loss of his wife and fortune in the previous few years had already left him morose and, in some respects, bitter. The FBI had heard a fair amount from Elias, who had quickly become impatient as the hunt for the killer had dragged on into the fall. They were told that he and the family were "quite stirred up" over the murder and especially eager to see the killer "brought to justice." Elias had written a furious letter after he had seen a report from Donner suggesting that Henrietta may have borne some of the responsibility for the murder through her behavior on the reservation:

My friends, all members of my family, and myself feel perfectly confident that the cruel murder was but a tribal affair,
while Mr. Donner has taken a different attitude from the first
day the body was found; an attitude which is encouraging
the Indians, so that other earnestly devoted research workers
might meet with the same fate.

It was only natural that the Justice Department would assume, as
it first contemplated bringing Golney Seymour to trial—and seeking
the harshest punishment—that Elias's presence in the courtroom
would work in the interest of conviction. Special Agent in Charge
Colvin wrote to the New York special agent in charge:

The U.S. Attorney is firmly of the opinion that Mr. E.
Schmerler, father of the deceased and who is supposed to
reside at 250 Fifth Ave., New York should be present at the
trial for the moral effect.

Colvin noted that the government would not be able to pay
expenses, but he believed "that Mr. Schmerler would be willing to
lend his moral support by coming to Globe, Arizona, at his own
expense, as it is understood that Mr. Schmerler is quite well-to-do."

There were a couple of surprises for the FBI when they
interviewed Elias in his apartment on Riverside Drive (not Fifth
Avenue) in Manhattan. First, according to information provided
(out of Elias's presence) by Elias's son-in-law Irving Meller, who
was also in the apartment for the interview, Elias would under no
circumstances be able to afford the trip to Arizona, "as he had lost
practically all his money," and would not appear without a subpoena,
in which case the government would have to pay.

But more significantly, Elias made it clear that he did not want
to be there:

He stated that he had lost his daughter, albeit [sic] a daughter
of promise, and that the life of one Indian or fifty Indians
would not recompense him for this loss, and that he would

feel no better than half savage himself if he were to ask a life for a life. Mr. Schmerler further stated that he was unable to see any good he could accomplish by lending his presence to the trial of this case and expressed a wish that it might be settled by compromise.

Shown this passage in the FBI report nearly 70 years later, Elias's son Sam Schmerler, Henrietta's younger brother—now nearing 90—became uncharacteristically emotional. His wife, my stepmother, later told me that he had cried at the revelation that, as he now saw it, he had been able to reverse his father's thinking on this subject. He remembers having gone to his father, as a 19-year-old, with a letter he had drafted asking for leniency in the punishment of the killer, but that his father, in anger, had torn it up. They had argued for some time about this, he recalled, but it was not until he read that FBI report over two-thirds of a century later that he learned that his father had subsequently changed his mind.

Justice Department preparations: anticipating the defense

The Justice Department anticipated from the beginning that a full-scale assault on Henrietta's research methodology, lifestyle, and character would be the cornerstone of the defense. Almost immediately upon Golney Seymour's capture —and before Street left the reservation—Special Agent in Charge Colvin and John Gung'l, the U.S. Attorney who would prosecute the case, began to seek witnesses who would be able to counter the allegations that would undoubtedly be raised.

In early December, Colvin raised the inevitable "horseback" issue:

Mr. Gung'l has stated that he is informed that one of the defenses will be that it is a tribal tradition among the Apaches that when a woman consents and agrees to ride on a horse with an Indian buck, she tacitly puts herself in his hands to do with as he will, and Mr. Gung'l desires us to procure several of the older Indians as witnesses to refute this alleged claim which will be put forth.

However, when Street was sent back to the reservation later that month to find some people to challenge the purported horseback taboo, his report indicated instead that those he had interviewed, like Tribal Chief Baha, said that "it was not the custom of Indian women to ride on horseback with a man unless she was his wife or his daughter, and that it was not the custom for a widow or single woman to travel around the country with a man, and if she did so, she would not be respected by the Indians." In fact, the five Apaches and two whites he quoted on the subject seemed to give remarkably similar testimony, with only slight variations, reflecting their personal perspectives. For example, the Reverend Edgar Genther, head of the Lutheran Mission in East Fork, added that it was *"entirely unethical* [emphasis added] for a single woman to ride horseback or accompany an Indian man alone."

The weight of opinion collected by Street would seem to confirm that Henrietta had egregiously violated tribal norms. However, no one seems in fact to have expressed any such concerns about Henrietta's behavior during her three-and-a-half weeks on the reservation. Moreover, Superintendent Donner—no defender of Henrietta—had himself said in a report soon after her death: "She had been quite familiar with Indian boys and would not hesitate to get on the same horse back of an Indian to ride to the dance, which procedure, if true, might be perfectly safe with some of our Indian boys especially when they are sober, but which procedure would not be safe with some of our Indian boys when partially intoxicated, especially with the suspects we have locked up."

Nelson Lupe, a former tribal chairman who, as a young man, spent some time on the reservation during the summer of 1931, told us in the late 1980s that he thought it was "too much of a temptation with a young girl riding in front of a man." When asked if it was specifically wrong to do so, however, he said, "No," (although he had added that "it is very unwise.") And the modern historians of Apache culture we have consulted have been hard pressed to identify a particular prohibition or explicit taboo in the practice, suggesting that the behavior might at worst be open to negative interpretation by censorious individuals.

The trial preparations of the Justice Department focused on two things: first, establishing that Golney Seymour had, in absolute fact, been seen by numerous people in the vicinity of Henrietta's house that Saturday afternoon (contrary to the story he originally told); and second, establishing the credibility of Robert Gatewood as a first-hand witness up to the point of Golney's departure with Henrietta and as an honest, accurate recounter of Golney's personal admissions to him. This was to assure that Golney's formal confession would stand up to the intense scrutiny to which it would undoubtedly be put during the trial—as in fact it was, especially when Golney later changed his story dramatically.

The Justice Department team was particularly wary of surprises. Colvin even suggested to Gung'l that he be prepared with witnesses to establish the identity of the dead body found as that of Henrietta. "I understand that the body was in a bad state of decomposition and it occurs to me that the question of identity of the corpse might be raised by a shrewd defense attorney."

But the character issue was the one they most feared. The charge that Henrietta was naïve and ill-prepared was not as worrisome as the suggestions that she was manipulative, exploitive, and headstrong to the point of arrogance. And even these allegations paled next to the charges of sexual impropriety and moral opportunism, which were now being widely spread. An early letter that Acting Special Agent in Charge Taylor—who had not been personally involved in the case—wrote to Hoover makes it evident that the FBI may have been quick to accept this slant on the story:

It is commonly known that the victim upon her arrival at Whiteriver, Arizona, became intimate immediately with the Indians and openly ignored and evaded all white persons. Her actions in this respect have prompted gossip of immorality with the Indians—even commercial prostitution. While there has not been an iota of evidence which would indicate sexual intimacy on the part of the victim, it is Mr. Street's firm belief that subject's defense will be that victim, a highly educated individual, came to the reservation, flaunted her virtues in the face of the Indian, became sexually intimate with the Apache, arousing his savage instincts which culminated in her murder.

Colvin's suggestion that the anthropologists at Columbia University be summoned to vouch for Henrietta's character was soon understood to be problematic: the Justice Department team learned that the stories about Henrietta's supposed indiscretions on the reservation had long since been making the rounds within the anthropology department and had been—to a surprising extent— believed. Nevertheless, Boas did write that, in the two years Henrietta had studied with him, "she was a very faithful student and appeared sensible in every way and I have the greatest respect for her character." And Benedict told Agent Shivers that "she considered her a girl of good moral character, brilliant, studious and devoted to her work."

In addition, in the same report in which Street wrote that numerous informants declared that a single woman on horseback might be considered a "boudwam," or prostitute, he also presented some testimonials to Henrietta's character from others on the reservation:

A number of Indians of the better class, as well as the white people of Whiteriver and vicinity, were interviewed regarding victim's character, and it is the general opinion of these people that victim was a lady. Quite a few of these people stated that while the victim may have been indiscreet among the Indians, that it is their belief that she was misled by Indian stories she had read, as she had in her possession a number of Indian Story Books which were stamped on the inside "The Property of Columbia University," in which a number of these books referred to the noble red man and how he had been mistreated by the white man, and how honest and truthful the Indians were, that victim in conversation with white people and when she was being warned that she should not live by herself and accompany the Indians out alone, would state to them that she felt that she knew the Indians better than they did; that they only knew them in an official way, leaving the impression that she thought that the Indians had been mistreated by the white man and all that was necessary was to give them good treatment...

Street concluded this February 2 report on a personal note:

... therefore, she was misled by some means, as it is a well known fact that the Indian will lie and is just as treacherous as any other race of people, in some respects more so.

The gossip continued unabated, however, and it became increasingly clear that an aggressive prosecution of Golney Seymour would undoubtedly be hampered by the belief in Arizona that Henrietta had been careless, at the very least. The prosecution team continued to talk about seeking punishment to "the maximum extent of the law" (i.e., hanging, in Arizona), but they realized that they might need to settle for the lesser penalty of life imprisonment.

Meanwhile, they were concerned as well about Seymour's confession, and in particular worried that there would be claims of coercion, or even torture. Five people, in addition to Street and the Apache interpreter who read Seymour the confession in both English and Apache, officially witnessed the confession, and they all would later emphatically reiterate that the signing was totally voluntary. Nonetheless, it was inevitable that questions would later be raised about the confession.

And there appeared to be no eyewitnesses to the crime, so the full story rested solely with Seymour, along with the parts of it he had allegedly told to Gatewood. This left the prosecution potentially quite vulnerable to a change of story as the trial approached. In fact, this is exactly what happened.

The defense makes its own plans

John Dougherty, an attorney from Globe who had never defended a murder case before, was hired by members of the Seymour family soon after Golney's arrest. According to Donner, Dougherty took the case "knowing perhaps that he would not receive a cent for his services." It was understood that the court "would have appointed an attorney to defend the boy at the beginning of the trial; but in view of the fact that there were many investigations to be made, prospective witnesses to confer with, and in fact a great deal of preliminary work to be done before the case came to trial, it was most necessary that this boy have counsel arranged beforehand."

Immediately following the trial verdict, Donner would make a strong plea for the BIA to compensate Dougherty for his "very able defense," particularly "considering the determined attitude of the Department of Justice to hang the defendant...to make a reputation by exacting the maximum penalty." With expressions of regret, Commissioner Rhoads denied the request. Instead, he wrote a carefully worded thank you to Dougherty: "I wish to thank you personally for the work which you did in connection with this case as you did without any assurance of a fee or compensation. That was indeed a splendid gesture of humanity and kindness." Dougherty never did receive any payment from the government, and only a very limited amount from other sources.

Gatewood would be the star witness for the prosecution, the centerpiece, in fact, of the case against Golney Seymour. Gatewood's statement had provided the basis for Golney's interrogation—and ultimate confession—and Gatewood was the only eyewitness who definitively placed Golney and Henrietta together on horseback as they headed off toward the dance. And he was, of course, Golney's brother-in-law and, prior to the evening of the fatal ride, his constant companion. Simon Wycliffe, the other person named in Golney's confession as possibly having seen him and Henrietta together was yet to be interviewed.

When word got out that Gatewood had informed on his brother-in-law, his life among the White Mountain Apache was effectively over. Donner and the BIA charged that Street and the FBI had revealed the identity of a confidential informant—whose instrumental role in the capture had originally been carefully withheld, as promised—to the press. Donner was outraged.

The veneer of cordiality that had marked the relationship between the two agencies began to fray quickly. When Gung'l asked Donner to give up custody of Gatewood so that he could be held in Tucson, Donner reacted:

I do not think it will be necessary for you to take Robert Gatewood to Tucson, or anywhere else at this time, as a matter of protection, *unless you have broken faith in exposing him* [emphasis added]. Robert revealed the information with the understanding that he would be protected. Thus far the Indians here are not blaming Robert for Max's confession.... Of course, the report has already gone out and came in over the radio that this boy is being held as a witness. Such information evidently has gone out by some of the people who were here Sunday.... It was the understanding, as Mr. Street will verify, that Robert was not to be brought into the case, at least for the present.

He went on to argue that Gatewood be allowed to make the choice himself of whether to return to the reservation or not. If, after public word is put out that he was not implicated, "the boy still feels that he would be in danger at East Fork," Donner wrote, "I will be glad to assist in keeping him away from the reservation in any manner Mr. Street sees fit."

Gung'l relented, for the time being, but imposed strict conditions:

This morning, I had an interview with Gatewood, and he is going to be a very material witness, as you know, and I was reluctant about allowing him to go back to the Reservation where it is possible and probable that some of his friends might get to him, telling him not to testify. However, as you have informed me that you and Mr. Street have promised that he would not be taken away, I am letting him go back, with the understanding that you will keep him under your direct and personal control, and under no circumstances is he to be interviewed by anyone (which, of course, includes the newspaper reporters), without written permission of myself. I wish you would see that he is confined at night in jail at Whiteriver, and a guard placed there, so that no one can talk to him, or throw anything through the window."

But tensions had been inflamed over this issue. Colvin would complain bitterly about this dispute several weeks later in a letter to

Hoover in which he asked, in effect, that Hoover do his best to have Donner fired:

> The U.S. Attorney advised me that Donner tried his best to keep custody of the material witness, Robert Gatewood, and has tried to have him released from jail to return to the reservation, where he would naturally be thrown among the other Indians and perhaps frightened into or influenced against giving truthful testimony.

As it turned out, Gatewood was not released until after the trial. At that point, he chose to live elsewhere.

It is significant that as late as March 8, only six days before the scheduled beginning of the trial, Dougherty, scrambling feverishly to prepare a legitimate defense for his client, was filing a petition in the United State District Court for Arizona, complaining that the government had "refused and still refuse[s] to permit the said John P. Dougherty to interview said witness [Gatewood]."

Chapter Twelve

The Grand Jury Indicts, But Issues Remain

Meanwhile, a grand jury was being hurriedly assembled to bring the indictment needed to move forward with Golney Seymour's prosecution. Gung'l asked Donner to bring Gatewood, Street, Dr. Hupp, stenographer Cobb, and interpreter Dosela to Tucson to appear before the grand jury. It took an extra day to put together a full grand jury, but Dougherty, recognizing the inevitability of indictment, announced he would be satisfied with any jury called. A reading of Golney's confession, confirmation by those who had witnessed his interrogation that he had signed the confession voluntarily, a presentation of a host of photographs of the crime scene and Henrietta's cabin, and a brief appearance by Gatewood as a corroborating witness provided the bulk of the government's case for indictment.

The *Tucson Daily Citizen*, in its November 20 account of Golney's appearance in the grand jury room, was preoccupied with his "stoic" demeanor. (The AP similarly described him as sitting "stolidly," in a theme echoed by virtually all the press.)

> The young Apache today appeared anything but the swaggering young cowboy of the fertile Whiteriver Valley as

he sat in the courtroom. He wore high heel boots of a select make, an enormous 10-gallon sombrero, dark trousers and a sweater. His heavy shock of jet hair indicated a recent military cut... As he took his seat with his attorney, J.P. Dougherty of Globe, he placed his headgear in a safe place on the table in front. Then he focused his beadlike eyes on the table and never once looked in another direction.

Mr. Dougherty, just back from Whiteriver region, conversed earnestly with the Indian for some time, but not once did the sinewy built young buck raise his eyes, and only once or twice nodded acquiescence to what his lawyer said.

On Monday, November 23, the grand jury returned an indictment alleging that "Golney Seymour, alias Max Seymour ... on July 18, 1931 on an Indian reservation in Arizona ... did kill and murder one Henrietta Schmerler."

A trial date of January 5 was floated and then pushed forward numerous times, until March 14 was settled on. Golney remained in the Pima County cell he had occupied since being sent to Tucson on November 5. Robert Gatewood was held in Tucson as well, in a separate section of the jail, as an "important material witness."

With Golney indicted, Dougherty beginning to prepare a defense, and the press still swarming the reservation, the prosecution tightened its control over the case. Gung'l fired off a telegram to Donner on January 13:

UNDERSTAND DEFENSE ATTORNEY AND OTHERS NOW ON RESERVATION RELATIVE TO SEYMOUR CASE STOP KINDLY INSTRUCT OUR WITNESSES IF APPROACHED NOT TO SAY ANYTHING NOTIFYING PARTIES THAT THEY ARE GOVERNMENT WITNESSES AND THE UNITED STATES ATTORNEY INSTRUCTED THEM NOT TO TALK ABOUT CASE.

Most of those who were later to testify had not yet been notified that they were witnesses, so the assignment was not an easy one.

Golney's character

With a case so far built primarily on a single confession, Gung'l went to work to buttress his prospective attack on Golney's character. He was hearing that the defense would try to parade a series of witnesses maintaining that Seymour was hard working, honest, and not particularly worldly—a typical, innocent, young Apache "buck."

Gung'l knew he could find more than enough witnesses to Golney's heavy drinking on the day of the murder—but Gung'l also knew that drunkenness might, in fact, be one of Golney's *defenses.* More importantly, Gung'l had hopes that the story he had heard about Golney having threatened Simon Wycliffe as a possible eyewitness would later be confirmed.

Gung'l also wanted testimony about Golney's questionable behavior as a schoolboy. Street, thus instructed, obtained information that Mrs. Carl Britton, who had taught at the Lutheran Mission School in Fort Apache, could speak about young Golney's "breaking into a chicken coop and chopping the heads and legs off a number of chickens with a knife." The Los Angeles FBI office located Mrs. Britton, now in California, and reported on its interview. While it turned out that Mrs. Britton did not remember Golney, her husband, Carl, was certain that it was Golney who had entered their chicken coop one night and "killed and mutilated twelve or fifteen chickens purely for the pleasure of slaughtering them."

Funding problems

If Dougherty encountered major problems with both access and funding in his efforts to prepare a defense for Golney, the prosecution did not have it much easier in their own trial preparations. Gung'l and his assistants ran headlong into a federal fiscal bureaucracy newly panicked by the Depression that had recently overtaken the nation, and found themselves needing to justify meticulously each penny spent—and even then not getting the support they needed.

Gung'l's later efforts to have a court reporter reimbursed $3.50 for taking down the statements of several witnesses against Golney were repeatedly challenged. (An assistant attorney general with responsibility for keeping the government's trial expenses low would not accept that the prosecutor's own stenographers could not keep up with the rapid questioning—and translating—and said, "The rapidity of the questions and answers... is a matter entirely within your control.") Later, following the trial, the Justice Department objected to paying $5 to each of the two bailiffs on the one day (Sunday) the jury was held over by the judge. Similar disputes over payments fill a large file of correspondence between the prosecution and their employers in the Justice Department, most prominently with regard to the compensation for the photographer who would document the murder site and surroundings and for the surveyor who would spend ten days mapping the terrain.

What may ultimately have had a more serious consequence—at least for two researchers pursuing the case 60 years and more later— was the inability of the prosecutors to persuade their funding agents to allow a full transcription of the court reporter's notes from the trial. (Since the case was not appealed, they were told, a transcript of the proceedings was not essential.) As of the first consideration of Seymour's parole in 1933, the Departments of Justice and Interior were still debating which agency was poorer and which had the obligation to pay for the still-unproduced transcript. The story of a complex, dramatic trial has therefore had to be pieced together instead from the daily local news coverage in the Arizona Record *of Globe, AZ, and Phoenix's* Arizona Republic, *and the even sketchier second-hand reporting of the New York City newspapers and the wire services.*

Finding an anthropologist to testify

The government wanted Franz Boas or Ruth Benedict (or both) to appear at the trial and was particularly interested in their ability to discuss the fieldwork instructions given to Henrietta before her trip. Boas was hospitalized for a heart attack in December, and although he remained closely involved in the anthropologists' response strategy, he made it known that he could not attend the trial. Benedict alone was subpoenaed. Margaret Mead, who was Benedict's partner in the June meeting held with Henrietta to prepare her for her fieldwork among the Apache, was not called.

Benedict was emphatic that she did not want to attend the trial. The idea of serving as a character witness for someone whose character she was now seriously doubting, of assisting in the very public prosecution of a member of the Apache tribe she was dedicated to studying, and, in general, of exposing the human vulnerabilities of the research methodology she was instrumental in developing—all of this made the trial an unbearable prospect.

Columbia's anthropology department searched, somewhat frantically, for someone to send to the trial in Benedict's place. Finally, Ruth Underhill, an assistant at Barnard and a confidant of Henrietta's former professor Gladys Reichard, allowed her name to be put forward. Underhill had worked that summer with the Papago tribe in Sells, Arizona. According to Benedict, she was more eager to attend the trial than she let on.

An astonishingly unguarded letter that Benedict sent to Mead on March 12, two days before the trial began, provides critical perspective on Underhill's decision and Benedict's role in bringing it about.

> Darling, I'm still here! Did you have a presentiment that in spite of all appearances I wouldn't have to go? And I didn't. Guess who they were persuaded to accept in my place: Ruth Underhill. They asked for someone who could testify to the fact that Schmerler was sent to the reservation by Columbia and as to the usual policy of the department. Fackenthal appointed Underhill assistant secretary to the department and she went out armed with records. She is excellent as it happened for giving the kind of testimony that's needed, for she can't remember that she spoke to a man alone all summer. Who'd have thought it?
>
> It was all arranged through the law firm that serves Columbia's trustees at Fackenthal's request. With Papa Franz ill and not too much said about Kroeber, it was a good plea for my being essential to the department. Anyway, it worked. Now I imagine that Underhill will imagine she's put me under obligation for life. But before she and Gladys realized that martyrdom was her appointed role in the matter, Gladys had already told me that Underhill was all agog over the scheme.

She is, too. She knows reporters out there and she'll be appearing as Columbia's representative, and she's interested. Technically, I protected myself well! I told Ruth Bryan that I couldn't possibly suggest Underhill, on account of treading on her and Gladys' toes, so she got Papa Franz to think that he suggested Underhill himself and he called me at the lawyer to tell me to see if I could get them to take her. So I did.

She's already departed. They let Bertha Cohen off, too, and I had a party in celebration last night. All the people around the department came down here to drink the cointreau that Bertha had given me as her bet on having to go and what with the additional alcohol I provided it was an excellent and convivial party.[13]

The public explanation for the choice of Underhill as Columbia's representative was given by Benedict in a March 6 letter to Jesse Nusbaum, a New Mexico anthropologist:

I expected until day before yesterday that I might very well see you while I was in Arizona at the Schmerler trial. I was subpoenaed, but as they wanted formal testimony on Columbia fieldwork customs, and not particularly testimony on Miss Schmerler's instructions, it seemed possible to have someone else go in my place. With Professor Boas' illness, it was exceedingly difficult for me to be away at this time for an indefinite period, as the trial would necessarily be. The district attorney was most cooperative, and it has been

---

[13] Benedict's letter of March 12, 1932, was found in a closed file among the Mead papers in the Library of Congress, opened to Evelyn with the special permission of Catherine Bateson, Mead's daughter. We wondered if she had read it. This discovery came over a year and a half after we had first begun to chafe at what we felt was haste on the part of the Columbia anthropologists to condemn Henrietta, an inclination to believe the worst about her, an over-eagerness to defend their own actions, and, in fact, a callousness toward the whole tragedy. But we were prejudiced, we knew: one person's self-interest is another's prudence; one person's insensitivity is another's scientific objectivity. Nevertheless, there was some vindication in seeing the nakedness of one scheme so clearly laid out. By one measure, at least, these great anthropologists were quite human.

arranged that Miss Ruth Underhill, assistant in anthropology at Barnard, go to give this testimony.

Underhill would ultimately testify at the trial for less than twenty minutes. She would leave Globe shortly after her dismissal from the stand. Columbia's formal role in the Schmerler murder case would end there.

Assembling witness lists

The prosecution was assembling its witness list. There would be routine testimony establishing Henrietta's presence in Whiteriver and the legitimate purposes for which she had come. Some of those witnesses would also have been able to testify to Henrietta's good character, if the defense had been successful in making that an issue at the trial. James McNeil would testify that he brought Henrietta to the reservation for the first time in his mail truck, and found her a "lady in every respect." Ruth Underhill would bring the weight of Columbia University to establish the seriousness of Henrietta's mission— although she was privately reluctant to say anything in defense of her character (she had not known Henrietta personally, but had heard the ugly rumors from her good friend Gladys Reichard). Drs. Ferguson and Hupp, Don Cooley, Gertrude Cobb, and Jesus Velesques would testify to seeing Henrietta's badly battered body in the creek bed where it was found, and leave no doubt that the murder was brutal—and sexual. Silas Classay, Paul Johnson, and Jack Perry could contribute their independent knowledge of Golney Seymour's whereabouts on the day of the murder and following. And finally, Gertrude Cobb, Tom Dosela, and William Maupin, who had witnessed the statements of Golney and Gatewood, would testify that those statements were recorded accurately and had been made voluntarily, not under duress.

Several of the witnesses on the government list were also sought by the defense for testimony about both Golney's *and* Henrietta's character. Jack Keyes was prominent among those who would be called to testify for the defense, despite his closeness to Henrietta during her stay on the reservation and his role in helping find her body.

Donner would, of course, be called as a government witness

both because he could provide the context for Henrietta's work and actions on the reservation, with which he had been centrally involved, and because he was the embodiment of the need for law and order on the reservation. By the time of the trial, however, it had long since been clear that Donner was highly resentful of the trouble Henrietta's attitudes had brought on all of them and eager to spare Golney from being executed. Donner therefore also appeared on the defense's witness list and undoubtedly would have testified for that side as well, if they had been successful in introducing the question of Henrietta's character into the trial.

Possibly most interesting of all was who did *not* testify, despite appearing prominently on preliminary witness lists. Simon Wycliffe, whom Golney feared (as reported in his confession) had seen him and Henrietta together on horseback as they headed through the woods to the dance—and who reported that Golney had later chased him with murderous intentions, for no reason Wycliffe could think of—was glaringly absent from the trial.

The absence of John Doane is the most inexplicable of all. Doane, it is quite evident from the FBI files, was more than someone who could testify to Golney's presence at Henrietta's house (he had seen them talking that day) and someone who could testify to Golney's drinking on the afternoon of the murder (indeed, he drank with him). He was also someone, notably, who would tell Gatewood (according to notes of Gatewood's interview) that he, Doane, had broken into Henrietta's cabin and stolen suitcases containing notes and clothing. And, remarkably, he was also reported (by a "squaw named Dora," who lived in Forestdale, where Doane moved immediately after the murder) to have told her that he *saw* Henrietta struggling desperately to escape Golney in the woods, at a time which would have been just prior to her death; this is the only report that even hints of anyone else having witnessed the murder. And Street himself, in a side note to his February 3 report, had written:

> This Indian [Doane] was half-drunk on tulapai when interviewed and was very nervous —seemed to be very much excited, and should be interviewed again before being used as a witness, as it is believed by agent that he knows more

regarding this matter than he has told.

In fact, there is no record of Doane ever having been interviewed again, nor did he appear at the trial. His name only came up once, in passing, in court testimony.

Without question, the key witnesses for the government would be Street and Gatewood. Gatewood's statement stood, along with Golney's confession, as the only formal evidence tying Golney to the crime, and—in view of the likelihood that Golney would seek to retract his confession—would undoubtedly need to withstand severe challenges. Street would need to both substantiate the voluntary nature of the two statements and to establish his own credibility as their conduit.

The defense begins early

Dougherty had actually orchestrated the public beginnings of Golney's defense on the Saturday before the trial began. An AP story dated March 12, 1932, is headlined "APACHE WITNESS DISCLOSES STORY OF KILLING OF GIRL" and subheaded: "Student Threatened Indian When He Refused to Marry Her and In Ensuing Fight Was Slain, Witness Relates In Account to Defense."[14] Dougherty had finally been authorized by Judge Albert M. Sames to speak with Robert Gatewood, after several days of angry complaint that he was being denied access to key prosecution witnesses. The interview with Gatewood, whose testimony would clearly be central to the government case, took place at the Pima County Jail two days before

---

[14] There was an odd, unexplained story we found in the Washington Herald under a February 15, 1932 "U.S." dateline in which Golney is reported to have repudiated his original confession, calling Henrietta's death an "accident." This explanation follows the general story line presented publicly for the first time a month later by Golney during the trial—with the suggestion of gentle, consensual love-making, followed by a quarrel, then a fight—except that it ends with "The injuries of which the girl died were caused accidentally when he took the knife away from her, the Apache declared." (In his trial testimony he said that he had no idea what caused the injuries and did, in fact, not know she was seriously injured when he left her.) Was this a very early, anonymous leak from Dougherty? From BIA or reservation authorities or sources? Could this have been a simple typo, we wondered, recording March as February? Probably not, since the earliest testimony to this effect in the trial would have been March 17. Besides, there is a Justice Department stamp on the document we found dated February 16.

the trial was to open, and Dougherty clearly didn't waste a moment before going to the press.

Gatewood "broke his 8-months silence today" and told Dougherty that Henrietta "was slain after Seymour had refused his [sic] hysterical demand he marry her,"[15] according to the account in the *Arizona Daily Star* of March 12, 1932, which further reported:

> Later in the night, the Apache witness declared, he saw Seymour alone, and Seymour told him he had a fight with the girl when she demanded he marry her. Seymour was married already, Gatewood said. When Seymour told her that and refused her plea, she tried to 'cut him' with a knife.

> Next morning, Gatewood related, Seymour told him 'I acted bad last night.'

The article also noted:

> Previous to his interview with Gatewood, Dougherty had expressed an opinion Miss Schmerler, misunderstanding Indian emotional reactions, had essayed flirtatious advances which, misunderstood in turn by Seymour, had led to reciprocations on his part, which evoked a fight and resulted in the death of the girl.

According to the *Arizona Daily Star*, Dougherty indicated that Seymour's defense would be based on such reasoning. Gatewood's story, "*if repeated on the stand* [emphasis added]" would not alter the defense he had planned.

In fact, Gatewood would say in his later court testimony that he had misunderstood some of the questions he'd been asked in his interrogation; but he still stood by his statement that Henrietta

---

[15] The pronouns here are confusing, but most likely either simply innocent typos or recorded incorrectly as a result of the translation from Apache to English. In addition, the article is presented as if the reporter had heard directly from Gatewood, which contributes to the difficulty.

reacted angrily to Golney's refusal to marry her.

This was to be one of many variations of the revised story that Golney and his lawyer would put out during the trial—and later during his relentless pursuit of parole. In the most astonishing of his accounts, found in a parole application handwritten in prison fifteen years later, he said, "I have been charged, convicted, and committed for a crime which in my opinion does not warrant the severe penalty imposed. I do not know who committed the crime. I was drunk at the time. If it were Golney Seymour, then Golney Seymour did not know what he was doing. It was not premeditated if Seymour perpetrated the act. A crime not planned, but committed out of passion, drink, fear or any other stimulant, should not have been first degree murder. At most the charge should have been second degree, and the sentence should not have been more than twenty or twenty-five years. Of course if Golney Seymour did not commit the crime, he should not be here at all." (When we read that, we thought of O.J. Simpson's proposed book and television special, If I Did It, Here's How It Happened, *released finally to disbelief and dismay and with the revised title* If I Did It: Confessions of the Killer, O.J. Simpson, New York: Beaufort Books, 2007.)

Golney would not get a chance to tell the details of his newest story until late in the fifth day of the trial, but Dougherty would meanwhile be previewing many of those details in both his statements to the press and to the jury.

Part Four:

THE TRIAL OF GOLNEY SEYMOUR

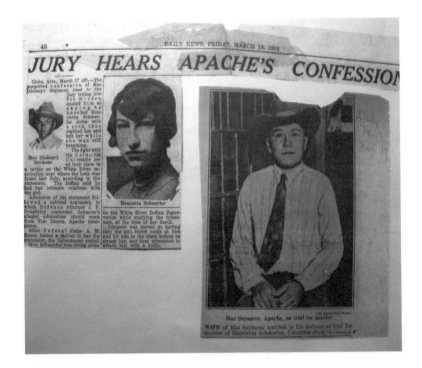

Chapter Thirteen

Seven Days in the Courthouse

Globe, Arizona, was incorporated in 1875 as a mining camp. In 1932, it remained a mostly dusty frontier town, with a population that had never exceeded 7,200. Now, its "downtown" featured two prominent buildings, both courthouses. The Gila County Courthouse was a huge gray stone structure, built on North Broad Street in 1905 primarily of tufa rock cut from the San Carlos Apache reservation. A three-story jail in the back, "behind which many were hanged," was connected to the courthouse by a bridge familiarly called the "walk of horror." The trial and conviction of the Apache Kid, legendary renegade, had been held in 1889 in the building's smaller predecessor—followed by the Kid's having overpowered and killed the sheriff escorting him to jail.

Less than two blocks away, on Hill and Sycamore Streets, sat the newer (1928) and smaller but still imposing U.S. Post Office and Courthouse, which, on March 14, was attracting far more than its share of local—and national—attention. The trial of Golney Seymour was in federal court because there is federal jurisdiction over the murder of a non-native on a Native American reservation. The main courtroom was overflowing that morning, and camped outside on the streets were dozens of White Mountain Apache, denied entrance to the trial but, in most cases, there to show solidarity with one of their own.

COLLECTION OF RICHARD S. MICKLE

U.S. Post Office and Courthouse (1928), Globe, Arizona. Building used by the U.S. District Court for the District of Arizona. Still in use as a post office. (National Archives, RG 121-BS, Box 3, Folder W)

Presiding at the trial was Judge Albert M. Sames, an Illinois native and long-time Superior Court judge in Arizona, who had just the previous year been appointed by President Herbert Hoover to the United States District Court in Arizona.

Day One: Jury selection

Barely into the opening minutes of the trial's first day, from the first questions asked of prospective jurors, the defense gave clear indication of the tack it would take. There would, despite the signed confession, be a claim of self-defense. That the defendant was intoxicated, and could therefore not have premeditated his act would be offered as a mitigating circumstance.

Dougherty announced he would ask potential jurors, "Would you be biased against the defendant if the evidence should disclose he violated a custom of his tribe by riding behind an unmarried woman on a horse?" And, "Would you require the defendant, who is an Indian, to exercise more discretion and more rectitude in resisting temptation to commit an illegal act than you would require if he were a white person?"

Gung'l's objections to these two questions were sustained, and the court ordered the records to show both that the questions had been raised and that the government had properly objected.

The quickest disqualifier, prospective jurors found, was to tell the prosecutor that they were opposed to the death penalty, or knew they would not vote for it in this case. According to a handwritten list of twenty-six potential jurors found in Golney Seymour's court file, four were eliminated for their stand on the death penalty—and one was eliminated from the list as "deaf-prejudicial." Several others were excused for having "already formed and expressed an opinion."

Court was extended—unusual for the customarily sleepy courthouse—into an evening session, so that the jury could be finally empaneled and testimony for the prosecution begin the next morning.

The twelve jurors selected were all men. In fact, it would seem that, as was the custom then, every one of the sixty-eight names in the original pool was male, although several were listed by their initials. The *Tucson Daily Citizen* said in a March 12 dispatch, "Dougherty has been handed a list of the venire from which 12 *white men* [emphasis added] will be selected to pass upon the guilt of Seymour." The paper also reported that the final jury "conspicuously excluded farmers and ranchers," a number of whom had appeared on the original list.

The potential jurors who were questioned—including both those who were excused and those who were ultimately chosen—were all clearly identified by name, residence, and occupation in the news accounts of the *Arizona Record* and the *Tucson Daily Citizen*. The reasons for their being excused were also given. *[Considerations of privacy and safety for jurors and prospective jurors have long since taken precedence over the public's right to know this information.]* The variety of occupations of the final jurors, if not of their gender or ethnicity, was impressive:

Samuel C. Foote, barber
Henry H. Hood, grocery clerk
J. Myron Allred, salesman
Andrew H. Crane, carpenter

Vernon Grade, oil truck driver
Paul Michaelson, contractor
George Mills, miner
G.D. Barclay, feed and fuel dealer
Benjamin T. Worley, laundryman
James F. Arillo, assayer
Charles Carrell, highway department employee
Fred Whitford, miner

Day Two: Establishing the body

Much of the earliest part of the trial would be spent, somewhat
bizarrely, establishing that it was indeed Henrietta's body that had
been found in the ravine. With the jury finally empaneled on March
14, the second day opened with a parade of government witnesses
detailing the finding and identification of the body and the conditions
surrounding the discovery. Dougherty continually questioned the
relevance of the testimony to the charges brought against his client,
while regularly denying that any of this showed the victim to be
Henrietta Schmerler.

Columbia's Ruth Underhill, as the prosecution's lead-off witness,
testified for less than twenty minutes. She reported that Henrietta,
as one of three young women sent by Columbia to southwestern
reservations during the summer of 1931, was assigned to "study
particularly women of the Apache tribe," and was to write a thesis
from the material thus obtained. She said Henrietta was given money
for her expenses and "to pay Indians who might give her information."
Much of Underhill's brief time on the stand was occupied by a back-
and-forth between the attorneys: Gung'l attempted to get her to
speak of the many other students who had been sent to reservations
for similar purposes, but Dougherty repeatedly objected on grounds
that this was irrelevant. The objections were sustained by Judge
Sames, and Underhill was dismissed shortly thereafter.

The driver of the "stagecoach"—or mail truck—who had
first brought Henrietta from Showlow, Arizona, to Fort Apache—
James McNeil—identified the suitcase in the courtroom as the one
Henrietta had carried with her on the ride. He said that he had later
delivered a cot to her cabin. Under cross-examination by Dougherty,

COLLECTION OF RICHARD S. MICKLE

Left to right, Golney's employer, Sid Earl; his lawyer, John Dougherty; Golney; his parents, Samuel and Alma Seymour ("Mr. and Mrs. H-4").

he admitted that the suitcase he had first seen was new and this one looked old and battered.

A surveyor and mapper, Charles Firth, established for the jury, with the use of a large map, the location of the death scene and the lay of the immediate surroundings.

Dr. John Hupp, one of two doctors summoned to the death scene, gave the most graphic testimony. Using Agent Street as a model, he described the position of the body as he had found it eight months earlier. According to the *Arizona Record*, he told the jurors "The body was on its back with the knees drawn up, the right knee being slightly higher than the left. The right arm was thrown out above her head, with the right hand clenched as if grasping something. The head was turned to the right. The left arm was lying by the side.

"From the waist to the knees, the body was bare, except for a band which held the bloomers in place," Hupp continued. "The right stocking was down over the boot, hunting boots, the rest of the clothing being drawn up over the head, exposing the breasts. The body was in a badly decomposed condition. There was a wrist watch on the left arm and a bracelet on the right. The body was removed to the carpenter shop where I made two more examinations."

Hupp described the cut over the right eye—"made by a sharp instrument"—and a bruise on the right temple. He described the face as decomposed, but said there was evidence that the nose was "mashed in." He said two front teeth were missing—"I think they were the upper teeth." At this point, Gung'l asked if he had his notes to refer to and Hupp began to read them. But Dougherty immediately asked if they were originals and, upon being told they were typed, objected. The objection was sustained.

Without reference to his notes, Hupp described the knife wound to the back of Henrietta's neck, which he believed to have caused her death. He said the wound was about four inches long and two inches deep.

On cross-examination, Hupp conceded that the body could have been moved before he arrived. He said, according to the account in the *Arizona Record*, that he had "examined the body for evidence of criminal assault but did not tell the results of his examination."[16] Hupp had, in fact, previously expressed his opinion—"from the position of the body"—that Henrietta had been sexually assaulted. The other doctor on the site, Ray Ferguson, had said he personally could not determine this from what he had seen of the body.

Day Three: Building to the government's chief witness

Special reservation officer William Maupin—or "Tulapai Bill"—testified for the prosecution at the beginning of the Wednesday session. His nickname came from his vehement, if sporadic, enforcement of prohibition policies, specifically regarding the drink most commonly used by the White Mountain Apache.[17] Maupin described his role in

---

[16] The word "rape" was virtually never used in any of the press accounts we reviewed of the murder. "Criminal assault" was only one of many euphemisms, with "ravished" being particularly common.

[17] The prevailing view of Apache drinking habits was presented in Edward S. Curtis's 1907 opus, *The North American Indian*: "The intoxicant and curse of their lives is tulapai, or tizwin as it is sometimes called. Tulapai means "muddy or gray water." It is, in fact, a yeast beer... As the tulapai will spoil in twelve hours, it must be drunk quickly. Used in

COLLECTION OF RICHARD S. MICKLE

Left to right, Golney Seymour; John Dougherty, personal attorney for Seymour; James McManus, Deputy U.S. Marshal, custodian of Seymour during trial. Below, Special Agent in Charge R.H. Colvin; prosecuting attorneys Clarence V. Perrin and John C. Gung'l. Pictures made in U.S. Courtrooms, Federal Building, Globe, Arizona. (ACME) 3/18/32.

COLLECTION OF RICHARD S. MICKLE

the discovery of the body and identified as Henrietta's the flashlight exhibited in evidence. He told also of having found the suitcase which was now sitting in evidence near the witness stand, already connected to Henrietta by stage driver McNeil. He and John Doane[18] had pulled it from a crevice between several rocks at a point about a mile and a half from where Henrietta's body was found, he said. He told of opening it at reservation headquarters in Whiteriver and seeing "a bunch of papers and yellow blocks [presumably for work with children]," then resealing them into a tow sack and transporting it to Globe, where he turned it over to Gung'l, Perrin, Donner, and Colvin for use in the trial.

Gung'l asked him to open the suitcase for the jury and Maupin complied. It contained assorted papers and yellow wooden blocks, as Maupin had said, plus a pocketbook, a Boy Scout belt, several notebooks, and some letters. At Gung'l's request, Maupin took out several letters with the name "Henrietta" or "Henrietta Schmerler" written on them.

Dougherty sat quietly, if tensely, until Gung'l moved to place the exhibit into evidence. Then he sprang to his feet, objecting loudly that the suitcase had not, in fact, been properly identified. "The grip when last seen by James McNeil, the stage driver, was brand new. This suitcase, found a mile and a half away, is old and battered. I don't know, and the records do not prove, that this suitcase is the one brought to the reservation by Miss Schmerler."

The judge overruled the objection and the suitcase was placed

---

moderation it is not a bad beverage, but by no means a pleasant one to the civilized palate. The Apache, however, knows no moderation in his tulapai drinking. He sometimes fasts for a day, then drinks great quantities of it—often a gallon or two—when for a time he becomes a savage indeed." (p.50)

[18] This casual reference to John Doane is one of only three we could find in the entire trial. What Maupin did not say here is that Doane, suspected of stealing and discarding the suitcase, had, under duress, led him to its hiding place. Nor was there any mention of Doane's drinking with Seymour and Gatewood on the afternoon of the murder. Nor of Doane's purportedly having spoken privately of having seen, from a distance, Henrietta running for her life from Golney. We learned of all these from the FBI reports—but they are not followed up in those files, either. (Today, this information would have had to be disclosed at the trial, under the subsequent "Brady rule.")

Left, Golney's wife, Elizabeth, holding their newborn son, at Golney's trial.
Right, Golney seated in front of holding cell.

into evidence. Dougherty then asked for permission to examine the contents himself—and spent the next twenty minutes doing so. In his subsequent cross-examination, Dougherty got Maupin to admit that he knew the victim only as Miss Schmerler, since that is how she had introduced herself to him.

"So the fact she told you she was Miss Schmerler is the only knowledge on which you have to base your testimony this dead woman was Henrietta Schmerler?"

"Well, she introduced herself as Miss Schmerler," responded Maupin.

"I ask on the strength of that answer that all this witness' testimony be stricken," Dougherty demanded of the judge.

"It is easy to prove Henrietta Schmerler." According to the AP account, Dougherty was now "shouting." "But the government has not done so. I'm surprised it hasn't."

Judge Sames ruled that he would allow the testimony.

George Woolford, a deputy sheriff of Navajo County, followed Maupin but had an easier time on the stand. He identified an Indian bag he had found hanging near where Henrietta's body was found, plus its contents. He had originally opened it in Donner's office and found, as he described them, "a conch [probably a conch hat], a notebook with writing, blank papers, a small handkerchief, a metal cup containing $1.40 in silver consisting of two half dollars, a quarter, a dime, and a nickel." Dougherty this time allowed the bag and contents to be placed in evidence without objection, but, in an interesting procedural sidelight, forced Woolford to concede that he, Maupin, Dr. Hupp, and Gertrude Cobb had rehearsed the exact position of the body, with Agent Street acting as a model, just before the trial began. He clearly was prepared to sow seeds of doubt about the integrity of the prosecution's case wherever he could.

The next few witnesses established the comings and goings of the various parties as they passed through East Fork on the way to the Canyon Day dance that Saturday night. Silas Classey, a neighbor of Henrietta's, saw Golney Seymour, Jack Keyes, and Jack Perry passing by Henrietta's cabin "around 6 or 7 o'clock." A little later, he said, he saw "Mrs. H-4" coming by on horseback at a fast pace, while her daughter (Bessie Gatewood) and daughter-in-law (Elizabeth Seymour) rode alongside together on a second horse. Paul Johnson, who was working on a car with Classey, corroborated his account, with a bit of help from court interpreter Donald McIntosh.

Jack Perry, according to the brief account in the *Arizona Record* which is our primary source of Perry's testimony, said he had stopped by Henrietta's cabin "the night before the killing" *[actually, all the evidence points to late afternoon or early evening on the day of the dance]* and asked Henrietta for a drink of water. She told him she had no water in her house, he said. The newspaper account made more of his dress and anxiety than it did of his specific testimony. He was "dressed in a gray shirt, Levi overalls, brightly colored scarf, leather cuffs, leather leggings." He began his testimony in English, "appearing very nervous, but soon asked for an interpreter. He used a colored handkerchief all through his testimony to wipe his face."

Gatewood

But it was Robert Gatewood who, as the *Arizona Record* put it, "provided the only excitement of the day." Gatewood had long been anticipated to be the "star witness of the prosecution" and "the main link in the chain of circumstances which the government expects to weave into a noose around the neck of Seymour." However, since Gatewood's ostensible change of story had been publicized by Dougherty just before the trial, suspense had been mounting around the courthouse. Had the powerful pull of kinship and the taboo against testifying against one's own—not to mention the fearsome prospect of returning to live among Golney's family and friends—gotten to Gatewood in the four and a half months he'd been kept incommunicado off the reservation? Or would the threat of facing whatever consequences had persuaded him to speak against Golney in the first place induce him to stand by the statement he had originally made to Agent Street?

Gatewood was summoned early Wednesday afternoon. He walked to the stand with his head lowered. There was a distinct buzz in the normally silent courtroom. It was understood that not only might Gatewood's testimony be important in contradicting whatever defense Golney would offer in his own behalf, but that the validity of Golney's confession would also invariably be judged by the reliability of Gatewood's original statement.

Gung'l's questioning was gentle and began slowly. In a quiet voice, mostly through an interpreter, Gatewood spoke of Golney's visiting him on the afternoon of the Canyon Day dance, their looking for a clean razor to cut Golney's hair, their ride past Henrietta's cabin, seeing Jack Perry there with a cup of water he had been given by Henrietta, and Golney's having gone in to speak briefly to her while he himself waited by the gate. *[One of many minor contradictions: Perry had testified that she had refused his request, saying she had told him she had no water.]* He described their return to his father-in-law's (H-4) camp and, a little more than half hour later, their departure—with Golney going in to visit Henrietta while he, Gatewood, continued down the road toward his own cabin. At this point, he testified, he went to bed.

Gung'l moved quickly to the heart of the testimony. Gatewood "was led to his startling revelation with dramatic suddenness" is the way the *Arizona Record* reported it. Gatewood was asked what happened next, after he had retired. "Early the next morning, Max came to my place with blood on his hands. 'I had to kill that white woman down there,' he told me," Gatewood answered, without expression.

If there was any remaining doubt that Gatewood would be the "star witness" for the prosecution, it was removed as Gatewood continued to quote Golney. "We were intimate and when she threatened to tell on me and have me sent far away, I had to kill her. If you say anything about it, I will kill you, too."[19]

Gatewood said that, in addition to the blood on Golney's hands, there was also blood on his sleeve—"more on the right than on the left." He reported that Golney went over to the fire to wash off the blood, dried his hands over the flames, and left.

Later that morning, Gatewood testified, Golney returned to Gatewood's camp. Golney asked, "Do you remember what I told you last night? I will kill you if you tell anyone!"

Dougherty began his cross-examination quickly. "Where do you live?" he asked Gatewood.

"I used to live at Cibicue, but now I live at the East Fork" was Gatewood's answer.

Dougherty persisted, "Where have you been living since November 1?"

Gung'l, seeing immediately where this line of questioning was heading, objected, requesting that the jury be excused while the admissibility of this question be argued before the judge only. Sames agreed to dismiss the jury and hear the objection.

At this point the acrimony between Gung'l and Dougherty reached its height. Gung'l complained bitterly that the defense counsel had "insisted on interviewing every government witness" and, according to the AP account, "branded his actions 'unprofessional and unethical.'"

---

[19] This language, as reported in the *Arizona Record* and featuring their word of choice for the sexual act—"intimacy"—is suspect, and makes the lack of a transcript even more meaningful.

"You scapegrace!" Dougherty shouted at Gung'l. "You talk to me of ethics!"

When Sames had calmed the attorneys, with the only threat of censure we could find in the trial, they got to the business of the sidebar. Gung'l maintained that Gatewood's detention at the hands of federal authorities was not germane to the testimony he was giving. Dougherty made clear that he wanted to show the jury that Gatewood may well have been under the influence of the district attorney during the months he was held incommunicado—and without counsel—in the Pima County jail. Sames said he would permit the question, but cautioned Dougherty against any suggestion that Gatewood had been improperly influenced. After a total of ten minutes, Sames summoned the jury to return.

"Where have you been living since November 1?" Dougherty asked again.

"In a hotel," Gatewood responded.

"Is that the hotel run by the sheriff?" asked Dougherty.

Gatewood paused briefly. "I was taken to Tucson November 19 and kept in a hotel for three days. I was then taken to the jail, where I spent 113 nights. I was brought here several days before the trial."

Dougherty, clearly unhappy with the testimony Gatewood had just given, then questioned Gatewood—"hammered," according to the *Arizona Record* account—about statements he had made to Dougherty in their meeting two days before the trial opened. Gatewood finally said he had misunderstood some of the questions. What he had meant, when he said that Golney had told him he killed Henrietta "because [s]he had refused to marry him" was that "marriage in Apache means having intimate relations over a period of time."

Dougherty was finally able to elicit from Gatewood that Golney had told him he killed Henrietta in self-defense when she attacked him with a knife "after [s]he had refused to marry him on the grounds he was already married."

Dougherty allowed Gatewood to stand down, having laid the groundwork for the most likely of defenses that Golney Seymour would offer, self-defense. But the certainty with which Gatewood had also affirmed Golney's having admitted to killing Henrietta was surely not good news for the defense case.

J. A. Street was called to the stand late Wednesday afternoon. The FBI agent's primary task was to authenticate the confession he had obtained, but Dougherty was on his feet the moment Gung'l mentioned Golney's statement. He asked Gung'l if the statement he was about to read into the record had been interpreted. When Gung'l said that it was and began to explain the circumstances, Dougherty interrupted. He objected that Street could not testify about a statement that had been interpreted—as such, it would be hearsay and therefore inadmissible. Gung'l countered that he would show beyond any doubt that the statement Golney signed was fully understood by him; he would further substantiate the confession with testimony authenticating the interpreter's services. When Sames asked both lawyers to cite authorities for their opposing positions on interpreted statements, however, Gung'l asked for extra time and the court was recessed until the following morning.

Day Four: The confession

The fourth morning of the trial, Thursday, was devoted to hearing the testimony of those who had witnessed the reading and signing of the confession on that hectic morning of November 1. The jury would remain out of the courtroom until the judge was convinced that the reading of the statement was appropriate.

Agent Street began with the admission that he "did not know the Apache language but had dictated the statement to Mrs. Cobb from notes he made while Seymour was confessing to Tom Dosela in the presence of William Maupin, Mrs. Cobb, William Donner, T.E. Shipley and Jesus Velesques that he killed Miss Schmerler during a fight." It is noteworthy that Gung'l restricted his questioning of Street to the reading, recording, interpreting, and dictating of the confession that morning, and did not ask about the involved process of interrogation which led to it—nor about the FBI man's three-month pursuit of the killer. Dougherty likewise withheld his questioning in these areas, quite possibly in anticipation of later introducing the ideas of coercion and fabrication.

Tom Dosela, the Apache who had been called from the San Carlos reservation to act as interpreter during the confession, testified that he spoke both Apache and English and that he first interpreted Mr. Street's reading of Golney's constitutional rights. He said Street told Golney that he "wanted him to make the statement voluntarily but that if he did make any statements, they must be the truth." He said that when he read the confession as it had been recorded to Golney—"the entire statement in the presence of witnesses"— Golney had signed it voluntarily. "He said it was all right but he had more to tell," Dosela testified.

In cross-examination, Dougherty pressed Dosela on the possibility that changes may have been made throughout the process of interpreting Golney's statement. Dosela conceded that the form of the confession as it appeared this day in court "might differ widely from statements made by Seymour in the clubhouse the day before the confession was typewritten." Asked by Dougherty if any persuasion had been used by Street to convince Golney to sign, Dosela quoted Street as saying: "If you come through, it will go a lot easier with you."

Jesus Velesques, who had known Henrietta through his daughter Mary (who had made the dress Henrietta would wear to the dance) and was also involved in the finding of Henrietta's body, testified that he had been present throughout Street's conversations with Golney, that he himself spoke both Apache and English, and that the confession was an accurate representation of Golney's statements.

Woolford, the deputy sheriff, had also been present at the signing of the statement. Furthermore, he said he had transported Golney from McNary, where he had been kept in jail the night before he confessed, to Whiteriver, where Street awaited. "Max, what do they have you in jail for?" he said he asked during the trip, and Golney replied it was "something about a white woman." Woolford further said that Golney, speaking about his time in jail, had told him, "The devil was there, too."

Donner, the reservation superintendent who was known as a hard-edged advocate for law and order, was originally seen by the prosecution as one of its important witnesses. But it became increasingly clear that Donner's sympathies now lay more with Golney Seymour, as his resentment toward Henrietta appeared to grow daily. He wound up on both witness lists, and in this struggle over the validity of the confession, which he had personally overseen, he was called by Dougherty. The defense lawyer here focused his questions to Donner on Golney's understanding of English. Donner said that, although Golney had finished fifth grade at the reservation's Theodore Roosevelt Indian School, he spoke little English."I am sorry to say that the Indians do not retain as much of the English as we would like for them to retain," he said from the stand.

The fact that Donner did not—either in his testimony or even in the behind-the-scenes correspondence we have been privy to—offer any hint that Golney might have been abused during his interrogation may be revealing. Either Golney had not, in fact, been coerced, as we had thought might be the case—or Donner's position in the hierarchy made it impossible for him to challenge the government in any public way. The record seems to indicate he came to believe some of the worst stories about Henrietta, and was eager for Golney not to be punished excessively.

Dougherty was careful throughout to establish wherever he could that Golney had been held by Street for over a day—approximately thirty hours, without food—before the confession was made public. Tulapai Bill Maupin was recalled to the stand to tell of his assignment to escort Golney to and from the jail in McNary and the agency headquarters in Whiteriver. Dougherty made sure that Velesques, who had been there much of the time, told of the many hours that Golney had been questioned at headquarters. Dosela, too, was asked to speak of the length of time Golney was held before the confession was delivered.

At every opportunity, Dougherty interposed his objections to the reading of the confession, both on the grounds of its unproven validity—especially due to Golney's weak understanding of English and the conditions under which his statement was obtained—and the fact that the body had not been proven to be Henrietta Schmerler's. This latter argument appeared increasingly to irritate the judge, who seemed to pick up the pace in overruling the objections.

Dougherty's insistence on keeping the identity issue afloat remains puzzling. The coroner's jury that convened on July 25 (six white citizens of Fort Apache and Whiteriver) had quite explicitly identified the body it was viewing as that of Henrietta Schmerler. No less than twenty other reservation officials, law officers, medical personnel, and assorted others who knew her had seen the body and had not expressed a single doubt that it was Henrietta. Was Dougherty intending to inject that one additional bit of doubt in the jury? Would the jury not respond as we did to this ploy, sensing a transparent attempt to distract from the weaknesses of the other defenses? Would this tactic not therefore be counterproductive? Certainly nothing in the subsequent actions of the judge or jury showed otherwise.

Gung'l moved once again to allow the reading of the confession before the jury. He asked only that several parenthetical, hand-bracketed comments that were added in the body of the confession to Golney's statement be excluded from the reading.

When Street wrote up the confession for Golney's signature, he had included several words not spoken by Golney to Dosela. He had added, for example, "[Henrietta Schmerler]" after "the white girl" for purposes of clarification. More tellingly, he had added in brackets several mentions of Golney's unwillingness to discuss the blood on his clothing. "[At this time subject was asked if he went into Robert Gatewood's camp to wash the blood off of his shirt, to which he would not answer.]" And later: "[Subject was asked several times with reference to blood being on his shirt and if he had not washed his shirt while at the camp of Robert Gatewood, to which he refused to answer.]" Finally, Street had added this: "[On being further questioned subject stated that he had never talked to his father and mother about this matter, but he believed that they knew what he had done.]"

None of these parenthetical comments came directly from Golney, as the rest of the signed statement was contended by the government to have been. Gung'l would offer the statement into evidence without them.

As the courthouse clock now approached three o'clock on the fourth day of the trial, Dougherty made his final plea to the court to exclude the confession. He would base his objection on six reasons:

"For the reason that the government had failed to prove that Henrietta Schmerler, named in the indictment, had been murdered."

"That the government had failed utterly to establish the corpus delicti."

Golney Seymour and Donald McIntosh, official court interpreter

"That the instrument contained matters not testified to by the defendant and is not a true confession."

"That the confession and statement upon which the exhibits were founded were obtained under circumstances that show that defendant did not make it freely and voluntarily."

"Further it appears that defendant made other statements in reference to this written statement not included therein."

"It is not a true, complete and accurate statement made by the defendant on the day previous."

A brief recess was called and the lawyers and judge conferred once again. Raised voices were heard coming from the judge's chambers, but there is no report of this conversation.

When court resumed, Gung'l asked to withdraw his original motion to admit the confession without the deleted portions, and—surprisingly instead—moved that the entire statement be admitted. Dougherty objected, perfunctorily this time—it was evident that he knew he had lost this round. Sames overruled the objection and declared that the confession could be read into the record for the jury.

Confession

Gung'l then read the confession aloud, pausing regularly for dramatic effect. The jury listened intently and showed no outward reaction.

Whiteriver, Arizona, November 1, 1931.

Reference the murder of Henrietta Schmerler at Fort Apache on July 18, 1931, I Golney Seymour, otherwise known as "Max" Seymour, after being informed of my constitutional rights that any statement I might make with reference to the murder of Henrietta Schmerler could and would be used against me in the prosecution of the case, after being so informed, it is my desire to make a statement and tell the truth regarding the matter to the best of my memory and belief.

My name is Golney Seymour, also known as "Max" Seymour, age 21. I reside with my father on East Fork near Whiteriver, Arizona. My father is known as H-4 (Samuel Seymour), my mother is Alva Seymour. I have a sister that is married to Robert Gatewood who resides on East Fork near where my father's camp is and where the white girl (Henrietta Schmerler) lived.

On July 18, 1931, I went from my father's camp over to my brother-in-law, Robert Gatewood's camp, with the desire of having my hair cut. Later on in the afternoon Robert Gatewood and myself returned to the camp of my father. We were on horseback. On arrival at the gate that goes into my father's place just near where the white girl lives, we saw Jack Perry standing talking to the white girl. The gate was opened by Robert Gatewood and we rode into my father's camp. Before going into my father's

camp, I had a conversation with the white girl and
she said that she desired to borrow a horse from
me to ride to the Canyon Day dance. I told her that
I had only the one horse, but she could ride with
me to the dance if she desired to do so. Later on
Robert Gatewood and myself left my father's camp,
passed out of the gate, Gatewood going down the
road and I stopping at the white girl's house. We
remained there a short time and we left, the white
girl and I both riding the same horse, she riding
in front in the saddle and I was riding behind.

Down the road a short ways from the white girl's
camp I saw Robert Gatewood off to the side of the
road as he was going toward his camp. We went down
the road further. It was getting dusk and we met
Simon Wycliffe who passed us going up the road in
the direction that we were coming from. I recognized
him but wondered if Simon recognized me. We went on
past eh [sic] seven-mile canyon and we turned off
on the trail that leads in south of the old Fort
Apache cemetery and goes south of the Fort Apache
town. We arrived at a little canyon where there is
a flume that crosses the canyon. It was muddy in the
canyon and we each got down and walked across the
canyon to the far side, when the white girl began
to hit me with her hand bag and tease me. I thought
from her movements that she desired to have sexual
relations with me. I took hold of her and we had
sexual relations at that time. After this was over
she got mad and commenced to fight me. She threw a
rock at me and hit me in the breast. She got a knife
out of her purse and also picked up another rock
and started to throw it at me, and just as she did
I threw a rock at her and hit her and knocked her
down. I do not know ehteher [sic] I hit her in the
head or not. She fell on her fact [sic], but as I
threw the rock she was facing me. After I hit her

with the rock I went over to her, took the knife
away from her, put my arm under her neck and stabbed
her in the neck and possibly about the head. After
I had stabbed her she got up and walked down the
canyon for a short ways and layed down. I walked
down to where she was and stood on the bank and
cried and felt very bad about what I had done. I
tried to talk to her and told her she was the cause
of me killing her. I stood there for a short while
and I picked up a stick and laid it across the body.
She was still breathing. I then got back to where
my horse was, which was standing on the west side
of the draw. I rode down toward Canyon Day and ran
into a fence and could not get through it. I turned
and came back, crossing the draw where the fight
first started. It is possible at that time that my
horse could have stepped on the girl's fountain pen
and crushed it, but I did not see any pen there.

I then came back up to Robert Gatewood's camp.
I called Robert Gatewood out and told him what
I had done and told him not to tell anyone. (At
this time subject was asked if he went into Robert
Gatewood's camp to wash the blood off of his shirt,
to which he would not answer.) While there I
talked to Robert Gatewood and told him not to tell
what I had done, as I knew he had seen me going
to the dance with the white girl. After talking
with Robert Gatewood I got back on my horse and
went back to the Canyon Day dance. After arriving
at the dance I sat out on the wood pile for quite
a while and my wife came out to where I was.

(Subject was asked several times with reference
to blood being on his shirt and if he had not
washed his shirt while at the camp of Robert
Gatewood, to which he refused to answer).

(On being further questioned subject stated
that he had never talked to his father and
mother about this matter, but he believed
that they knew what he had done.)

(Signed)   Golney Seymour

Witnesses:
Jesus Velesques,
Geo. Woolford,
Wm. Maupin
Wm. Donner
T. E. Shipley,
J. A. Street, Spl. Agt., Bureau of Investigation,
Dept. of Justice, El Paso, Texas

I hereby certify that I read the statement
to Golney Seymour in the Apache language
and he stated to me in the presence of
others that it was true and correct.

(Signed)   Thomas
Dosela, Interpreter

[Reproduction of these signatures is on page 259.] When the reading was completed, Gung'l announced that the government would rest its case.

The defense takes over

Almost four days into the trial, it was the defense's turn to make its case. Dougherty took the floor and was silent for several poignant minutes, as he shuffled through his papers. "Here's what I believe to have happened. And I will prove it to you, beyond a shadow of a doubt, through the testimony of the witnesses who will appear next on this stand," he began, finally.

The *Arizona Record* of March 19, 1931, provided Dougherty's opening remarks at length. They tell a story at variance on many points—and in emphasis—with the purported confession that had just been read to the court. More remarkable, however, is the most salient difference between this version of Dougherty's and the one presented over the following two days in Golney's own testimony and in Dougherty's closing argument: the admission here that Golney had killed Henrietta and knew it, while Golney himself subsequently and explicitly denied that he had.

"I expect to prove that Seymour replied to Miss Schmerler when she asked him to take her to the dance on his horse that it wouldn't be proper for him; that she invited him into the house to have a drink; that he followed her inside the house and she brought out a pint bottle of whiskey.

"When he complained that it burned his throat she put sugar and water in the bottle and they both took another drink. That after two or three drinks he felt merry and generous and when she asked him again to take her to the dance he said, 'All right.'

"She was in Indian costume, the first time he had ever seen her so dressed. They got on the one horse, she in front and he behind; that they met Robert Gatewood on a burro. They went on down the road. She talked to him, some of which he understood and some of which he did not understand.

"She appeared very happy, turning every once in a while to chuck him under the chin. They came to a trail after passing Simon Wycliffe and when she wanted to go up it to do some exploring he turned his horse's head that way. They went up the trail a little way and got off. She had brought the bottle along and they had another drink. They got on the horse again. By that time he was feeling very good. They went up the wash and decided to get off and cross it on foot.

"She kept on teasing and tantalizing him and hit him with the Indian bag she was carrying. He grabbed her. She went over beside him and sat down. She kept teasing him. So he finally became intimate with her and she made no strenuous objection. After it was over she cried.

"He felt badly over not doing right by his wife. He told her he had done wrong and was going to the dance alone. She insisted on going with him. *Rocks were thrown* [author's emphasis]. She drew a knife. They wrestled. She was cut but he doesn't know how many times.

"He got on his horse and started off but ran into a fence, turned down the trail and went to Gatewood's home. He told Gatewood he had killed the white woman and left there for the dance. He was still intoxicated when he got to the dance. His wife came out to where he was sitting and made a bed of hay for him. He slept the rest of the night and went to his father's house the next morning. He told Gatewood he had been bad the night before.

"Afterward he went to his own home five or six miles away. When he was sent for he went to the agency. He was put in the jail in McNary. The next time he talked to Street several officers were present. He was kept there a long time before the paper was brought in for him to sign.

"He was stupid and felt from the attitude of the officers that he had to sign it but it was not complete. He remonstrated with Dosela, the interpreter, who talked to Street and Street said it is not all there but go ahead and sign it."

It was apparent that the defense was now relying on several major threads: Golney was drunk. Henrietta helped make him drunk. Henrietta provoked the sexual attack and/or participated willingly. She was harmed by accident. Golney struck back in self-defense. Golney's confession was coerced. He didn't understand what he was signing and didn't mean what they said he said. Looming over it all was the suggestion that Henrietta was of loose moral character.

The first witness called, as the Thursday afternoon session ended, was H-4, Samuel Seymour, Golney's father and, as it turned out, an unwitting key to Golney's having been identified as the murderer. Dougherty drew from him that he "knows very little of the ways of the white man"—not even, noted the *Arizona Record*, incredulously—"how to convey the time of day." Dougherty asked him how old his son was, and H-4 said he did not know. "The white men have the papers," said H-4. "I don't know anything what the white men read and write." On cross-examination Gung'l could get nothing further of significance, and Samuel Seymour was dismissed. Court was recessed until Friday.

Day Five: Golney Seymour

The trial's fifth morning, Friday, featured a series of defense witnesses called to prove, somewhat paradoxically, that Golney was a good, stable man… and drunk on the night of July 18.

Golney's wife, Elizabeth Seymour, led off. If anyone was led to anticipate any drama—or any new information—in her testimony, they would be disappointed. She repeated the already-familiar account of her afternoon: going to her father-in-law's home with Golney, of Golney's leaving with Gatewood to get his hair cut, and of her going on to the Canyon Day Dance without Golney. She said he drank beer and tulapai during the afternoon, and that he arrived at the dance later on in the night in an intoxicated condition. At that time, she said, she made him a bed of blankets that he immediately curled up to sleep in, waking only in the early morning hours the next day. Gung'l, in his cross-examination, asked gently who had told Ms. Seymour to say that Golney was drunk. She denied that anyone had asked her to say this, but conceded that she had only actually seen him drink half a can of tulapai.

Under Gung'l's questioning, she said she was pregnant the night of the Canyon Day dance and that her baby, now six months old, had not yet been born when Henrietta Schmerler died. The newspaper accounts of Ms. Seymour's court appearance dwelt unusually heavily on her manner of dress. The *Arizona Record* described her as wearing "a long, flowing skirt of blue and red, a waist of a different color, her long black hair flowing down her back and partly hidden by a blanket shawl of red, purple and pink."

Several witnesses were then called briefly to establish that Golney was a solid citizen. Sid Earl, who had hired Golney for several cattle-herding jobs, said he had known Golney for fifteen years, that Golney had always proved a reliable worker, and his reputation was good. Walter Anderson, an Apache friend, testified he had known Golney all his life and that his reputation had always been good and he was law-abiding. There was no cross-examination of either witness, although Sames at one point chastised the courtroom spectators for an eruption of sustained, audible laughter during Anderson's testimony. (Dougherty had asked Anderson what his occupation was, and Anderson had said he has none, that he does nothing.)

Sames acidly announced that "this trial is not entertainment" and threatened to clear the courtroom if the spectators made noise again.

Character testimony

Reverend E. E. Genther, a missionary long residing on the Fort Apache reservation and pastor of the Lutheran Church at East Fork, testified he had known Golney all his life, and had, in fact, given him his name. As a former teacher of Golney's, he said that Golney had made slower progress in school than other Apache boys his age. Yet, Genther said that Golney had never been in any serious trouble before and that his character was "good."

Later, in cross-examination, Gung'l would get Genther to admit that he had earlier told Agent Street in a February interview that Golney was a "bright pupil." What he had meant, Genther said, was that Golney "was bright in his student activities, his actions on the playground, his associations with other youth, but that he was slow in his academic work." What was at play here, it seemed to us, was that the job of a character witness was to say complimentary and sympathetic things about the defendant; the other, contrasting role of a defense witness in this case was to help establish the possibility that Golney did not understand the confession he was signing.

When Dougherty asked Genther about his acquaintance with Henrietta, the prosecution lodged a strong objection. Any such discussion would be precluded as hearsay, they said. Sames allowed the objection and pronounced that he had "not changed his mind on the ruling he made earlier in the trial that any testimony offered by the defense on the character of Miss Schmerler or her activities on the reservation would not be admissible." Dougherty responded, "But since I have put the defendant on the stand, your honor, I thought you might have changed your mind. I ask that an exception to your ruling be noted." "All right," the judge agreed, and the jury was removed from the courtroom.[20]

---

[20] Judge Sames, it turns out, was acting on long-established Arizona legal precedent in excluding character testimony against Henrietta. There being no Uniform Federal Rules of Evidence at the time, applicable law in federal crimes resorted to whatever state law was in effect when the state was incorporated into the United States (in the

"For the record," Dougherty announced, now out of the jury's presence, "I desire to offer evidence to show that Miss Schmerler did not confine her activities to the study of anthropology, as indicated in evidence given for the government by Miss Underhill [of the Columbia anthropology department].

"I also want to prove Miss Schmerler was engaged in the study of abnormal sexual impulses of savages. Her conduct was such as to arouse indignation among the Indians and cause them to question her morals.

"I want to show, also, that on one occasion she met George Wallen, the Indian missionary youth, at the mission and asked him to accompany her home. That when they started out, she prevailed on him to go up the road with her. After going a few miles, she invited him to sit down and quizzed him about sexual life of savages. Her attempts to fondle him were most reprehensible to students of anthropology."

That Genther did not get to say more from the stand was a likely testament to the tight trial that Judge Sames was running. Genther had spoken at length to Agent Street prior to the trial and had made his skepticism about Henrietta's character clear. He admitted that he had not actually met her, but he "saw her in company with some of the Indians, and from what he saw at the time he thought she was acting foolishly—going around alone with different Indians... He also remembered hearing some of the Indians when in conversation about the white girl refer to her as a boudwam (prostitute)." Genther also told Street, when he was interviewing various Apache about the propriety of an unmarried woman riding horseback with a man, that he "knows" the practice "is entirely unethical." He went further: "It is unethical for a single woman or a widow to even travel around the country alone [emphasis added] or with some Indian man." In fact, his was the only statement on this subject to use the word "unethical," although many of

---

case of Arizona, 1912). "Character of deceased is not in issue in trial for murder, unless some evidence has been given tending to show that the defendant acted in self-defense" (Territory v. Harper, 1 Ariz. 399, 25 Pac. 598) is the applicable court ruling, according to the Digest of Supreme Court of Arizona Decisions, published in 1915. Thus, only a penchant for violence on Henrietta's part, had it existed, would have been admissible as evidence.

the respondents did say that it was unwise.

Genther's statement in his FBI interview that "he had not actually met" Henrietta struck us as strange. On the first page of Henrietta's field notes —which were never introduced at the trial—was this June 24 entry (the day after she arrived, and in the first paragraph of her notes, in fact): "This story about the Lutherans (from a Franciscan father, claiming that the Lutherans told the Apache horrible, ghoulish lies about the Franciscans) seemed highly improbable after meeting Mr. Genther, the Lutheran missionary who has been here for twenty years." Could the good reverend have innocently misspoken to the FBI, we wondered?

Genther's harsh opinion of Henrietta's actions, as he expressed them in the trial, had an oddly familiar ring to us. Nearly sixty years after the trial, Evelyn had spoken to Arthur Genther, son of Pastor E. E. Genther and himself a missionary to the Apache, and asked him what he himself had heard of the murder and of her aunt. He would not answer. "I have to live here, you know," he told her.

The pattern had now been established for the rest of the defense witnesses. Dougherty would walk them through their identifying information, have them explain how they knew Golney, elicit some testimonial to his good character, and then ask them something about Henrietta. At this point, the prosecutors would leap to their feet to object —"hearsay" or "inadmissible" or "prejudicial," they would complain—and the judge would sustain the objection. Several times his "Sustained!" would be accompanied by an admonition to Dougherty that his ruling on the issue of character testimony was quite clear and a warning not to try raising it again.

One of the defense witnesses was Chester Cummings, the government farmer at Whiteriver who had been friendly and protective toward Henrietta while she was alive but who was obviously now much disturbed by her having failed to follow all his cautionary advice. The sum of his testimony was a nod to Golney's good "general reputation" and a brief description of his relationship to Henrietta and of her cabin. When he was asked about the conversation he had with Henrietta on the afternoon of the dance, the prosecution objected, the objection was sustained, and Cummings was not allowed to speak of any of his conversations with Henrietta.

Jack Keyes had taken some personal responsibility for Henrietta's welfare from her first week on the reservation and was instrumental in many of the connections she made—most prominently, it would seem, her July 18 introduction to Golney Seymour. He was later, of course, suspected of concealing from the law his knowledge of the events of July 18 and Henrietta's murder. Now, when Dougherty brought him to the stand to speak on Golney's behalf, Keyes was silenced almost immediately. The government objected to the first question directed toward Keyes, which concerned discussions he had had with Henrietta. Ultimately, he spoke only of Golney's "good reputation"—and was dismissed.

But it was the testimony of fourteen-year-old George Wallen that was most notably abbreviated by the legal wrangling. This was the boy whom Dougherty said Henrietta (in what would have been a direct contravention of her instructions—as reported by Ruth Underhill—to study the lives of women) had questioned about the sexual life of a young Apache male, and then attempted to fondle. This was, to this point, the most flagrant of the accusations raised about her behavior. But Wallen was allowed to say on the stand only that he met Henrietta in Whiteriver on June 23 or June 24—in her first days on the reservation—and that he had seen her at an Apache dance on July 4. When Dougherty began to ask Wallen about other dances he had attended, Sames sustained the government's objections that this was leading inexorably to character testimony, which had been disallowed. Dougherty tried several other tacks, equally unsuccessful, and then voiced his increasing frustration with the court's refusal to allow him to make his case. Wallen was then dismissed.

It is to the testimony of this young man—and interviews with several other young informants—that Henrietta's field notes, never introduced or discussed in court, most interestingly speak. We obtained a copy of the field notes, after presuming them lost forever, more than a decade after we completed preliminary research for this book. The field notes were referred to as being in the possession of the "government" among Henrietta's effects, but were not returned to her family in New York with the other trial materials, and our various efforts to track them down had come to naught. We found them sitting, uninspected for decades, in the Arizona State Museum.[21]

The portrait of Henrietta that was reflected in them deeply enriched our understanding of her work, spoken of elsewhere in primarily abstract terms, but manifested here in great scholarly detail. It also gave us increased perspective on the methodology she employed—and something about her mindset and, in the words of Ruth Benedict, "ambition to do good work."

She records in considerable detail interviews with several young men, telling stories of adolescent rituals and behavior. Her persistence in pursuing this information did, indeed, raise some concerns with us, especially considering subsequent events. Her notes on her June 25 interview with George Wallen, however, on her third day on the reservation, spoke only of his concern with "gan," described as "supernatural beings that live in wind, air, caves, or anywhere inside of big mountains... and get out long knives to punish people who said or thought anything against them or made fun of them."[22]

When Golney Seymour was finally called to the stand, at 1:55 on Friday afternoon, it was increasingly evident that his defense was now hanging by the thin thread of his ability to present a story quite different from the confession he had signed, as well as Gatewoood's and Street's testimony in support of that confession. The prosecution had successfully blocked—with the judge's full participation—discussion of Henrietta's character or behavior. It also may not have helped that Golney himself, as several of the press accounts had it, appeared "sullen" and/or "emotionless." Golney entered the courtroom without expression, accompanied by an armed bailiff but otherwise not restrained. He looked neither right nor left as he took

---

[21] We finally found the field notes through Alan Ferg, archivist at the Arizona State Museum, who had gone out of his way to provide and explain the papers to us. They had come to the Museum from the collection of Bernard (Bunny) Fontana of Arizona State University, who could not explain to Ferg how he had happened to come by them. But the papers had the name John Gung'l stamped on them in several places, and Ferg theorized—undoubtedly correctly—that they had been typed up for the trial.

[22] Selected field notes, including those described above, appear in this book as Appendix A, page 250. The complete set of field notes can be found at *henriettaschmerler.com*.

the stand, but focused his attention totally on the judge as he was being sworn in, and on both Dougherty and the interpreter as he was led through the direct examination. His voice was low but audible. As it had when he first appeared months earlier before the grand jury, the press called him "stolid" and "impassive" and "stoic" in most of its stories. Alternatively, he was called "meek" and "docile" when that better fit the story line. He would retain this equanimity throughout the afternoon, as Dougherty helped him tell his story.

In response to his attorney's patient questioning, he described his activities during the day of the Canyon Day dance. Much of what had occurred that afternoon was by now familiar to those who were following the story—the signed confessions of both Golney and Gatewood had agreed in their accounts of that time period—but Golney now filled in some details of the morning. According to the *Arizona Record* of March 19, 1932 [the only record that appears to exist of his verbatim testimony], he testified, mostly in Apache:

"I was living on the east fork of the Whiteriver last July 18. I left my home and arrived at my father's place around 10 am. My father was telling stories. All my relatives were there, including my father and mother, my sister, Bessie Gatewood, Robert Gatewood, Iris Seymour, my little brother, and John Doane.

"I remained there about an hour and I left because my father told me they were having a dance at Canyon Day that night. I told them I would go home and ask my wife if she wanted to go. I started for home on horseback but joined a group of Indians who were drinking beer. I bought 50 cents worth and drank two before I went home.

"I stayed at home for about an hour before my wife and I started for my father's place to join the family to go to the dance. I drank some tulapai at the invitation of my brother-in-law. I asked Robert Gatewood to cut my hair. We went over to his house to get the scissors and razor and then started for my father's house."

Golney told of joining Jack Perry and Jack Keyes along the way and passing Henrietta in her yard, just before they turned in to H-4's place, just across the road from Henrietta's.

Here, a small difference can be noted. In the prior accounts, they came upon Jack Perry standing near Henrietta, who had a cup of water in her hand and may or may not have given Perry a drink.

This discrepancy does not appear to have bothered any of the lawyers, and it was unremarked upon during the trial. But what was far more significant, in trying to piece together an understanding of what truly happened that night, was his omission of the brief private conversation that he, Golney, had with Henrietta before following Gatewood into the Seymour camp. It was mentioned in Golney's confession, in this way: "Before going into my father's camp, I had a conversation with the white girl and she said that she desired to borrow a horse from me to ride to the Canyon Day dance. I told her that I had only the one horse, but she could ride with me to the dance if she desired to do so." This brief exchange with Henrietta was not mentioned during the trial, nor did it seem to be remembered either in Golney's later testimony nor in the press coverage of that testimony, which conflated what appears to have been two separate encounters with Henrietta into one.

It was Golney's story of his meeting with Henrietta as he and Gatewood left his father's camp, about half an hour later, that cut to the heart of the defense strategy.

He told of Gatewood leaving on a burro and he himself starting toward the dance on a horse. "I got as far as the white woman's house when she called to me. I had already passed her gate when she called out. 'Come here, I want to tell you something.' I turned my horse and rode back up to her gate.

"'You got horse to loan me?' she asked. I told her the horse I was on was the only one I had. She said, 'I hear dance. That's why I'm asking you. One horse might carry us both. I see lots of Indian men and women riding on one horse.'

"I replied to her that Indians that are married ride on one horse together, but that I did not like to do that. She then invited me to go into her house. I followed her to the porch and then inside. There was a table. She placed a chair for me and told me to sit down and then gave me a cigarette.

"She went out to a little house and then came back to the house. She came toward me again, held out a glass, said it was whiskey and asked me to take a drink. I took one drink and told her it burned my throat. She had a pint bottle with just a little bit gone. I drank some and she took a drink.

"When she asked me again to take her to the dance, I told her 'all right.' After we had left the house, she went back and got her Indian handbag. She was dressed in a yellow dress such as the Indian women wear. She wore white man's shoes. I left the house first, then, and she followed me through the gate. She got on the horse in front and I mounted behind. She hung the bag on the saddle horn.

"When we started, she kissed me, and then we started on to the dance."

The *Record* writer here seemed to need to make his reportorial presence felt, lest he seem merely a stenographer. He interjected a description here of Golney, the witness, "continuing in the unemotional monotone he had been using for an hour in his Apache tongue to the interpreter" and relating further details of "the night which changed the even course of his desert bred days."

Golney testified that, right after they left the white woman's house, they passed Robert Gatewood riding his burro and "further on down the road," Simon Wycliffe. [It may be speculated that, if Golney had tarried for any length of time at Henrietta's, as he said he did, Gatewood's burro would seem to have been extraordinarily slow—even for a burro.] He said that she kept talking to him all the time, with his understanding part but not all of the conversation.

"She had the whiskey with her, and we took some more drinks. When we got to the wash, she told me she wanted to get off. She went behind a tree and when she returned and asked me where the trail we were on went. I told her to the dance. She said she asked me about the trail because she was thinking of buying a horse and going over the trails." [Henrietta was expecting the horse she had already paid for to be delivered on Monday.]

"We took another drink. She kissed me again and we went on down the trail. We got off the horse to go across the wash, and when we came to the bridge she hesitated. We walked across the wash and led the horse.

"She took the bag and hit me on the legs. She held my hand and scratched my palm. Then we sat down and she kept on tickling my hands and neck. I thought she was thinking a different line of thought."

Different from what? *a partisan observer might ask here. In this description and that which immediately follows, given to the jury in response to his lawyer, there is no indication of the possibility of any other line of thinking by Henrietta, or actions with anything other than seductive intent. There was no discussion of any immediate fear or anger on Henrietta's part. There was no suggestion that hitting him on the legs or scratching his palm or "tickling" his neck might just have been physical resistance to a sexual overture—or, more directly, a powerful, violent, sexual attack.*

Golney went on to give "details" of the sexual encounter to the jury, but they are undoubtedly forever lost to us through the conventions of public discourse in 1932. Neither the *Arizona Record*, nor the AP, nor even the FBI in its confidential reports, would be explicit about any of the act, avoiding even the word "rape" in any of its accounts.

The *Arizona Record* reporter could bring himself to say, only, that "finding it hard to express himself even in his native Apache tongue, Seymour, under the coaching of Mr. Dougherty, related details of his intimacy with Miss Schmerler."

"After it was over I threw up. I knew I had done wrong and decided it would be best to go to the dance alone. I told her. She got mad. Hit me with a rock. I hit her with rock. Then she say 'I kill you —I stick you with knife.' She start toward me—I dodge. She say 'I stick your horse with knife' and go to horse. I run after her—her hand raised up to stick horse—I catch her wrist in back. I wrestle with her for a while—don't know how long—was drunk—took knife—threw it away—got on horse—made horse go fast away from here."[23]

Dougherty wanted there to be no chance the jury would misunderstand the implications of this version of the story. "What was the white woman doing when you left?"

"She was going toward where I threw knife away?"

---

[23] It seems that the *Record* reporter was attempting to capture the specific language used in the courtroom—the words of Golney Seymour as interpreted by Donald McIntosh. The Associated Press reporter appears to have further translated the words into more formal English, and published the final part this way: "I hit her. She said she'd kill me and started after me with a knife. She then said she'd kill my horse and started, with her right arm upraised, to stab my pony. I ran after her and grabbed her right wrist from behind. We wrestled. I got the knife and threw it away. I then ran to my horse, mounted and started to the dance."

"Did you see her again after that?"

"No."

"Did you think you had killed the white woman?"

"No."

"Did you tell Robert Gatewood you killed the white woman?"

"No."

It should be noted that, as Golney relates the story here, she did not get angry until he told her he would go on to the dance alone. In this version, there was no knife to the throat of the young woman. In this version, Henrietta was very much alive when Golney left the scene.

Yet it remained the confession itself, now entered in evidence and supported by government witnesses, that stood as the greatest barrier to disproving Golney's guilt. Dougherty, as anticipated, began to hammer away at the conditions Golney faced in custody prior to his confession.

Sowing doubt in the confession

Golney, in response to Dougherty's questioning, told of having eaten at about 7 a.m. on the Saturday of his arrest—and then being without food until signing his "confession" at about 1 p.m. on Sunday, thirty hours later. He was first questioned in Whiteriver—having been called into Street's headquarters at least three different times, finally with the interpreter Dosela present—but gave up no information about his encounter with the white woman. He said he was transported to the jail in McNary for the night, then brought back to Whiteriver for a Sunday interview with Street. Dosela was there, and so, too, were Cooley, Velesques, Cummings, and "two white officers," according to Golney's testimony. "I first told about the fight with the white girl about 13 o'clock, about two hours after I was taken in there. But, he said, "they were doing all the talking," referring to Street and Dosela.

"I admitted I had a fight with the white girl when they told me I was under arrest and would have to go to El Paso and they didn't know what would happen to me... They told me I would have to tell... I did not tell them I killed the white girl. I did not tell them I intended to kill the white girl. I first learned the girl was dead about one Sunday after the dance. I never did know the white girl's name."

Dougherty asked Golney to identify his signature on the confession, which he did. But he said he had only been in the office a short time before Dosela began reading him the confession. "I told him there were lots of words missing," Golney explained from the stand, "and that there was more I wanted to tell. But Mr. Street told me to hurry and gave me the pen to sign it."

"Were you advised of your constitutional rights?" Dougherty asked.

"I do not know what 'constitutional rights' are," Golney replied.

What was never mentioned—and there is no specific evidence to suggest it happened—was any type of physical coercion in extracting the confession. However, it would not be far-fetched to speculate that a detailed murder confession given by a solitary young Apache man in the hands of very determined lawmen (and later retracted) might in the traditions of white man's law in Indian country be accompanied by some rough play, or the threat of it, at the least. But, interestingly, nothing of this nature was ever mentioned in any of the files, articles, or letters we read.

Effectively, Golney's direct testimony ended with this description of how he came to give the confession he was now denying. Gung'l told the court he would need all day Saturday to cross-examine the witness, and the fifth day of the trial came to a close.

Day Six: The cross-examination

The trial was picking up a significant national following as it wore on. The Associated Press, United Press International, and the International News Service were filing daily reports from the Globe courthouse, publishing not only in the New York City newspapers—the *Times*, the *Herald Tribune*, the *Daily News*—but also, if less consistently, in most large city newspapers around the country. The *Arizona Star* and the *Tucson Daily Citizen* followed the story breathlessly with their own coverage, some taken from the wire services and some from their own reporters. But it was the tiny, biweekly *Arizona Record*, published in Globe, that recorded the trial in greatest detail. This proved particularly important to us, the researchers, when the depression-era court decided the trial transcript would be too expensive to reproduce.

When we first took on the project, in Belle's apartment, there were scrapbooks full of clippings about the murder, the search, and, most prominently, the trial. Every file we obtained, whether from universities, museums, FBI, prison system, or individuals, had its own large, motley assortment of articles—with many of the newspapers from which they came unidentified, but most often bearing an AP or UP dateline. Nevertheless, our most important find came very shortly after leaving the Arizona Record office in Globe on our first trip to Arizona, quite discouraged, having just been told that old newspaper archives would be too difficult to find, if they indeed still existed. Then, shortly after, the young editor came racing down the street to find us, waving copies of several issues he had just found. They were from Tuesday, March 15; Saturday, March 19; and Tuesday, March 22, 1932. They just happened to be the three issues published during the trial, and they contained recordings of trial dialogue far more precise and detailed than anything the wire services were producing. They remained our best source of trial material throughout our own search.

Not surprisingly, the stories had many different emphases. Sometimes, it was the lawyers who dominated the reporting—they were loud, combative, and blunt. The enduring travails—and usually stoic patience—of the Apache people provided another emphasis. The naïveté of Henrietta and the foolishness of all the adults surrounding this case was yet another recurring theme. Still others focused on Golney Seymour, naturally at the heart of controversy and depicted as taciturn and unemotional as the battle raged on around him. The drama preceding his appearance built: What would he say? What could he say, since he had previously confessed the murder so explicitly? But as reporters realized his defense was building toward a repudiation of his confession, with his lawyer promising to discredit it completely, the possibility of actual innocence increasingly excited the newspaper-reading public.

Maybe it was because the cross-examination was on a Saturday, and the Monday closing arguments, jury deliberations, verdict, and sentencing followed so rapidly and overwhelmed the news cycle, the reporting of the cross-examination turned out to be the least specific rendering of all the key courtroom dialogue. What was clear from the news accounts was that prosecutor Gung'l and his assistant Clarence Perrin were unable to get any retraction from him of the specifics of Golney's new courtroom version of the fateful horseback ride to Canyon Day: his temptation at the hands of Henrietta, his unpremeditated sexual encounter with her, their fight, and his departure while thinking Henrietta was still alive.

What the grilling did accomplish, however, was getting Golney to *strengthen* his statements of innocence—to the point that the prosecutors undoubtedly decided that he had clearly crossed into the realm of unbelievability.

Challenging Golney's trial testimony

During the cross-examination leading to this moment, Gung'l had tried every tack to get Golney to waver from the story of innocence he had just given in direct testimony.

Did he not stab her, as the confession stated? No, to the contrary, it was Henrietta who had produced the knife, threatening to kill Golney and stab his horse. Golney had, in fact, wrestled the knife from her and "threw the knife away."

Did he not hit her in the head with a rock? No, it was Henrietta who hit him with a rock, after he told her he regretted their "intimacies." Yes, he "threw a rock at her also," but he did not know whether he hit her and "did not see her fall down at any time."

Was she not lying on the ground, motionless, when he rode away from the scene? No. In fact, she was running into the bushes to find the knife when he "made horse go fast away from there."

Indeed, Golney remained consistent with the story he had told in direct testimony the previous day, describing the particulars of his confrontation with Henrietta, in contrast to the details of his confession and to his lawyer's opening statement at the trial. It was in what might have been more peripheral issues—Golney's level of intoxication and his understanding of English—that the prosecution seems to have placed its more immediate emphasis. Or at least that's what the press appears to have believed.

The AP said that "United States Attorney John C. Gung'l, his horn-rimmed spectacles tapping the table menacingly in front of the abashed-appearing defendant on the high witness stand, started a battering slashing attack, which he intimated might last all day." (The cross-examination did indeed occupy all of Saturday's session.)

Intoxication

Golney said, in response to Gung'l's questions about his drinking during the day of July 18, that he had drunk two bottles of beer at noon ("Did it make you drunk?" "No, make me feel good,") and, a bit later, some tulapai at his father's camp. "Did you get drunk there?" asked Gung'l. "Not very drunk," answered Golney.

He said of the whiskey he accepted in Henrietta's house that he had "two swallows—make me feel good." He made it clear, however, that he had become fully intoxicated while drinking with Henrietta from her flask on the ride to Canyon Day.

"Was the white girl drunk?" Gung'l asked, referring to the time of the confrontation in the ravine.

"I was drunk," responded Golney. "Don't know if the white girl was."

"Oh—you were drunk?"

"Yes—I was drunk."

By this time, it was more than clear that Golney's intoxication was part of an explicit strategy of the defense. But neither was the prosecution about to lose this opening. Toward the end of the cross, after Golney had again denied cutting and killing Henrietta, Gung'l declared: "And you were drunk!"

"Yes, I was drunk," Golney replied.

"You were so drunk you didn't know what you were doing," said Gung'l.

"I was not so drunk I cannot remember. If I was too drunk, I could not remember."

Here, the defense was bolstering its claim of drunkenness while, simultaneously, the prosecution was raising serious doubts about the defendant's ability to recall accurately the details of his deadly confrontation with the victim.

Golney's English

Gung'l then confronted an until-then unvoiced—but critical—

issue in the trial, Golney's command of English. The signed confession stood squarely and emphatically in the way of Golney's contention of innocence during the trial. The defense leaned ever more heavily on what they hoped would appear to the jury as a highly questionable process of obtaining Golney's statement and signature. Street's tactics and impatience in demanding the signature, the failure to properly inform Golney of his rights, and the ambiguous role of the translator raised questions about the integrity of the process. That Golney required the services of an interpreter throughout the trial would elicit even more doubts from jurors that Golney knew what he was signing.

Here's the way the March 19 *Tucson Daily Citizen* reported the government's attempt to expose what it considered Golney's "pretended ignorance" of English:

> Through an interpreter, Seymour said he attended school at the reservation—but did not know for how long—and was required to speak English in school.
>
> "Can you speak English?" Gung'l demanded.
> "Don't know," Seymour answered, through the interpreter.
> Gung'l signaled the interpreter aside and attempted direct conversation in English. "Did you go to the Canyon Day dance?"
> "Yes," Seymour answered in English.
> "Did you go in an automobile or on a horse?"
> "On horse."
> "Who went with you on the horse?"
> "White girl."
> "Do you know where the white girl lived?"
> "Yes."
>
> The interrogation switched back to Apache. Seymour explained he thought he could understand some English words, but when he tried to speak English "not always could make words go." Seymour repeated his story of passing the girl's house on his way to the dance and being called back by her.

"You weren't drunk when you passed the white girl's house, were you?" Gung'l asked through the interpreter.

"No," said Seymour in Apache.

"You knew what you were doing?"

"Yes."

"Then you can speak English, can't you?"

"Thought was talking English—maybe didn't say words thought said."

Gung'l demanded the defendant tell the jury in English what he told the white girl when she asked to ride with him on his horse, as she had seen the Indian men and women do.

After a pause, Seymour said haltingly: "That man riding horse with wife—don't want to do that way."

The sparring lasted most of the day, with virtually nothing from Golney's direct testimony changed. When he finally said, at 4:45 p.m., "I did not kill her," Gung'l quickly and emphatically rested his case. Both the prosecution and defense knew they had done what they could. Sunday would be a welcome day off and closing arguments were set for Monday.

Day Seven: Closing arguments and jury deliberations

The jury box was filled long before the scheduled 9:30 a.m. Monday opening of what was promised to be the final day of the trial. Sunday must have been an awkward, sometimes uncomfortable day for the jurors. While still sequestered, they were under tough strictures not to discuss the proceedings of the trial. Although they were able to move relatively freely around the boarding house in which they were lodged, they generally sought to avoid each other's company for more than short periods of time. The bailiffs who usually watched over them were not to be seen that Sunday, since they would not be paid—a clear manifestation of the Great Depression that law enforcement here, like the rest of the nation, found itself in the midst of. Consequently, the prohibition against discussing the trial had to depend even more heavily on the self-discipline of the jurors. Judge

Sames' warnings not to discuss the facts of the trial were clearly in their minds. Nonetheless, the situation was uneasy.

The courtroom audience also filed in earlier than on the previous days. There was the usual hush when they entered, although the halls had buzzed more loudly than usual. Most of the observers had been in attendance—generally occupying the same seats—for the entire week's proceedings, and were well aware that only closing arguments of the lawyers for each side, and the judge's instructions to the jury, would precede the case passing directly into the jury's hands.

Judge Sames opened the session by exhorting the jurors to listen extremely carefully to the lawyers' closing arguments, so they could reach the correct decision. He listed the five possible verdicts they might reach: guilty of murder in the first degree, without recommendation of leniency, making the death penalty mandatory; guilty of murder in the first degree with recommendation for leniency, fixing the penalty at life imprisonment; guilty of murder in the second degree; guilty of manslaughter; acquittal.

Gung'l, Assistant U.S. Attorney Clarence V. Perrin, and Dougherty spent the next six hours reviewing the facts, the testimony, and the possible interpretations—interrupted only by a brief break for lunch. As might have been anticipated after the prosecution suddenly rested its case on Saturday without calling all its witnesses, Gung'l and Perrin were much more measured and confident in their approach and tone. Dougherty, in what was increasingly looking like an uphill struggle, was more fevered—and sometimes strident.

Perrin began for the government by discussing Henrietta's selection for this assignment "from among a great number of students" by Columbia, "one of the biggest schools in the nation." He brought the jury in deliberate fashion through the days of trial testimony, which described Henrietta's arrival on the reservation, her purposeful and extensive research work, and her eagerness to get to the Canyon Day dance. He stopped just short of discussing her friendliness with many of her informants and her deeply inquisitive nature, since he knew this might open the door to character testimony, which Judge Sames had closed.

Perrin traced Henrietta's movements up to the final ride she took with Golney, with some trepidation, toward the dance. He asked,

"Do you really think, gentlemen, that she asked Golney Seymour, whom the evidence shows she had not met before, into her house to give him a drink and that she took some of the raw stuff herself and then kissed him?"

Gung'l and Perrin, in alternating presentation for the government, predictably emphasized Golney's graphic confession. They described at length the careful process of translation and repetition and witnessing that went into its attainment. Perrin reminded the jurors that Golney's English was proven on the stand to be a lot stronger than he had let on. Finally, Gung'l pointed out that Golney's courtroom repudiation of the confession differed even from the story his own lawyer had presented to the court earlier in the trial.

Second in importance only to the confession itself, Gung'l offered the testimony of Robert Gatewood as proof of Golney's guilt. Gung'l reviewed this testimony in detail and asked why a young man with so much to lose in the process would testify against his own brother-in-law and regular companion.

Gung'l discussed the condition of the body when it was found and the crime scene in general and suggested that forcible rape would be a far likelier cause for the havoc at the site than consensual sex and a post-coital fight.

When it was his turn, immediately after the forty-minute lunch break, Dougherty attempted to make clear the underdog status not only of his client but his own. He pointed to Golney: "This poor young man does not have a powerful Uncle Sam with all its resources to provide an elaborate defense for him. He has only what one lawyer with a limited amount for expenses can do."

He wasted no time in establishing the uniqueness of Henrietta's murder, in the entirety of time: "Never before has the Apache Indian's history been marred by a case like this. White women have gone into their strongholds year after year and none has had their chastity violated."

There was no rebuttal at the trial to this distortion of history. One reason that researchers in the years prior to Henrietta's visit were not welcomed to the reservation may have been precisely the earlier history of harassment and assault and, in at least one documented episode in the previous decade, significant physical violence.

Dougherty presented the run-up to Henrietta's death in stark contrast to the prosecution. In his version, Golney was a responsible, well-meaning innocent, and Henrietta was a desperate, scheming temptress. "Little did this Indian youth think, when he left his tepee on this fateful morning, that he would be in need of the well-known prayer, 'Lord, leadeth me not into temptation.'" To serve her base purposes—maybe just to cajole a ride to the dance but more probably to satisfy her carnal needs—Henrietta plied Golney with drink and subjected him to physical temptation which no red-blooded man could resist. Henrietta got what she wanted, in the ravine, but then got mad only when Golney "was stricken with remorse" and said he was going to the dance alone. Then, "thwarted in her desire to go to the dance, where she could show off the special costume she had made," she tried to stab Golney, then his horse, and then picked up a rock and threw it at Golney. Dougherty paused for effect and turned directly to the jurors. *"What was more natural than that he should fight back? He may have knocked her teeth out. He doesn't know."* [Emphasis added.]

To the prosecution's contention that Henrietta, who had displayed her scholarly credentials and attributes in so many ways during her time on the reservation, would never have offered whiskey to Golney, Dougherty's ire—and eloquence—reached a crescendo.

"I hope," he spoke directly to the jurors, "you are not fooled into believing all women sent to Indian reservations by a great university are angels. I hope you gentlemen are not bamboozled by college students as to believe they never take a drink. She was out on a lark!

"This poor savage would not have acted as he did, without the greatest provocation. This was not a modest, unsophisticated schoolgirl coming out here among the Indians without knowledge of ordinary facts of life. She went on a strange and lonesome trail, in the arms, we might say, of this young buck. Was she wise? Was she discreet?

"Let us not, because of the 18th Amendment, turn our backs upon facts. There is nothing unusual, in this day, in a university student having a flask of whiskey.

"First she offered him a glass of water—she was getting her trap ready to ensnare some poor Indian—but it was not potent enough. So she tried whiskey.

"This white girl came to the reservation in June," Dougherty pointed out. "She had been without the association of men. Having no white men available, she sought the association of this Indian kid and threw herself into his arms."

"But give her the benefit of the doubt—say she did everything proper. She was a canary released from a cage, seeking refuge in the paws of a domestic cat. Would you kill this cat because it could not resist natural instincts?

"He's an Indian, and according to witnesses you cannot doubt he's a good Indian. You are to judge his intent—what did he intend to do?"

Had he never been in trouble? This suggestion (from Donner's testimony that "he knew of no complaints against him ever having appeared in his office") also went unchallenged during the trial. However, the FBI had in its post-trial report said that Golney "has once or twice been reported to the superintendent of the Indian agency where he resided for misconduct." This latter was unbelievably, inexplicably excised from the original material the FBI would provide us, until Judge Gesell's order.

Dougherty also denied the prosecution's straightforward contention that Henrietta's body, as it was found a week later, showed evidence of her struggle with Golney—and clear signs that her attacker had cut her throat. He told the jury that it had rained three or four days in the intervening time and that the body would have been washed a considerable distance in that time, and that animals and other natural forces could have altered the body dramatically. "Woolford, in his trial testimony for the prosecution, admitted that government witnesses had staged a rehearsal to show the revolting position and all it would indicate to you. I hope you won't be deceived by that."

As for Gatewood's testimony, Dougherty was derisive. He suggested, quite directly, that the testimony was grievously tainted. "What about this witness Robert Gatewood? He was arrested at Whiteriver by government officers November 1 and kept in custody and in jail under the dominion of the district attorney's office all the time until the trial. He tried to deceive me and he tried to deceive you by telling me he was at his home in Whiteriver from November 1, when the confession was supposed to have been made. He then said he was at a hotel in Tucson. Finally he admitted he was kept in jail. And who was with him? Jesus Velesques, who found the body."

He was even more peremptory about Golney's alleged confession. "Put yourself in his position," he urged the jury. "If you had been surrounded by hostile men as he was and kept without food for thirty hours, you would probably have said, 'For God's sake, give me that thing, I'll sign it. Give me my death warrant, I'll sign that. Let me go.'"

He spoke to Golney's understanding of English or lack thereof. The issue was particularly significant for the government's contention that he knew more of the language than he let on during the trial, which would lessen the doubt about his knowing what he was signing. According to the *Arizona Record* of March 22, 1932, Dougherty "pointed out the young Indian is a man of the forest, living in solitude disturbed only by the howls of the wind and wild animals and being embarrassed by the presence of so many unfamiliar faces about him in the courtroom.

"Not many generations ago," Dougherty continued, "the very ground upon which this building stands was the happy hunting grounds of Indians. Though they fought doggedly to prevent it they were forced back farther and farther into the wilderness, finally being overcome by Uncle Sam's armed forces.

"This man was confronted with a graver menace—not guns or armed forces but lipsticks, attractive dresses, and other embellishments."

Dougherty stopped one final time, looked mournfully around the room, and made his final plea: "Apply your yardstick," he told the jurors, "that the Indian be given a square deal. Give this poor savage the same break you would a white man!"

Gung'l seized on the defense attorney's final words as he began his own plea: "Yes! I ask you to give this Indian the exact same consideration you would give a white man under similar circumstances.

"So long as juries continue to listen to sob stuff and forget the deceased, so long will we have crime. Tell the world by your verdict we of Arizona are not going to have people from outside come here and be murdered. Swerve not from your sworn duty—protect the people in Arizona!

"Too easily do juries forget about the deceased—their attention is attracted by the living—and listen to the appeal of the defendant to save his neck. I tell you in all sincerity this is a case that deserves the death penalty, and you should not be swerved from your duty."

Instructions

No sooner was Gung'l seated than the judge began his instructions for the jury. He was fervently hoping the jury part of the trial could be finished that evening—a verdict in hand—and the courtroom clock was now creeping toward 4 p.m. He repeated the five possible verdicts, pausing for effect after each one. "You may select one—and only one," he said. "You will need a unanimous vote for whichever verdict you decide upon. Every single one of you must agree on any decision that is reached."

He warned the jurors specifically against any trace of racial prejudice in their decision-making. "You have heard the lawyers for both sides agree on this one point: the guilt or innocence of the defendant must be judged on the evidence alone. Apply the same yardstick, they both said."

He asked if there were questions, and there were none. He thanked the spectators and the witnesses, and the jury was led by a bailiff to the jury room, where they were to remain until a verdict was reached. It was exactly 4 p.m.

Verdict

At 9:28 p.m. the foreman of the jury informed the bailiffs they had agreed on a verdict. Golney Seymour was brought into the courtroom at 9:39, Judge Sames arrived at 9:45, and court was called back to order at 10:00. When Judge Sames asked if the jury had arrived at a verdict, the foreman, G.D. Barclay, said they had and handed the written sheets to the judge. Sames, in turn, handed the sheets to the Deputy Clerk of the Court, Edward W. Scruggs, who read in a low, deep voice:

"We the jury, duly empaneled in the case of the United States Government versus Golney Seymour, find the defendant guilty of first degree murder, without the death penalty."

Today, we would know through the media exactly how many holdouts there had been during the deliberations, and their reasons. Several jurors would be granting TV interviews during the following week, and at least one would be negotiating for the book rights to the story of the trial. From 1932 we are able to piece these facts together primarily through the reporting of the Associated Press and stories in the Arizona Record *and the* Tucson Daily Citizen:

The jury had spent about four and a half hours in its deliberations. They had taken a one hour break for dinner. From the very beginning of their discussions together, it was quickly apparent that all of the jury thought Golney to be guilty. On their first ballot, everyone marked Guilty of First Degree Murder—but there was considerable disagreement as to whether that warranted the death penalty, or whether there should be "leniency," with a sentence of life imprisonment.

It took seven more ballots for them to sort out the punishment, but by the eighth ballot they had come to agreement: life imprisonment. The extent of their differences will never be known; to courtroom observers, including several experienced reporters who prided themselves in being able to read the faces of jurors, there was a united front.

Golney heard the verdict "without visible emotion," the *Arizona Record* reported. His parents listened from their seats in the courtroom "without changing their expressions." (The newspaper explained this as the result of a background of "hundreds of generations of stoicism to pain or expressing emotion.") The jurors were thanked for their service by the judge and sent home. The judge asked that Golney be brought before him the following morning at 11 a.m. for the pronouncing of sentence. Golney was escorted back to his cell at 10:09 p.m.

Chapter Fourteen

Sentencing and Departure for McNeil Island

On the morning of Tuesday, March 22, 1932, the courthouse was, after a week of intense bustle, quiet and relatively empty. A handful of officers escorted Golney to his seat. His defense attorney was there, of course. So were his parents, while his wife and six-month-old son, Harry, waited outside. A few resolute members of the Apache tribe remained in attendance, to bear witness. The prosecution team was all there, and several reporters were there for the last chapter of the story. Judge Sames gaveled the proceedings to order just after 11 o'clock.

Any remaining thoughts that the sentence might be delayed by an appeal were dispensed when Golney's lawyer was immediately recognized by the judge. "We will not at this time be filing a motion for a new trial," announced Dougherty. "We do reserve the right to file an appeal to this decision if Mr. Seymour's family or tribesmen decide to do so, and if the appeal can be financed." It was obvious at that point that defense funds—whatever there had been *[and Dougherty would still be trying to collect his fees years later]*—had been used up, and that a later change of circumstance was highly unlikely.

The judge acknowledged Dougherty's remarks, and turned to

Golney Seymour. "Do you have anything to say at this time, or can you provide any reason why you should not be sentenced?" he asked. Golney stood—moving more quickly than he had during the trial—and, through the court interpreter, asked permission to address the court before sentence was pronounced. "You may speak," said Sames. "Or you might have your attorney speak for you."

"No, must speak for self," Golney said, in language reported just this way by the Associated Press.

"I was real good Indian. I did not think ever would be criminal like I look now. I just always tended to my work—was fourteen years of age when commenced work." (The *Arizona Record* reported the same message in slightly different words, for whatever the journalistic or linguistic reasons: "'I have always been a good Indian,' the young brave said, without trace of emotion. 'I never expected to be the criminal as I appear now to the world. I always attended to my own business. I started work at the age of 14 years and have worked ever since.'") He went on to explain that his English was not better because he was sick—"in the hospital"—most of the time he was in Indian school.

Golney had barely returned to his seat before the judge pronounced the sentence that had already been decided by the jury: Imprisonment for life—"the rest of your natural born days"—in federal prison. The penitentiary in which Golney would serve was not mentioned during the sentencing phase of the trial, but it was well known to be McNeil Island, off the coast of Washington[24].

Golney followed U.S. Marshal George Mauk out of the courtroom and back to the holding cell in the back of the building. In his brief moments outside, he was met by his wife Elizabeth, who handed his infant son to him for a brief, emotional farewell, before Mauk insisted that mother and baby turn back. Golney continued, eyes forward, back to his cell. That afternoon, he would be transported

---

[24] McNeil Island served as a federal pen from 1904-1976, known for its inaccessibility to the mainland, except by boat or air. Charles Manson, Creepy Karpis (of the Barker gang), and Mickey Cohen were only a few of the well-known gangsters/murderers who served there. For many years, Native Americans found guilty of federal crimes were routinely sent to McNeil Island.

to the Maricopa County Jail in Phoenix, handcuffed to another prisoner, on the first leg of his trip to McNeil. The AP reported that he was smiling as he left for Phoenix, "apparently happy over refusal of the jury... to fix the penalty at death."

National press would be quick to include as fact, in its stories announcing Golney's guilty verdict, this bit of lore, apparently first reported by the Associated Press the evening the verdict was read: "Imprisonment for more than three or four years is looked upon by officials as a virtual sentence of death for Arizona Apaches, since only one has lived as long as seven years in confinement." This wisdom was ascribed to "Federal Court attaches," and explained in that "Apaches appear unable to live without their freedom and the companionship of their tribesmen."[25]

The public's direct view of this case would end with Golney temporarily in Phoenix, awaiting his long trip to McNeil Island. He told a reporter for the AP that he believed "his particular guardian spirit—the benevolent shade from the happy hunting ground each Apache must placate to work in his behalf—has deserted him, and left him at the mercy of white man's law." He told the reporter he is going to "be a good boy," in hopes that "his spirit" will guide events in his favor and win him a pardon. He said, however, that had he been a "white man," he would have had "a better chance" in the trial. The reporter said that Golney "held aloof from other prisoners in the country jail, but smiled and attempted to answer in broken English when any essayed conversation with him. Only since the verdict was returned Monday night, removing the shadow of the gallows, has he allowed an occasional smile to flit across his usually somber features."

---

[25] This particular exercise in myth-making may have had a tinge of credibility, stemming from the high death rate of incarcerated Apaches in the late 1800's, particularly during the "Apache Wars" that ended with the capture of Geronimo in 1886. However, Geronimo himself lived as a "prisoner of war" for most of twenty years; numerous Apaches served sizeable sentences in the early part of this century; and, we cannot help but note, Golney Seymour himself was healthy when he was finally released from prison in 1962—thirty years after he had originally been locked away, with twenty-five of those years behind bars. (He was first paroled in 1952, but was then re-arrested for violating parole—amazingly, having allegedly molested a 10-year-old girl—and served five additional years.)

Part Five:

ENDING THE STORY

Chapter Fifteen

Making Sense of Henrietta, 85 Years Later

The story of Henrietta Schmerler's life and death and its immediate aftermath effectively ended in late March of 1932 with the departure of Golney Seymour to serve a life sentence in a Washington State penitentiary. The reverberations, however, did not end there.

It is not hard to see why there have been so many different versions of Henrietta's story. Whenever there is a public tragedy, as this was, all the players have powerful self-interests in presenting one perspective or another. Since the reservation and other government officials, the anthropology community, and the writing community (both journalistic and creative) all had a stake in suggesting that Henrietta brought at least some of this tragedy on herself—whether through naïveté, carelessness, or manipulation—it is not a surprise that the dominant narrative that has endured portrays Henrietta as more than just an innocent victim.

We ourselves, immediate relatives of the victim (and children of a man who idealized the memory of his sister, Henrietta, until his own death over seventy years later), have our own interests, of course, in seeing her portrayed as serious, capable, concerned—and innocent. We will never be certain we have all the facts, or reproduced the events exactly as they happened. We do, however, try to explain here, as fairly as we can, why others believed and spoke and wrote what they did. But then, in this account at least, the final word rests with us.

Officials

William Donner, the reservation superintendent; the Bureau of Indian Affairs, in the person of Commissioner C. J. Rhoads; and the FBI, most prominently Special Agent J. A. Street, Special Agent in Charge R. H. Colvin, and Director J. Edgar Hoover, were all quite voluble about the case.

Among the officials on the reservation and in the government who commented extensively on the case, Reservation Superintendent Donner was in the most complex, and often conflicted, position. How he acted toward Henrietta directly and what he said during her time on the reservation was one thing. Resigned and wary acceptance—and maybe even an occasional trace of gruff affection—were his most visible responses. What he said after her death, faced with many conflicting pressures, was another story.

First, there was the need to show he had personally advised her to take actions quite different from those which seemed to have led or contributed to her death: "I advised her that I did not think it possible or advisable for her to live in the type of camp and with the Indians that she desired." Equally, it was quite important to him not to allow the impression that the reservation in his charge was run in a loose or permissive—and therefore ultimately dangerous—manner: "Of course the press has published all kinds of ridiculous stories, even to the extent of the Apaches being hostile, simply to make good newspaper propaganda…We also regret the wide publicity it has brought on and the ungrounded reports as to there being any trouble with the Indians."

As more negative reports about Henrietta's behavior began to circulate, Donner's tone changed apace. "At first I did not suspicion the girl of any immoral actions… I do not care to personally condemn the girl either then or now," he said initially. This soon became "Even the older Indians advised her against her actions… The Indians were perfectly safe while sober but should she be among them or meet up with them when they were drinking or partly drunk with tulapai or moonshine it was dangerous. She advised me that the only thing she was afraid of around on the reservation was rattlesnakes."

Condemnation from Donner became more generalized and personally resentful: "They [anthropology fieldworkers, particularly young women] come in with the attitude that the Indian is a superior being, that he can do no wrong and will do no wrong, that he has been abused and with proper treatment will be a perfect angel. They are harmless even when drunk if those working among them and with them will use discretion, know their place and keep it… Neither do I know of a single instance where a white woman has come onto the reservation and has been so extremely careless as the facts brought out prove this woman to have been."

Finally, as Golney Seymour's trial approached half a year later, Donner felt himself walking a fine line between making sure that an Apache in his charge was not too harshly punished for a crime that may have been incited by a provocative woman and, at the same time, sending a message that bad behavior (particularly murder) would not be tolerated. Donner's perceptions were echoed regularly in the press and continually during the trial. There would be few dissenting voices to this narrative.

By the time former Governor H. J. Hagerman, "Special Commissioner to the Indians," broadcast the results of his August visit to the reservation, there was no longer any attempt to find complexity in the circumstances: "The girl was most frightfully indiscreet—provocative would put it plainer—to the Indians, and what happened in her cabin prior to her murder is scarcely a matter of conjecture. She openly danced with the Indians all night—rode on the same ponies with them—and what she did at her cabin—seems, according to Donner's investigations, not uncertain. Horrible—horrible—and these awfully dirty Indians! Her cabin when they found it was a filthy place. When she came in there, Donner warned her in as plain language as he felt he could against too great familiarity with the Indians—but probably not plain enough for one with her complexes."

Now, after the arrest of Golney Seymour, the narrative was fixed. The FBI, in the person of Acting Special Agent L. C. Taylor, was reporting to Director J. Edgar Hoover that "It is commonly known that the victim upon her arrival at Whiteriver, Arizona, became intimate immediately with the Indians and openly ignored and evaded all white persons. Her actions in this respect have prompted gossip of immorality with the Indians—even commercial prostitution."

Anthropologists

The anthropologists who had been Henrietta's mentors and facilitators and (at least from their previous public expression) admirers were instantly put on the defensive by the press, law enforcement, government officials, and her family. The natural first question—"What instructions did you give her?"—put them in an immediate bind. The briefing(s?) that Benedict and Mead held with Henrietta were noted, but without much specificity about the content or the length of such meetings. "Both Ruth and I spent hours advising her and she disregarded every bit of the advice," Mead later explained to Boas. But only one such "advisement" session was, in fact, ever reported by Henrietta, and it can be questioned whether academics of the stature and wide responsibilities of Benedict or Mead would have been able to give more than an hour or two to the young graduate student.

In fact, the prevailing practice of the day was to give as much license and freedom as possible to fledgling fieldworkers. Ruth Underhill, who testified for Columbia at Golney Seymour's trial, quoted Boas in her memoir, *An Anthropologist's Arrival*, [Ruth Underhill, Tucson, AZ: The University of Arizona Press, 2014[26]] as sending her into the field with these words, "Just find out how these people live and come tell us about it." Mead herself later exalted the "liberality which characterized the formative period of American anthropology, when no one who wished to [do fieldwork] was turned away on account of sex or race or age." She described this time as a "dramatic emergency," when "every month's delay meant that… some record of what man had been was being irrevocably lost, because there were no field workers there to write down the vanishing culture." (Speech at Gladys Reichard memorial, December 1955.)

---

[26] Underhill died in 1984 at the age of 101, and this memoir, published ultimately in 2014, "edited by Chip Colwell-Chanthaphonh and Stephen E. Nash, is based on unpublished archives, including an unfinished autobiography and interviews conducted prior to her death, held by the Denver Museum of Nature & Science."

It was evident from the moments immediately following the discovery of Henrietta's body that the future of anthropological fieldwork might be very much at stake, especially among the Indian tribes of the American Southwest. Within two weeks, the Bureau of Indian Affairs was floating the possibility that fieldwork permits would subsequently be dramatically restricted, with women in particular being limited. C. J. Rhoads, BIA commissioner, wrote that, "It has been suggested that the following paragraph be included in all permits to research workers and archeologists working on Indian Reservations: 'The bearer of this permit shall not hold the Department of the Interior or any officer or employee of the government responsible in any manner for accidents of any nature.'" (August 5, 1931, "Memorandum for Mr. Burlew.") And Superintendent Donner, in Whiteriver, had been even blunter: "Under no consideration would I again permit a woman of her age to take up the branch of ethnology she was working on while here."

The continuing narrative

It is easy—if profoundly ironic—to understand why Mead, Benedict, Reichard, Boas, and Underhill, preeminent among contemporary anthropologists, might be eager to believe—and perpetuate—the more critical accounts of Henrietta's excesses, naïveté, and/or willfulness. It would thus follow inevitably that the story of this event would be told and retold in this light and that several generations of historians and writers would accept this narrative uncritically.

In one prominent example, Karen Louise Smith Wyndham, in her 2001 dissertation on "ethnographic fictions," has accepted without question the perspective of an earlier and more self-interested generation of anthropologists. "Clearly," Wyndham writes, "Schmerler wanted adventure more than fieldwork, with its boring rigors and careful dictation." The evidence cited in Wyndham's account—Benedict's objection to her going in the first place, Reichard's advice to her to avoid the men of the tribe, Henrietta's unwillingness or inability to practice "normal" female roles and behavior at Columbia, her romantic involvement with an Apache—is all totally unsubstantiated by our extensive research. For instance,

Henrietta never spoke to Reichard about her trip to Arizona, as far as we could ascertain. And there was no physical relationship with an Apache man even remotely hinted at in Henrietta's notes or in later accounts. Yet Wyndham, a self-declared feminist, seems never to have questioned this version of the narrative, much of which came from the post-murder, pretrial stories that were spread widely.[27]

Fictionalization

Beyond what might be called the "Columbia version" of the circumstances that led to Henrietta's rape and murder, accepted so readily by academics and scholars, there lies the world of imaginative literature. The Henrietta Schmerler story has been used by various other media to create their own tales, however different from the original events. The fiction market, not surprisingly, was fertile ground for her story. Writers for the pulp men's magazines of the '30s, '40s, '50s, and '60s reveled in the image of a coed beauty being ravished by a "savage" of uncontrollable lust, either as payback for her calculated, exploitive opportunism or as a result of her—paradoxical for a New York intellectual—innocence and naïveté. Cover stories from *Argosy*, *True Detective*, and *Saga*, among others—heavily embellished by both drawings and photographs—told the tale from a variety of titillating perspectives. In almost all of those stories, though, Henrietta is the agent of her own death. And often the story of the FBI's subsequent pursuit of the killer is dramatized as a superhuman, sometimes even mystical, feat, especially to the extent that magazine writers were allowed access to government-created and "authorized" versions of the murder, the investigation, and Golney's subsequent trial.

Ten years after Golney's trial, one extensive account of Henrietta's actions before the murder, along with the details of the investigation that led to Golney's confession and arrest, appeared

---

[27] Contacted in late 2015 and offered a contrary view of the historical events, Dr. Wyndham declined the opportunity to reconsider, writing, "I still don't have anything substantial to contribute to the conversation." [*Traffic in Books: Ethnographic Fictions of Zora Neale Hurston, Salman Rushdie, Bruce Chatwin, & Ruth Underhill*, Karen Louise Smith Wyndham, CCLS, University of Arizona, Tucson, AZ. Doctoral dissertation, 2001, p. 315.]

in *True Detective* (May 1942, pp. 49–51, 73–75). Under the title, "The College Girl Murder Mystery"—framed with the blurb, "when her research called for attendance at an Indian dance it was bad medicine"—Edmond Van Tyne's account begins with Henrietta on the train to Holbrook, Arizona, proclaiming, "'I'm not afraid of a little dirt. My work is more important than any consideration of personal comfort.'" And then comes the first of a number of warnings that this inexperienced woman should tone it down and know her proper place. "'I hope for your sake, that you will change your mind,' her knowing train companion said slowly. 'It is most dangerous.'" The crime eventually occurs because Henrietta refuses sensible direction, and the remainder of Van Tyne's narrative focuses on just how the government agents pursued the case before cleverly tricking Golney into spilling the beans. In closing, Van Tyne claims that while at the beginning of the investigation it was "'Apache no talk, white man learn nothing,' after the apprehension of Seymour… the slogan was changed to, 'Indian no talk, G-man know everything.'" Apparently G-men are capable of solving any mystery, but the implication is that absent Henrietta's willful behavior, there need not have been any tragedy in the first place.

In contrast to Van Tyne's version—which certainly questioned Henrietta's behavior but did not specifically feature her misconduct—nineteen years later the narrative appeared once again, this time in *Saga* under the following frame: "'If sex appeal helps in my research,' said the lovely white girl, 'then I'll use it.' This was before she watched the Dance of Death" (April 1961, pp. 20–23, 97–100).

The author of "The Case of the Apache and the Curious Coed," West Peterson, spares nothing in heating up the case: "She probably would not have been slain if only she had known the peril of riding astride a horse with a hot-blooded Apache of the opposite sex… It is an Apache legend that if a girl forks a horse in front of a brave she is clearly expressing a desire to mate with him." Further, in Peterson's account, Henrietta boasts, "A few drinks might make them reveal their tribal secrets to me. Don't worry, I've seen plenty of inebriates right on the streets of New York. I know how to take care of myself." And, of course, the more Henrietta resists "good advice," the more she appears at fault.

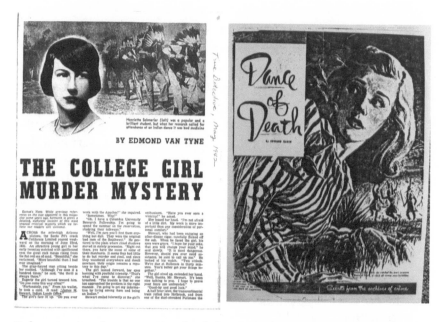

Pulp magazines have sensationalized the story of Henrietta's death through the years. Edmond Van Tyne published his lurid account in True Detective in May 1942. Edward Radin re-imagined the dance at Canyon Day in the September 26, 1946, issue of the Sunday Mirror (pp.10-11 © King Features Syndicate, Inc.). And the story still resonated in 1961 when West Peterson wrote "The Case of the Apache and the Curious Coed" for the April issue of Saga.

Even on the Columbia University campus in 2006, an incriminating portrait of Henrietta suddenly appeared. Jen Spyra related her own version of Henrietta's story, "Indian Burial Ground," in a campus publication, *The Eye: Columbia on the Street*. Spyra portrays Henrietta as "a thoroughly modern Millie in both style and spirit. Her chic, sheared bob, sumptuous lips and Roman nose conveyed the sense of style, seriousness, and progressive thinking for which she was reputed." Thus we have the picture of a fearless young woman who "had no qualms about leaving Columbia's academic candyland for wild rural living." Further, we're told that "Schmerler liked to drink and dance, ride postilion, and research. She was the kind of girl who walked around with a flask of sugared whiskey pressed against the flesh of her thigh... The kind of girl who, according to an Apache man drunk on tulapai (aboriginal moonshine), was looking for trouble." Aggressively forward, Spyra's Henrietta exhibits behavior that is questionable for an anthropologist, let alone a woman in a male arena.[28]

As recently as 2013, Maida Tilchen—who describes herself as writing "primarily to preserve and/or dramatize lesbian history"— published a novel, *She's Gone Santa Fe* [Maida Tilchen, Salem, NY: Savvy Press, 2013], which uses Henrietta as the basis for dramatizing relationships that existed between anthropologists and Indians on reservations in the southwest. Henrietta was, indeed, as Tilchen writes, a young Jewish woman from New York City who, during her studies in anthropology at Columbia, had been inspired by Ruth Benedict. Tilchen, however, shifts the setting from an Apache reservation in Arizona in 1931 to a Navajo one in the late 1920s, with strategic stops at a lesbian dude ranch in New Mexico and the lavish quarters of Mary Cabot Wheelwright, an older, wealthy, eccentric Bostonian, intent on recording Indian customs and rituals. Golney Seymour, Henrietta's killer in real life, does appear briefly as an unsympathetic character in the novel, but this time the murderer is a white man named Sack, who

---

[28] Spyra said, in a December 2006 interview with me, that she was glad to hear of the true story behind the embellishments she created for her article, which drew its facts primarily from the "pulpy magazines." She did not personally believe most of the things she wrote, but felt the dramatization was expected of her. Most significantly, she offered: "You can use my article as an example of how people distorted Henrietta's story."

in the novel was connected to "Ree" back at Columbia University and who appears at opportune deus-ex-machina moments throughout the novel. Although Tilchen refuses to accept Golney as the murderer, she also makes it clear that her character, Henrietta, is not at fault for what happens to her at the end.[29]

Finally, in *Euphoria* [Lily King, New York: Grove Press, 2014], a loosely fictionalized account of Mead's time in New Guinea with Reo Fortune and Gregory Bateson—Mead's current and future husbands, respectively—author Lily King portrayed Mead sympathetically, although with full acknowledgement of the dangers of her occupation. Once again, Henrietta is employed to point out the risks at hand, but also to represent the very fearless qualities that Mead sought to impress upon other female anthropologists. When Nell [the Mead character] described her adventures visiting several nearby tribal villages, the Bateson character asked if she went alone.

"There's no danger."

"I'm sure you heard about Henrietta Schmerler."

She had.

"She was murdered." I was trying to be delicate.

"Worse than that, I hear."

What do we think?

What are we finally to think of this woman whose story at the time—and through the years—has been told in so many ways, by so many people, to serve so many purposes? Indeed, it does not seem

---

[29] Tilchen's late 2015 correspondence with us makes clear the distance between her novel and the actual story of Henrietta Schmerler. "Please remember it is a work of fiction and very very loosely based on Henrietta's life. I did all the research I could, but little is factual in my story of my character Ree." She elaborated on a key plot point she had devised: "I saw such conflicting accounts of whether she had permission to go, but if I went with the version in which she did, I wouldn't have had much of a plot."

Tilchen had made all of this clear in the book itself, in her Author's Note: "Since so little is known about what Schmerler did during her brief time in Columbia and in the southwest, I made it up. Changing the character's name to 'Ree,' which was my creation, gave me more artistic license. My character, Ree Schmerler, is attracted to women, but I have seen no evidence that the real Henrietta Schmerler was... I choose to believe that Golney Seymour did not kill Henrietta Schmerler, but was a victim of a racist justice system. I don't know who might have done it."

grandiose to ask: Just what might history say of Henrietta Schmerler?

What happened to Henrietta, for instance, has been offered as a warning to anthropological fieldworkers and others who pursue their ethnographic science among indigenous peoples. In one version of this cautionary advice and guidance, the tone is mostly sympathetic: "Don't be naïve and trusting." "Know the people you are studying well, and especially know their language." "Stay close to others for protection." "Don't show blind faith in the goodness of anyone." "Be careful when dealing with the opposite sex." "Prepare thoroughly."

Yet another, more cynical, version exists. "Don't use your sexuality to obtain information." "Don't drink or carouse among the people you're studying." "Don't be overt in your manipulation of less sophisticated peoples." "Be particularly wary of the opposite sex." This cataloging of dangers similarly ends with the injunction to "Prepare thoroughly," but in this instance the emphasis is on the specific cultural behaviors the fieldworker brings to the situation.

It pained and angered us to learn early on that Henrietta's story was sometimes told—often by people who, above all, should have gotten their facts straight—in the latter manner. From this perspective, a tale is woven portraying an insensitive, exploitative, and ultimately very foolish opportunist who brought tragedy upon herself. Neither our pain nor our anger is any less now, at the end of this investigation, even with the understanding that Henrietta may not always have acted as prudently as we ourselves might have, in hindsight, given our current perspective.

Henrietta's exact behaviors on the reservation—her various discussions with the white people who later contended that they gave her frequent warnings, warnings she dismissed in a manner some described as headstrong; her reputed social interactions with the young Apache men; her interviews with informants, some of whom worried about the confidentiality of their answers; and, most centrally, her dealings on July 18, 1931, with Golney Seymour, who was the center of an extensive, widely publicized trial and continuing speculation—cannot be described with total certainty.

We've had our own moments of pause, particularly as we've contemplated the breathtaking courage—or audacity—it took for Henrietta to choose to spend her summer in such lonely, alien surroundings, not to mention what it took to persevere through the darkening days, right up to her final, desperate attempt to visit a dance that could well have seemed beyond her reach. And, as we read and reread her field notes, we could see them not only as abundant proof of the depth, intensity, and integrity of her scholarly pursuits but also see in them possible indications that she may have pushed some of her interview subjects, especially the adolescent boys, a bit beyond the point of sensitivity.

But these concerns mostly pale alongside the respect we felt for her enormous professional skill and determination, the affection we felt for her noble intentions and her human vulnerability, and the sympathy we felt for someone whose life's labors and particularly her crowning achievement on the reservation were so quickly and thoroughly undone by a single violent act. The ugliness of the subsequent tarnishing that took place in some academic circles, in the press, and even in court, promoted by numerous individuals protecting and promoting their own reputations and livelihoods, seemed far out of proportion.

We are far more convinced, after our years of research, of what Henrietta *did not do*. We are quite clear she did not willfully disregard all advice from her mentors. In fact, she received little guidance in her field activities, for this was the prevailing practice in those heady, boundary-stretching times; students were encouraged to figure things out for themselves. What advice she did receive, she generally tried her best to follow: She made several efforts to find an Apache woman to live with or to locate a more central place to live among the Apaches before settling for the lonely, secluded shack where she ended up staying alone. She worked diligently to find women to interview before concluding that many of the Apache women simply would not speak with her, while the men would.

At the same time, we are convinced that she was never advised to interview women exclusively, as was later suggested, and never told to avoid sexual topics. In fact, from all we can gather (including the all-important precedent established by Mead in Samoa), information on virtually all manner of human and societal behavior, very much including courtship and kinship patterns, sexuality and mating behaviors, and age-specific rituals, was specifically prized in such research. Further, we do not believe for a moment that Henrietta ever used sex or alcohol as lures for information or access. Neither seems to have been much a part of her prior life. Indeed, all we know of her personality would indicate her strong aversion to such conventional manipulations.

Throughout our long search, we have frequently disagreed with each other about the extent to which Henrietta's risk-taking exceeded legitimate boundaries (and particularly whether the term "foolhardy" could appropriately be applied), or whether her innocence and trustingness were excessive to the point of dangerous naïveté. With the benefit of hindsight, we can, of course, see that they were. But placed in the context of a time when anthropology was at the height of exuberant, unpredictable expansion, and fieldworkers were at the very heart of this volatile enterprise, we doubt that Henrietta's decisions were really outside the mainstream of expected behavior.

We prefer to listen instead to the perspective of one modern historian, the biographer who wrote *Margaret Mead and Ruth Benedict: The Kinship of Women* [Hilary Lapsley, Amherst, MA: University of Massachusetts Press, 2001]. Lapsley concluded, "In Ruth's and Margaret's views, it seems, anyone who violated the norms of a culture was fully to blame for the consequences. Yet their lack of outrage at women's relationship to male violence seems a little surprising, viewed from the present. Schmerler was not alive to tell her story, there were no witnesses except the accused, and the supposition that, among the Apache, it was perfectly natural to murder following sexual rejection seems not to have been contested in their circles. Moreover, their private attitudes suggest a callousness about the victim that was uncharacteristic, perhaps demonstrating just how threatened women anthropologists felt about their legitimacy as fieldworkers" (p. 207).

The Henrietta we will remember was probably neither entirely innocent nor entirely naïve. She understood, certainly by the latter part of her time on the reservation, the challenges of the work she had undertaken—and probably the dangers, as well. She persisted with work that she took very seriously, even in the face of increasing evidence that her efforts were not all appreciated. She was doing the best she could—diligently gathering family and kinship data from whatever sources she could find, attempting to honor every cultural signpost—and seemingly doing it quite well, as her extensive field notes demonstrate. On July 18, 1931, it turns out, she was in the wrong place at the wrong time.

Afterword

A book that is thirty years in the making brings its own obvious set of problems. Paramount among them is exactly how and when to finish. Although this is an historical account centered around the year 1931, the most applicable research was completed within the first five years of the project's inception, and mostly by the beginning of the 1990s. Henrietta Schmerler, the main subject of the story, was dead in 1931, and her murderer, Golney Seymour, was shortly after headed off for a life sentence in prison.

The book took a lot longer to write than expected, to say the least. Meanwhile, we got hold of a huge parole file that told a great deal more about the twists and turns in Golney's post-trial life. There was new and fascinating information about the FBI and the way its director, J. Edgar Hoover, spun this particular story for maximum favorable publicity. There was continuing evolution in the way anthropological fieldworkers could do their jobs, more insight into the anthropologists, and new fiction based on this long-ago event. And then, of course, the internet and Google happened, assuring a never-ending stream of pertinent addenda to the story.

But the book—at least the hard-copy version—must be published, and the time to end work on it is now. Another technological "innovation," the website, becomes the vehicle to provide for the release of information beyond the scope of the central chronological tale; for additional details and perspectives that only the most interested will follow; for the development of the story into new directions, if that's where it goes; and for the views of others—maybe supportive, maybe contrary—to be included, as well. The book will be supplemented—and extended—at *henriettaschmerler.com*.

The last chapter of this book, "Making Sense of Henrietta,

85 Years Later," has been written as originally intended, as a brief summary of Henrietta's legacy—and what we know of the woman herself—over the years. Included in this chapter are perspectives from government officials, anthropologists, the press, historians, and, finally, some writers of fiction. But we have been selective, and deliberately abbreviated, in our use of each of these perspectives. Margaret Mead, as one particularly prominent example, is briefly contextualized as an enduring public figure, and quoted in what she says was her advice to Henrietta. But further insight into Mead's own history—a model in some ways for Henrietta—and her views and vulnerabilities will need to be read elsewhere, lest her own outsized personality exert disproportionate influence on the story. Similarly with other anthropologists, historians, and pulp writers—as with FBI Director Hoover, who has filled many volumes on his own. More on these figures, and others, will be coming to the website.

Appendix A:
Selected Field Notes

Henrietta's field notes are discussed in this book as examples of both the intense and earnest scholarship she conducted in her three and a half weeks on the White Mountain Apache Reservation as well as the openings she may have offered for misinterpretation of her methods and motives.

The field notes that survived total thirty pages, typed. (We can only assume they were handwritten originally and typed by someone else to be used in the trial.) Most of the entries involve the domestic practices and spiritual beliefs of the Apache interviewees, as well as descriptions of various tribal and social dances. We provide several examples here. The full set of field notes will be found in the *henriettaschmerler.com* website.

Here's a July 6 note on "Jewelry," based on Henrietta's general observation (no informant identified):

Everybody wears sp,e. [?] from little children up to old men. Every little girl has her bead bracelets and necklace. Some of the women wear earrings, tho I haven't seen many. The men wear a good deal of silver on their belts, rings, hatbands and even in a sort of necklace down the front which looks like "medicine." Many of the older men wear a medicine bead in their coat buttonholes—it's a turquoise and some other beads. Many of the men wear beaded hatbands. The women have beautiful beaded necklaces which are worn close around the neck and come down the front this way [schematic attached].

They are usually a few inches wide and these are usually worn only on dress occasions and have very pretty designs on them. They also wear long beaded necklaces made of a great number of single strands of different colored beads. When dressed up, they often wear a colored comb in the hair and one of these wide collar necklaces and a bunch of single necklace strands besides.

And several with Mary Velesques as her informant, dated July 16 and 17:

Inheritance customs—At his death a man's children inherit. They all divide the property, the eldest son receiving the most. The father has the usufruct of the property during his lifetime, but cannot dispose of any of it. His brothers and sisters frequently receive a share in the property if the property is large, but it is similarly dependent on the will of the children of deceased. The relatives all come together in a friendly way and discuss the whole matter peaceably. Whether or not the sister and brother get any (provided there is plenty for deceased children) seems to depend on their eloquence. In any case a sister would get more than a brother. The wife gets nothing, but because she is the wife of a brother, he may get her to [sic]. This is all the old tribal law.

Her [Mary's] baby is nearly 2 and is not yet weaned. Many mothers do not wean them until they are 3 years old. When they wish to wean them they put chili on their breasts and that does the trick.

My camp dress is made of:
13 yards of blue calico
7 yards of orange calico
2 yards of red calico
1 ½ yards of white calico
6 spools of white thread

There is no difference between the dress of the unmarried women and that of the married women. When women are in mourning, they wear only dark dresses and wear a cloth loose around the shoulders (cape fashion).

At husband's death wife stays in mourning for about 2–4 years. During that time she cannot have anything to do with a man—if she did her husband's spirit would come back and kill her. During that time she must keep particularly clean—wash herself frequently. She then becomes wife of her husband's brother if he wants her. If he does not, it is up to him whom she shall marry. Nowadays of course the husband's brother is frequently married and thus has to hand her over to someone else. Man whose wife dies must stay content for same period of time, no matter how many wives he has at the time.

And here's a portion of Henrietta's first-hand observation of a "puberty ceremony dance" (for fifteen-year-old Bessie Hosby) on June 26:

Girl dressed in beautiful orange and black native costume with hair down her back and feathers in her hair. A sea shell hangs from her head over her forehead.

Girl holds a crooked staff with three eagle feathers and two bells on it. Same kind of feathers in her hair. Surrounded by two young women parallel to her on one side and one on the other side. She dances with back to east with them (to fire). On east side of fire sit medicine men and many others (only men) singing songs—a fluctuating group. They dance only while chanting accompanied by drums goes on. They really dance in place (swaying from side to side and shifting weight from one foot to another). Laughter goes on even in inner circle of chanting during it.

She also quotes a June 25 interview (her third day on the reservation) with George Wallen in a paragraph on the first page of her notes. *Wallen would later testify briefly at her trial, and be mentioned by her lawyer as the victim of "reprehensible" treatment at the hands of Henrietta.* In the notes, their discussion is confined primarily to Wallen's perceptions of Gan, who are, she gathered from their conversation,

> the plural of supernatural beings that live in wind, air, caves or anywhere inside of big mountains. They have painted masks to represent them—these can be handled only by very powerful medicine men. Long ago the people thought these Gan know exactly what one says and thinks. They would go to their dwelling place and get out long knives in order to punish people who said or thought anything against them or made fun of them."

That is the only mention of George Wallen in her notes. But then there were two extraordinary entries where she describes extensive interviews with young men, which a critical observer might interpret as pushing for details about adolescent sexuality. One of these is George Clantz, whom she describes as a "sixteen yr. old school boy whom I met on the road on the way to see his girl."

Clantz tells about fighting with his father (sometimes physically), his relationship with his girlfriend (and with two other girls he was also "paying attention to"), boys' adolescence ceremonies, and his relationship to ghosts that he much feared. Remarkably, Henrietta writes,

> When asked whether the boys had to go thru something just as the girls did at adolescence, he said yes, but was mortally afraid to tell me more. Only after repeated promises not to let a soul here know anything about it did he tell me more, and then only by replying to the questions I asked. When asked if the women know about it, he said that they do, but it's evidently a careful secret from whites. I had asked several men whether there was such a ceremony and they had promptly answered no and switched the conversation.

We wondered if Clantz could somehow be an alternative name—or a mistaken reference to—Wallen, since the description in Henrietta's notes was so similar to some of the description of George Wallen in court testimony.

And there is another intriguing account of an interview with a young man, this listed as

Conversation with _____ *[blank included in notes]*, an Apache boy of 18 whose identity I had to promise repeatedly never to reveal, as he was terribly afraid and reluctant to divulge the information I drew out of him. He told me about the puberty ceremony, answering my questions rather than daring to volunteer information. The men who visit the boys during the period of fasting threaten to kill him if he should ever tell anything about it, which explains the uniform reluctance on everyone's part to even speak about it and the hurry to change the subject.

This young man goes on to describe the puberty ceremony in considerable depth and tells of seeing during his own ceremony the Gan who would become his guardian spirit for life. He also

told me that sometimes at the dances things happen to the girl and then there are hurried marriages after that. For example after the dance on the 4th of July (Saturday nite) one couple got married on Monday. In such a rather forced case, the boy's parents pay the bride price just the same. But it doesn't make for happy marriages. The man doesn't respect the girl whom he has to marry in this way and whenever he gets drunk will throw it up to her and beat her whenever he gets drunk."

Then she described a walk with this boy which had eerie echoes of Henrietta's later ride with Golney Seymour: "When he walked me into White River we took a short-cut, a narrow rocky foot trail over the mountains, probably used by none but the Apache as a rule." We wondered here again if this boy, recorded age (18 instead of 16 or 14) notwithstanding, might have been George Wallen. Or whether there were numerous such conversations with Apache adolescents.

Finally, although this was an older informant, we worried about her description of a July 10

> Conversation with Charley, a man of 26 who is still unmarried and has no particular desire to get married as he can have too good a time without being married. He says he can have plenty of girls without getting married, so why should he get married. He told me of the existence of secret societies—medicine societies which a boy joins after his puberty ceremony. *He was drunk when he came to see me or he probably wouldn't have given me this information so freely.* [Emphasis added.] It was the first inkling I had of the existence of secret societies among the Apache, altho I had fished several times for just such information.

Appendix B:
Selected Documents and Photos

Here are a few of the documents obtained during the research for this story. A more extensive collection can be found at *henriettaschmerler.com*.

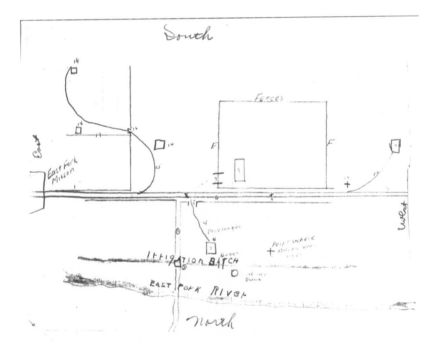

A schematic of the murder site, used at Golney's trial. The small box toward the center bottom indicates where the body was found.

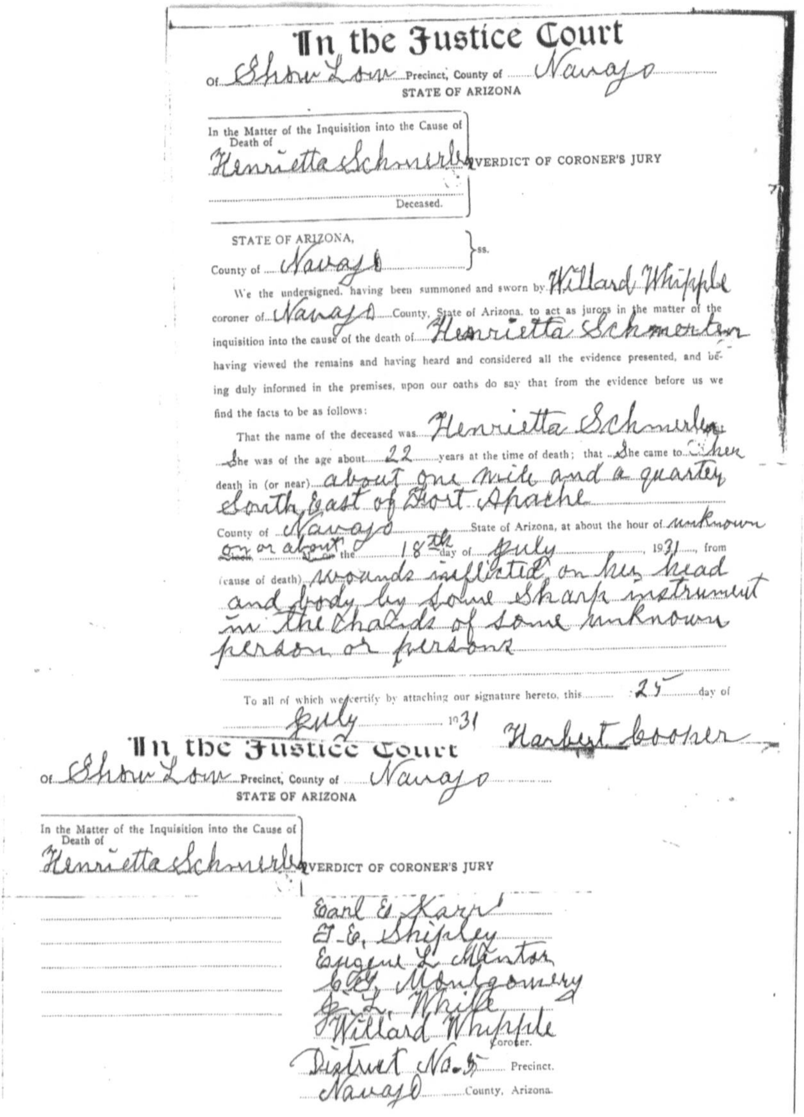

In the Justice Court

Of Show Low Precinct, County of Navajo
STATE OF ARIZONA

In the Matter of the Inquisition into the Cause of Death of
Henrietta Schmerler
Deceased.

VERDICT OF CORONER'S JURY

STATE OF ARIZONA,
County of Navajo } ss.

We the undersigned, having been summoned and sworn by Willard Whipple coroner of Navajo County, State of Arizona, to act as jurors in the matter of the inquisition into the cause of the death of Henrietta Schmerton having viewed the remains and having heard and considered all the evidence presented, and being duly informed in the premises, upon our oaths do say that from the evidence before us we find the facts to be as follows:

That the name of the deceased was Henrietta Schmerler; She was of the age about 22 years at the time of death; that She came to her death in (or near) about one mile and a quarter South East of Fort Apache County of Navajo State of Arizona, at about the hour of unknown on or about the 18th day of July 1931, from (cause of death) wounds inflicted on her head and body by some sharp instrument in the hands of some unknown person or persons

To all of which we certify by attaching our signature hereto, this 25 day of July 1931 Harbert Cooner

In the Justice Court

Of Show Low Precinct, County of Navajo
STATE OF ARIZONA

In the Matter of the Inquisition into the Cause of Death of
Henrietta Schmerler

VERDICT OF CORONER'S JURY

Earl E. Karr
T. E. Shipley
Eugene L. Minton
C. E. Montgomery
J. L. White
Willard Whipple Coroner.
District No. 5 Precinct.
Navajo County, Arizona.

The coroner's report of Henrietta's death.

(On being further questioned subject stated that he had never talked to his father and mother about this matter, but he believed that they knew what he had done.)

Golney Seymour
Colney Seymour

Witnesses:

Jesus Velasquez
Geo. Woolford ja strut
Wm Haught
T. E. Shipley

i certify that i read the statement to Golney Seymour in the Apache language and he stated to me in the presence of others that it was true and correct. *Thomas Dosela* interpreter

Signatures of Golney Seymour and the witnesses to his confession.

The telegram to FBI Director J.Edgar Hoover indicating the murder had been solved and Henrietta's killer had confessed. The name of the killer was whited out, despite Golney Seymour having been identified in dozens of newspaper articles.

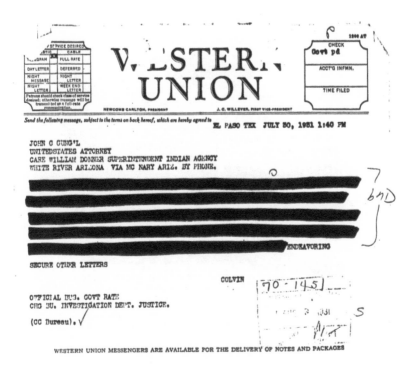

An example of heavily redacted documents in the FBI's original release to Gil Schmerler. The Freedom of Information Act filing against the FBI later produced unredacted copies.

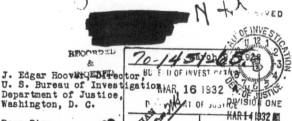

RECORDED
&
J. Edgar Hoover, Director,
U. S. Bureau of Investigation,
Department of Justice,
Washington, D. C.

Dear Sir:

Recently I have been in communication with
Mr. Ralph Colvin, Agent in Charge, Department of
Justice at El Paso, Texas, regarding the case of
an Indian named GOLNEY SEYMOUR, or SEYMOUR GOLNEY,
who murdered Miss Henrietta Schmerler on an Arizona
Indian Reservation.

has written, asking whether or not I could
submit a true account of this case, which would
include a number of actual photographs.

Mr. Colvin advises me that it is necessary
that I obtain permission from you to write this
story under the official name and title (as co-author)
of one of the investigating officers in the case.
If you find you can grant me such permission, I
should appreciate it very much if you would author-
ize Mr. Colvin or Mr. Street or others connected
with the investigation and prosecution to assist
me in obtaining true and accurate details in order
than an ungarbled story may be submitted to the
magazine for publication.   This, of course, at the
conclusion of the Indian's trial.

I have sold a number of crime stories
to the above named magazine, which is, incidentally,
the highest class of its type.

I shall be very grateful for a reply from
you, or any assistance you may give me.

Sincerely yours,

*This exchange with Director J. Edgar Hoover is just one example of the very
active role of the FBI in assuring that the Henrietta story told to the world would
highlight the centrality—and skill—of the FBI in resolving the case. The Freedom*

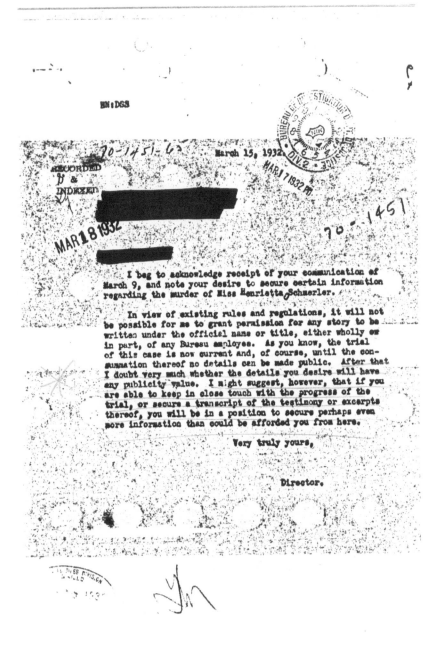

EN : DSS

70-1451-42   March 15, 1932

RECORDED
& INDEXED

MAR 18 1932

70-1451

    I beg to acknowledge receipt of your communication of
March 9, and note your desire to secure certain information
regarding the murder of Miss Henrietta Schmerler.

    In view of existing rules and regulations, it will not
be possible for me to grant permission for any story to be
written under the official name or title, either wholly or
in part, of any Bureau employee. As you know, the trial
of this case is now current and, of course, until the con-
summation thereof no details can be made public. After that
I doubt very much whether the details you desire will have
any publicity value. I might suggest, however, that if you
are able to keep in close touch with the progress of the
trial, or secure a transcript of the testimony or excerpts
thereof, you will be in a position to secure perhaps even
more information than could be afforded you from here.

                    Very truly yours,

                    Director.

of Information Act suit in this case provided abundant evidence that many of the pulp magazine stories involving the case were based on information provided directly by the FBI.

U. S. Department of Justice

Bureau of Investigation
P.O. Box 771,
El Paso, Texas.
Feb. 20, 1932.

70-1451-61X

DIVISION (

FEB 23 193...

Director,   APR 20 1932
Bureau of Investigation,
Department of Justice,
Washington, D.C.

APR 20 1932 A.M

DEPART... OF ...

NATHAN   Div. Tvº   FILE

Attention: Mr. Nathan.

Dear Sir:

In Re: Golney Seymour - Murderer,
E.P. File #70-180.

70 - 1451

Having reference to your letter of Feb. 3, 1932,
relative to publicity in regard to the Henrietta Schmerler
or Golney Seymour case, I am enclosing herewith a fifteen
page story of the case which I have compiled from the files
and from conversation with Agent Street, which contains in
narrative form most of the facts, and a little other stuff,
concerning the case. My literary ability and imagination
are not sufficiently developed to have put out any better
story,   and I submit it "as is" for such censorship or embellishments as the Bureau may deem appropriate for publicity purposes.

I am also enclosing some pictures of the victim,
the murderer, Agent Street, and the writer, in case the Bureau should desire to use any of them in a story which may
be released. Some time ago I sent also to the Bureau postcard photograph of Agent Street, Tom Dosela, interpreter,
and others who assisted in the investigation.

In accordance with the suggestions in your letter,
I am again writing Miss Madeline Kelley Hannah advising her
that she will have to secure her information from the Bureau.

At the present time this case is set up for trial on
March 14, 1932, and it might be best to hold up the story until the trial is over, although I do not see that any particular harm could come from the release of the story at this
time after it had been censored or edited by the Bureau. However, if we are successful in convicting Seymour, the story
would be more complete if put out after the trial and sentence.

At the time I talked with Mr. Nathan about this story

70-1451-61X p.1

in Washington, I thought I could turn out something real good,
but it seems that I have been dealing with facts for so long
that the old imagination just won't work.

                        Yours very truly,

                        R.H. Colvin,
                        Special Agent in Charge.

RHC/wc
Encs.

Cover letter from the Special Agent in Charge of the FBI's El Paso office, R.H. Colvin, contributing his own 15-page imaginative version of the Henrietta story, "from most of the facts, and a little other stuff."

Evelyn on the White Mountain Apache reservation, with a wickiup behind her, 1987.

Mary Velesques Riley, at right, who as a young woman sewed the dress Henrietta would wear on her death ride, and who later served as a tribal elder and one of the first women on the tribal council, sits in her driveway with Evelyn in 1987.

Reprinted from The Journal of American Folk-Lore,
Vol. 44. April-June, 1931. No. 172.

TRICKSTER MARRIES HIS DAUGHTER.[1]

BY HENRIETTA SCHMERLER.

The myth of the trickster who lusts after his daughter and by the
feigning of death achieves his end is told by the North American Indians,
with variations, over a large area, embracing the Central Woodlands, the
Plains, the Great Basin, California, the Plateau and Puget Sound. The
story has also been recorded among the White Mountain Apache and the
Navajo, but in the latter it is known as a tale of the origin of the Utes,
and as incest tales are exceedingly rare in the Southwest, we may consider
these as sporadic occurrences in this region. It is unusual for a tale to
have so continuous a distribution over the particular area covered by
this myth, especially as analysis of its elements shows comparatively
little variation in versions from widely separated tribes. The only
surprising gap in the distribution occurs in the region occupied by the
Kutenai, Coeur d'Alene and Nez Percé tribes, from whom no variants
have been recorded, although the Shoshonean, Plateau and Plains
peoples by whom they are surrounded and from whose cultures they
have borrowed extensively possess very detailed versions. An excellent
and representative version of the myth, recorded by R. H. Lowie among
the Southern Ute, runs as follows:

Sunawavi had two daughters and a son. One day he was lying down
in a little brush lodge. It was raining and the roof leaked so he asked his
daughters to fix it. While they were doing this he caught sight of his
elder daughter's genitalia, which were large, and began to lust for her.
He thought of possessing both his daughters and considered how he
might do so. He went out to hunt rabbits. He found an old rabbit bone,
and stuck it up in front of his tipi. There was snow on the ground, and in
cleaning it from his feet he purposely stepped on the bone. He cried out
and his family came out. His wife pulled out the bone, but he pretended
to be sick. He continued ailing for a long time, at last he said he was about
to die. He told his family that after his death they should move far away
to a big village. When they were there, some visitors were going to come
from another part of the country. One was going to ride a gray horse,
and he was the one his elder daughter should marry. There would be
a lot of gambling there. This visitor would stand there. He would be
good-looking, have his hair wrapped with otterskin and carry an otterskin quiver. "He is a good fellow, and if my daughter marries him she
will never starve." He pretended to get worse. "When I die, I want you
to burn me up. Roll me up in blankets on a pile of wood and burn me.

[1] The tragic death of Miss Schmerler, during a field trip at Whiteriver,
Arizona, occurred while this article was in press. Her death was a loss to
anthropology, to which she had devoted her best efforts.

Henrietta's story, The Trickster Marries His Daughter, *was published in the*
Journal of American Folklore.

The author, left, with Edgar Perry, Apache translator and curator of the Fort Apache Culture Center, who tried to help us locate Henrietta's cabin.

About the Author

Gil Schmerler has had a long and consuming interest in alternative schooling, the creation of teacher-centered supervisory models in leadership preparation, and, in addition—for the last three decades, with his sister Evelyn—the 1931 murder of their aunt, Henrietta Schmerler.

Their research brought out a story quite at odds with the one accepted by the public in this once-celebrated—and then mostly forgotten—case. J. Edgar Hoover's FBI and Franz Boas's Columbia University anthropologists were among the many who accepted, and perpetuated, an inaccurate picture of the crime and its aftermath.

Gil is a graduate of Amherst College and Columbia University, practiced as an English teacher and school administrator, and has been on the faculty at Bank Street College in multi-various roles such as advisor, instructor, chair, and program and center director. He is co-author, with Mary Anne Raywid, of *Not So Easy Going: The Policy Environments of Small Urban Schools and Schools-Within-Schools*.